Contemporary Poetry

Edinburgh Critical Guides to Literature
Series Editors: Martin Halliwell, University of Leicester and Andy
Mousley, De Montfort University

Published Titles:
Gothic Literature, Andrew Smith
Canadian Literature, Faye Hammill
Women's Poetry, Jo Gill
Contemporary American Drama, Annette J. Saddik
Shakespeare, Gabriel Egan
Asian American Literature, Bella Adams
Children's Literature, M. O. Grenby
Contemporary British Fiction, Nick Bentley
Renaissance Literature, Siobhan Keenan
Scottish Literature, Gerard Carruthers
Contemporary American Fiction, David Brauner
Contemporary British Drama, David Lane
Medieval Literature 1300–1500, Pamela King
Contemporary Poetry, Nerys Williams
Victorian Literature, David Amigoni

Forthcoming Titles in the Series:
Restoration and Eighteenth-Century Literature, Hamish Mathison
Crime Fiction, Stacy Gillis
Modern American Literature, Catherine Morley
Modernist Literature, Rachel Potter
African American Literature, Jennifer Terry
Postcolonial Literature, Dave Gunning

Contemporary Poetry

Nerys Williams

Edinburgh University Press

© Nerys Williams, 2011

Edinburgh University Press Ltd
22 George Square, Edinburgh

www.euppublishing.com

Typeset in 11.5/13 Monotype Ehrhardt
by Servis Filmsetting Ltd, Stockport, Cheshire and
printed and bound in Great Britain by
CPI Antony Rowe, Chippenham and Eastbourne

A CIP record for this book is available from the British Library

ISBN 978 0 7486 3884 0 (hardback)
ISBN 978 0 7486 3885 7 (paperback)

Contents

Series Preface

The study of English literature in the early twenty-first century is host to an exhilarating range of critical approaches, theories and historical perspectives. 'English' ranges from traditional modes of study such as Shakespeare and Romanticism to popular interest in national and area literatures such as the United States, Ireland and the Caribbean. The subject also spans a diverse array of genres from tragedy to cyberpunk, incorporates such hybrid fields of study as Asian American literature, Black British literature, creative writing and literary adaptations, and remains eclectic in its methodology.

Such diversity is cause for both celebration and consternation. English is varied enough to promise enrichment and enjoyment for all kinds of readers and to challenge preconceptions about what the study of literature might involve. But how are readers to navigate their way through such literary and cultural diversity? And how are students to make sense of the various literary categories and periodisations, such as modernism and the Renaissance, or the proliferating theories of literature, from feminism and marxism to queer theory and eco-criticism? The Edinburgh Critical Guides to Literature series reflects the challenges and pluralities of English today, but at the same time it offers readers clear and accessible routes through the texts, contexts, genres, historical periods and debates within the subject.

Martin Halliwell and Andy Mousley

Acknowledgements

Firstly, my immense gratitude to both editors of the series, Martin Halliwell and Andy Mousley, for their original interest and subsequent support for this project. Their patience, alert editorial eye and encouragement were appreciated throughout. I would also like to thank the work of Jackie Jones and staff at Edinburgh University Press.

Thanks go to colleagues at the School of English, Drama and Film at University College Dublin. In particular I would like to acknowledge my lively conversations with Michelle O'Connell, Porscha Fermanis and Ron Callan – and the support of Maria Stuart and Mary Clayton. I am also grateful to Nick Daly for encouraging research life in the department in such a productive way. Pauline Slattery's wonderfully efficient management of undergraduate academic life in the school (with the help of Marguerite Duggan and Anne Cleary) made this process less painful. The experience of teaching the MA in American Literature and a course on 'Poetry and Poetics' at UCD has informed this project greatly. To those lively and inspiring students who offered interpretations that opened up the poems again (particularly Jean Hogan, Ciaran Lawless, David McCarthy and Tobias Ryan) – my thanks!

Much of the initial writing took place in the lofty space of the Irish National Library, and I would like to thank the staff at this precious establishment. Bob and Becky Tracey very generously enabled a space at Berkeley where the final tidying up of the manuscript took place. I appreciate their thoughtfulness.

Close friends and family outside of Ireland – Sally Perry, Una a John, Ifor Owen, Sue Currell, Ciara Hogan and Sarah MacLachlan, Gaynor Jones – provided necessary words of wisdom, especially when there seemed to be far too many poets in one pot.

Special thanks go to my super furry animal, Cal, for witnessing the process and keeping her feline eye on tea breaks. A final *diolch anferth* to my husband, Myles Dungan, for being in sync with the vagaries of a writing timetable, and acting with such grace, good humour and affection.

Chronology

Date	Historical Events	Literary Events
1950	President Truman announces that the USA is to proceed with the building of the hydrogen bomb; the Korean War breaks out.	Charles Olson, 'Projective Verse'
1952	Dwight Eisenhower is elected President of the USA with Richard Nixon as his Vice President.	
1953	Soviet troops suppress strikes and an uprising in East Germany; the Korean War comes to an end.	
1954	The defeat of French forces by the Viet Minh at Dien Bien Phu effectively ends French colonial involvement in Indo-China.	
1955	In Montgomery, Alabama 42-year-old African-American Rosa Parks refuses to give up her seat on a city bus to make room for a white passenger.	Philip Larkin, *The Less Deceived*

Date	Historical Events	Literary Events
1956	The Hungarian Revolution is crushed by the Soviet Union after three weeks; Elvis Presley has his first number one hit with *Heartbreak Hotel*.	Allen Ginsberg, *Howl and Other Poems*; Robert Conquest, *New Lines*
1957	The Treaty of Rome establishes the European Economic Community.	The *Howl* obscenity trial results in the acquittal of publisher Lawrence Ferlinghetti; Ted Hughes, *The Hawk in the Rain*
1959	Fidel Castro assumes power in Cuba after his guerrilla forces defeat the army of President Battista.	Robert Lowell, *Life Studies*; Frank O'Hara, 'Personism'; Gary Snyder, *Riprap and Cold Mountain Poems*
1960	Cuba aligns itself with the Soviet Union; Penguin Books is found not guilty in the *Lady Chatterley's Lover* obscenity trial.	Donald Allen, *The New American Poetry*; Sylvia Plath, *The Colossus*
1961	John F. Kennedy becomes the youngest and the first Roman Catholic US President; the attempted CIA-led incursion into Cuba comes to grief at the Bay of Pigs.	Allen Ginsberg, 'Prose Contribution to Cuban Revolution'
1962	A Russian missile site is identified in Cuba by a US military overflight, precipitating the Cuban Missile crisis; The Beatles' first single *Love Me Do* reaches no. 17 in the British charts.	Al Alvarez, *The New Poetry*
1963	President John F. Kennedy is assassinated in Dallas, Texas; Vice President Lyndon Baines Johnson is sworn in.	Amiri Baraka, 'Expressive Language'

Date	Historical Events	Literary Events
1964	The Civil Rights Act becomes law in the USA, outlawing the unequal application of voter registration requirements and racial segregation in schools.	Ted Berrigan, *Sonnets*; Philip Larkin, *The Whitsun Weddings*; John Berryman, *77 Dream Songs*
1965	American Civil Rights campaigners march from Selma to Montgomery on 7 March and 9 March, they finally complete the journey at the third attempt on 21 March; militant African-American rights activist Malcolm X is assassinated in New York.	Amiri Baraka, 'State/ Meant'; Sylvia Plath, *Ariel*
1966	England, the host nation, wins the World Cup by defeating Germany 4–2 at Wembley stadium after extra time.	Amiri Baraka, *Black Art*
1967	Israeli military forces win the Six-Day war fought against its Arab neighbours in Egypt, Syria and Jordan; race riots in Newark, New Jersey, USA; The Beatles release *Sgt. Pepper's Lonely Hearts Club Band*; hippies and other counter-cultural elements descend on San Francisco for the 'Summer of Love'; in Britain the Abortion Act legalises abortions by registered practitioners.	Roland Barthes 'Death of the Author'
1968	The Viet Cong and North Vietnamese army strike against American forces in the 'Tet offensive' with limited military but huge propaganda success; Richard Nixon is elected President of the USA – defeating the Democratic	Michel Foucault, 'What is an Author?'

Date	Historical Events	Literary Events
	candidate Hubert Humphrey; Spiro Agnew becomes Vice President; Soviet forces crush the 'Prague Spring' peaceful uprising against communist rule in Czechoslovakia; presidential candidate Robert Kennedy and African American leader Dr Martin Luther King are assassinated; Pierre Elliott Trudeau becomes fifteenth Prime Minister of Canada.	
1969	Neil Armstrong and Edwin 'Buzz' Aldrin become the first men to walk on the surface of the moon; the My Lai massacre in Vietnam is revealed due to the journalistic work of Seymour Hersh; the Woodstock open-air concert takes place at Max Yasgur's farm in upstate New York.	Adrienne Rich, *Leaflets*; Tom Leonard starts *Six Glasgow Poems*, completed 1979; Alberto Baltazar Urista, 'El plan Espiritual de Aztlán'
1970	The Brazilian soccer team beat Italy 4–1 in the final to win the World Cup in Mexico City; The Beatles announce that the group is to break up.	Ted Hughes, *Crow*
1971	Battles between India and Pakistan erupt into full-scale war when India invades East Pakistan (now Bangladesh) in support of the independence movement.	Geoffrey Hill, *Mercian Hymns*; Adrienne Rich, *The Will to Change*
1972	Richard Nixon is re-elected president of the USA; five men are arrested for breaking and entering Democratic party offices in the Watergate complex in Washington DC; Labour leader Gough Whitlam becomes Prime Minister of Australia; Clyde shipworkers strike.	Edwin Morgan, *Glasgow Sonnets*; Seamus Heaney, *Wintering Out*

Date	Historical Events	Literary Events
1973	The Yom Kippur War fought between Israel and the Arab countries on its borders results in co-ordinated action by Arab members of the Organisation of Petroleum Exporting Countries and the first Energy Crisis; under the Paris Peace Accord signed by Henry Kissinger and Le Duc Tho, the USA agrees to withdraw its ground troops from Vietnam; the US Supreme Court in the case of *Roe v. Wade* lifts most federal and state restrictions on abortion.	Mutabaruka, *Outcry*; Robert Hass, *Field Guide*
1974	Richard Nixon becomes the first US President to resign, his resignation comes about as a result of the Watergate scandal 'cover-up'; Vice President Gerald Ford assumes office; a series of strikes, including a major action by the National Union of Mineworkers, brings down the Conservative government of Edward Heath in the UK.	
1975	NBC's long running game show *Wheel of Fortune* premieres on American television; South Vietnam falls to the combined forces of the North Vietnamese Army and the Viet Cong; the Khmer Rouge take power in Cambodia, which they rename Democratic Kampuchea, a reign of government terror begins; Australian Prime Minister Gough Whitlam is controversially removed from office by Governor General Sir John Kerr.	Seamus Heaney, *North*; Derek Mahon, *The Snow Party*; John Ashbery, *Self Portrait in a Convex Mirror*; Iain Sinclair, *Lud Heat*

Date	Historical Events	Literary Events
1976	Democrat Jimmy Carter defeats Republican President Gerald Ford in the US Presidential Election; Harold Wilson resigns as British Prime Minister and is replaced by James Callaghan; the Sex Pistols play Manchester's Lesser Free Trade Hall on 4 June, in the audience are fans who will go on to form the Buzzcocks, Joy Division, The Fall and The Smiths.	
1977	Elvis Presley dies.	
1978	Polish Cardinal Karol Wojtyla becomes Pope John Paul II.	Tony Harrison, *From the School of Eloquence*; Andrew Motion, *The Pleasure Steamers*
1979	Shah Reza Pahlavi is deposed as ruler of Iran – the Ayatollah Khomeini becomes the spiritual leader of a new Islamic Republic; Iranian Revolutionary Guards seize sixty-six American hostages when they take over the US Embassy in Tehran, the 'Hostage Crisis' continues for 444 days; Vietnam invades Cambodia and forces the removal from power of the Khmer Rouge, widespread famine affects the country; Conservative leader Margaret Thatcher becomes the UK's first woman Prime Minister after the defeat of the Labour party government led by James Callaghan; the Soviet occupation of Afghanistan begins.	Amiri Baraka, *AM/TRAK*; Robert Hass, *Praise*; Iain Sinclair, *Suicide Bridge*; Adrienne Rich, 'Blood and Bread Poetry'

Date	Historical Events	Literary Events
1980	Republican candidate Ronald Reagan defeats Jimmy Carter in the US Presidential election, George Bush becomes Vice President; John Lennon is shot dead in New York; the Iran–Iraq War begins. It continues until 1988.	Lyn Hejinian, *My Life*
1981	American hostages in Iran are released six minutes after the inauguration of Ronald Reagan as fortieth President of the United States of America; Provisional IRA volunteer Bobby Sands dies after sixty-six days on hunger strike in the Maze prison; influential Jamaican reggae singer-songwriter Bob Marley dies at the age of 36; Brixton riots in Lambeth, South London, England.	Lorna Dee Cervantes, *Emplumada*
1982	The UK and Argentina fight the Falklands War.	
1983	South Korean Boeing 747 jetliner bound for Seoul apparently strays into Soviet airspace and is shot down by a Soviet SU-15 fighter.	Paul Muldoon, *Quoof*; Rita Dove, *Museum*; Cathy Song, *Picture Bride*; Jorie Graham, *Erosion*; Iain Sinclair, *Flesh Eggs and Scalp Metal*; Anne Szumigalski, *Doctrine of Signatures*; Jerome Rothenberg (ed.), *Symposium of the Whole: A Range of Discourse Towards an Ethnopoetics*

Date	Historical Events	Literary Events
1984	The Miners' Strike begins in the UK, it ends with the defeat of the National Union of Mineworkers, led by Arthur Scargill; Ronald Reagan is re-elected President of the USA.	Grace Nichols, *The Fat Black Woman's Poems*; Kamau Brathwaite, 'Nation Language'; Linton Kwesi Johnson, *Making History*
1985	Reagan and Gorbachev meet at summit and agree to arrange arms control talks.	Lyn Hejinian, 'Rejection of Closure'; Liz Lochhead, *True Confessions and New Clichés*
1986	The Space Shuttle *Challenger* explodes and disintegrates shortly after lift off in Cape Canaveral in Florida, killing all seven crew members.	Mutabaruka *The Mystery Unfolds*; Li-Young Lee, *Rose*
1987	Gestapo wartime chief Klaus Barbie, aged 73, sentenced to life for war crimes.	Paul Durcan, *Going Home to Russia*; Jorie Graham, *The End of Beauty*
1988	George Bush defeats the Democratic party candidate Michael Dukakis to become forty-first President of the USA; testimony to the US Congress by NASA climatologist James Hansen highlights the threat of climate change.	Michael Palmer, *Sun*; Yusef Komunyakaa, *Dien Cai Dau*
1989	Communist regimes collapse in Poland, Hungary, Czechoslovakia (the Velvet Revolution), East Germany, Bulgaria and Romania; the Berlin Wall is dismantled and the year ends with the execution of the Romanian dictator Nicolae Ceausescu.	The Ayatollah Khomeini issues a *fatwa* against Salman Rushdie's novel *The Satanic Verses*, forcing Rushdie to accept round-the-clock protection.

Date	Historical Events	Literary Events
1990	German Federal Republic Chancellor Helmut Kohl proceeds with the early reunification of Germany; John Major replaces Margaret Thatcher as Prime Minister of the UK; the Iraqi forces of Saddam Hussein invade Kuwait.	Derek Walcott, *Omeros*; Joy Harjo, *In Mad Love and War*
1991	The Gulf War, militarily codenamed Operation Desert Storm, begins as American, British, Saudi and Egyptian forces succeed in dislodging the Iraqi army of Saddam Hussein from Kuwait.	Anne Szumigalski, *Rapture of the Deep*
1992	Democratic candidate William Jefferson Clinton becomes forty-second President of the USA, defeating President George Bush and third party candidate Ross Perot in the Presidential election, Clinton won 43 per cent of the popular vote.	Derek Walcott wins the Nobel Prize for Literature; Maya Angelou, 'On the Pulse of Morning'; Benjamin Zephaniah, *City Psalms*
1993	The European Union is established by the Treaty of Maastricht.	Carolyn Forché, *Against Forgetting: Twentieth Century Poetry of Witness*; Jackie Kay, *Other Lovers*; Paul Durcan, *A Snail in my Prime: New and Selected Poems*
1995	The US-led war against the ruling Taliban begins in Afghanistan.	Seamus Heaney wins the Nobel Prize for Literature; Gwyneth Lewis, *Parables & Faxes*; Sujata Bhatt, *The Stinking Rose*

Date	Historical Events	Literary Events
1996	John Howard leads the Liberal–National coalition to victory to become twenty-fifth Prime Minister of Australia.	Charles Bernstein, 'Poetics of the Americas'
1997	Labour leader Tony Blair becomes British Prime Minister.	
1998	President Bill Clinton is impeached by the House of Representatives but is subsequently acquitted by the US Senate; the Good Friday agreement signed in Northern Ireland clears the way for a power-sharing executive; a bomb planted by the Republican splinter group the Real IRA kills twenty-nine people and injures two hundred in Omagh, Co. Tyrone.	Lee Harwood, *Morning Light*
1999	Hugo Chávez becomes President of Venezuela.	Jennifer Moxley, *Imagination Verses*; Li-Young Lee, *The Winged Seed*; Simon Armitage, *Killing Time*; Caroline Bergvall, *Goan Atom*
2000	George W. Bush narrowly defeats Vice President Al Gore, after a number of recounts in Florida and a case taken to the US Supreme Court, to become forty-third President of the United States of America.	Michael Palmer, *The Promises of Glass*

Date	Historical Events	Literary Events
2001	Two hijacked airliners destroy the Twin Towers in New York, and the Pentagon in Washington DC is similarly damaged in a successful Al Qaeda terrorist operation; the US-led invasion of Afghanistan begins and the ruling Taliban government is overthrown.	Lorna Goodison, *Travelling Mercies*; John Cayley's *windsound* wins *Electronic Literature Award for Poetry*
2002	The Euro, already formally in existence, becomes an active currency in daily use in sixteen European Union countries.	Kate Fagan, *The Long Moment*; Sujata Bhatt, *A Colour for Solitude*
2003	The USA and UK invade Iraq in search of Saddam Hussein's 'weapons of mass destruction', none is found; the Space Shuttle *Columbia* disintegrates on re-entry into the Earth's atmosphere, killing all members of its crew.	Jennifer Moxley, *The Sense Record;* Don Paterson, *Landing Light*; Todd Swift (ed.), *100 Poets Against the War*
2004	Indian Ocean earthquake results in Indonesian tsunami killing nearly 230,000 in 14 different countries.	Choman Hardi, *Life for Us*; Claudia Rankine, *Please Don't Let Me Be Lonely*; Tusiata Avia, *Wild Dogs Under My Skirt*
2005	The Kyoto Protocol on global warming goes into effect but without the signature of the USA.	Eliot Weinberger, *What I Heard About Iraq*; Gary Snyder, *Axe Handles*; Juliana Spahr, *this connection of everyone with lungs*; Jackie Kay, *Life Mask*

Date	Historical Events	Literary Events
2006	A few months after test firing missiles, North Korea announces it has tested its first nuclear weapon.	Charles Bernstein, *Girly Man*; Joshua Clover, *the totality for kids*; John Kinsella, 'The Ocean Forests'
2007	Opening of Northern Irish Assembly Stormont with First Minister Ian Paisley and Deputy First Minister Martin McGuinness; former Pakistani prime minister Benazir Bhutto is assassinated.	Laynie Browne, *Daily Sonnets*; Lawrence Ferlinghetti, *Insurgent Art*; Jennifer Moxley, *The Line*; Robert Hass, *Time and Materials Poems 1997–2005*
2008	President of Cuba Fidel Castro resigns; Lehman Brothers file for bankruptcy, acting as a catalyst for a global financial crisis.	Robert Minhinnick, *King Driftwood*; Geraldine Monk, *Ghost & Other Sonnets*; M. NourbeSe Philip, *Zong!*; Daljit Nagra *Look We Have Coming to Dover*
2009	Barack Hussein Obama becomes the first African-American President of the United States of America.	Carol Ann Duffy becomes the first woman, first Scot and first openly bisexual person to become British Poet Laureate; Elizabeth Alexander, 'Praise Song for the Day'; Paula Meehan, *Painting Rain*; Mark Nowak, *Coal Mountain Elementary*

Introduction

I love reading all those optimistic things that people say about poetry. Those sweeping statements about poetry being all about love, or poetry being all about countering the oblivion of darkness, or poetry being the genre to comfort in times of trouble. They make me feel good about poetry.

But poetry doesn't really work that way for me. For me, poetry is a troubled and troubling genre, full of desire and anger and support and protest, primarily useful because it helps me think. Lyn Hejinian's essays, her explorations of inquiry, have been really helpful to me on this. My theory is that poetry helps me think because it is a genre that is so open right now. There are so many rules about how to write poetry, that there might as well not be any at all.[1]

Juliana Spahr's statement, taken from an anthology *American Poets in the 21st Century: The New Poetics*, gestures towards two seemingly antithetical directions for contemporary poetry. Poetry can be seen as a salve for troubled times and a medium of comfort. From another perspective, poetry offers a means for examining and exploring the world. Spahr suggests that the form of analysis offered by poetry may even provide discomfort. Her statement valorises contemporary poetry's openness as a genre, yet paradoxically she suggests that the proliferation of alternative rules liberates our understanding of what poetry might be.

The aim of this book is to introduce students to a broad span of ideas and movements, as well as essays and debates that surround and inform contemporary poetry. By examining a range of contemporary Anglophone poetry, the book seeks to promote adaptive reading strategies and to create links between a variety of poetic forms and genealogies. Interpreting 'poetics' as the thought, strategies and statements 'behind' the poetry, this guide aims to introduce key manifestos as enabling devices for interpreting individual texts. In offering a range of different poetries, I show the differing ambitions of authors for their poetry, and how the work of contemporary poets interacts with politics, culture and society by questioning boundaries and often transgressing assumptions. My discussion considers how poetry comments upon the world and the status of representation itself, as well as how poetry might develop in the twenty-first century and the interaction of media with poetic forms. A central consideration for contemporary Anglophone poets is how to consider the complexity of asserting differences in a global culture without resorting to didactic definitions. In this aim, the book considers poetry from the USA, United Kingdom, Ireland, New Zealand, Australia, the Caribbean, Canada, India and Kurdistan. My overarching intention is to illustrate how a plurality of approaches to poetic form and linguistic textuality enables innovative modes of thought. American poet Lyn Hejinian may well suggest this multiplicity of poetic approaches when she states 'where once one sought a vocabulary for ideas, now one seeks ideas for vocabularies'.[2]

'NEW, NEWER AND NEWEST' POETRY

It often seems that Ezra Pound's rallying cry 'make it new' is still very much in circulation and with it the dangers of fetishising the next new paradigm for writing.[3] From a modernist perspective, one can read Pound's calling as the need for literary endeavour to find new forms in which to address the material of the modern. New ways of representation may defamiliarise the everyday, or break down what the Russian Formalist Victor Shklovsky referred to as the automation of perception in which the ordinariness of everyday objects remains uninterrogated.[4] Even a brief snapshot of poetry anthology titles since the 1950s indicates the predominance of the 'really really' new. Take as examples the following cross-section: Robert Conquest's *New Lines* (1956), Al Alvarez's *The New Poetry* (1962), Donald Allen's *The New American Poetry* (1960), Michael Schmidt's *New Poetries* (1994), Michael Hulse, David Kennedy and David Morley's *The New Poetry* (1993), and Claudia Rankine and Lisa Sewell's *American Poets in the 21st Century: The New Poetics* (2007).[5]

A key question is how do we read 'new' and can the word 'contemporary' be substituted for 'new'? Gertrude Stein reminds us that the term 'contemporary' denotes a complexity of time frames. As Stein proposes in her early essay 'Composition as Explanation' (1926), World War I necessitated that art forms needed to be 'so [. . .] completely contemporary and so created the completed recognition of the contemporary composition'.[6] Stein insisted that as a result an acknowledgement of the contemporary occurred since 'Every one but one may say every one became consciously became aware of the existence of the authenticity of the modern composition.'[7] We might also be warned that perceiving literary forms as a simple dismantling of what has already preceded can be problematic. American poet Ron Silliman, using an analogy of the athlete, notes how an emphasis on the zeitgeist can seem to reject a present perception of writing:

> The production of novelty, of art objects that could not have been predicted, and cannot be accounted for, by previous critical theory, is the most problematic area in aesthetics. Like a record in sports made only to be broken, a poetics is articulated in order to be transcended.[8]

Remarking particularly on the evolution of form in American poetry, Silliman notes that what we are witnessing is a form of 'acceleration in literary historicity' where a poet's aim can often be seen as a vague commitment to 'Make it Different, if not New'.[9]

With this in mind I will be considering the 'contemporary' as poetry written in English produced over the past forty years. Wherever possible I gesture towards a historical context, especially regarding the evolution of poetic forms, conceptualisation of the poets' ideas through essays and manifestos, and a critical consensus regarding tendencies in recent contemporary poetry. But in order to understand what the implications of what being 'contemporary' might mean for poetry written since the 1960s, it is important that we broach initially what we can understand by a 'poetics', as well as some important historical precedents, tendencies and movements that impacted upon the writing of contemporary poetry in English.

POETICS?

Jerome McGann in a recent collection of his essays on poetry *The Point is to Change It* (2007) identifies his central concern: 'this book is about the ancient quarrel between philosophy and poetry. When their dispute involves a claim to critical thinking, the question is usually decided in favour of philosophy'.[10] It is useful to consider 'poetics' as a philosophy of poetry, the thinking of the art of poetic composition. Key early philosophers and thinkers whose work is associated with the creation and discussion of a poetics would be of course Aristotle, Horace and Dante. *The New Princeton Dictionary of Poetry and Poetics* states that poetics is at its most specific 'a systematic theory of poetry'. Poetics in effect 'attempts to define the nature of poetry, its kinds and forms, its resources of device and structure, the principles that govern it from other arts, the conditions under which it can exist, and its effects on readers or auditors'.[11] M. H. Abrams, writing in 1953, identified four directions that poetic theories address:

> Toward the work itself (objective or formalist theories), toward the audience (pragmatic or affective theories), toward the world (mimetic or realistic theories) and toward the poet creator (expressive or romantic theories).[12]

Remarking on the momentum of twentieth-century philosophy with its post-World War II emphasis on language philosophy and the impact of French deconstruction, McGann suggests that poetic writing found itself suddenly in favour: 'this kind of writing was energized', since philosophy's linguistic turn 'made the scene of writing itself the source and end and test of the art of critical thinking' (p. xi). McGann notes that the most significant poetry after 1848 'has been consciously language oriented as opposed to content driven' (p. xi). Central to McGann's consideration of more recent and radical contemporary poetries is that they imply 'a marked change in the way we think about our poetic tradition on one hand and the way we might engage a critical practice, on the other' (p. xii).

One can consider twentieth-century poetics as a 'thinking through' of ideas and declarations of intention. Essays and manifestos by poets from the 1950s onwards provide a context for understanding current poetic thinking. This book introduces ideas – from American poet Charles Olson's consideration of poetry as kinetics or energy in his famous essay 'Projective Verse' (1950) that is central to understanding ideas of poetic performance, to Kamau Brathwaite's consideration of the development of 'Nation Language' which provides alternative approaches for considering the plurality of Englishes in Caribbean poetry. In addition Charles Bernstein's examination of what he poses as 'ideolects' in his provocative 'Poetics of the Americas' (1996) creates a mode of poetry reliant less on a multiplicity of identities than a plurality of different languages. We might add to these essays, ideas taken from Lyn Hejinian's proposal of an 'open text' in her essay 'The Rejection of Closure' (1985) where the reader's participation is key in the construction of poetic meaning, or in an alternative and more immediate key Mark Nowak's reflection upon poetic writing as performing a form of activism through a documentary impulse. We could also gesture towards Caroline Bergvall's attempts to articulate what poetic 'performance writing' entails and John Cayley's propositions of 'electronic writing'. Many of the ideas that can be said to form a 'poetics' are not made as explicit as a manifesto essay; these can be remarks made by the poets during an interview or reflections in prose that are not quite as didactic as a programmatic description of poetic intent. Here one might include M. NourbeSe Philip's reflections upon her use of legal archives in her volume *Zong!* (2009) for examining the slave trade, as well as the volume's glossary to the African languages she incorporates into her text. We might also consider Gwyneth Lewis's reflections upon the impact of bilingualism upon her work, or John Kinsella's considerations on the intersection of poetry and the environment and the creation of what he terms a 'poisoned pastoral'. A central concern motivating the majority of these poets is their analysis of poetic language as a method of examination or, as Hejinian notes, poetry as 'a language of inquiry'. Hejinian notes that the distinctions between theory and poetry in her own work are indeed negligible:

> Theory asks what practice does and in asking, it sees the connections that practice makes. Poetic language, then, insofar as it is a language of linkage, is a practice. It is practical. But poetry insofar as it comments on itself . . . is also theoretical.[13]

My discussion of essays, manifestos and reflections on poetry in this volume considers the relationship between poetic theory and practice to discern how a poetics can be mediated through composition.

BEFORE THE 1970S: POETIC PRECEDENTS

In their collaborative essay 'Leave the Manifesto Alone: A Manifesto', Juliana Spahr and Joshua Clover playfully propose that poets need 'To stop wringing [their] hands over poetry's lost popularity, that autocritique more stirring than any Maoist's. The manifesto is obligated to say *There are other countries where poetry still matters!*'[14] For all the whimsy of Spahr and Clover's positions, they both believe that contemporary poetry matters, as both a disseminator of ideas and an enquiry about the world. My division of the field of contemporary poetry in this book into five chapters – (1) subjectivity, (2) politics, (3) performance, (4) place and environment, and (5) global Englishes – illustrates the expansiveness of poetry's responsiveness to the world around us. While my project begins with the poetry of the late 1960s, it will be useful to map out some important precedents to the manifesto essays and groupings which emerge in the twenty-first century. Romana Huk in discussing the relationship between Anglo-American poetries notes that there is an American tendency 'to read radical British and Irish poetics not as *different* but as lagging behind American versions'.[15] Equally I am aware there is a danger of reading global Anglophone poetries through the lens of Anglo-American poetries. There is a similar pressure, as Rey Chow observes, in world literatures which are held together by 'investigating multiple literary traditions on the assumption that there ought to be a degree of commonality and equivalence and thus comparability among them . . . [yet] the assumption of parity/sameness is premised on a requirement of linguistic sameness/difference'.[16] The following outline of movements and tendencies emerging after World War II is intended as a backdrop and introduction to the poetries discussed in the subsequent five chapters, and *not* necessarily as an abiding framework for their interpretation.

NEW LINES, THE NEW POETRY, THE NEW AMERICAN POETRY

Different approaches to developing a 'new' poetry are evident in three key anthologies that appeared in the late 1950s and 1960s, two in UK and the other in the USA. The first is *New Lines: An Anthology* (1956) edited by Robert Conquest, which grouped together elements of a tendency which would later been known as 'The Movement' and included John Holloway, Elizabeth Jennings, Thom Gunn, Kingsley Amis, D. J. Enright, Donald Davie and John Wain. These poets tended to see their work as continuing in an English tradition. Peter Finch proposes that this impetus reflects something of 'the English suspicion of modernism and insistence on form, often at the expense of content, that has sidelined it on the world stage'.[17] In his introduction, Conquest proposes that *New Lines* is an attempt to restore 'sound and fruitful attitude to poetry, of the principle that poetry is written by and for the whole man, intellect, emotions, senses and all' (p. xiv). His ambition moreover is to regain a form of empiricism in poetry, the poetry present in the anthology 'submits to no great systems of theoretical constructs nor agglomerations of unconscious commands. It is free from both mystical and logical compulsions and like modern philosophy – is empirical in its attitude' (p. xv). Conquest adds that in terms of

form the poets refuse 'to abandon a rational structure and compre-
hensible language, even when the verse is most highly charged with
sensuous or emotional intent' (p. xv).

Compare this gesture towards formal control with the introduction by Al Alvarez to *The New Poetry* in 1962. Alvarez's opening
essay 'The New Poetry', subtitled 'Or Beyond the Gentility
Principle', considers that behavioural niceties and politeness has
strangled the evolution of British poetry. Alvarez comments that
'Gentility is a belief that life is always more or less orderly, people
always more or less polite . . . controllable; that God is more or
less good.'[18] Passionately, he argues that our lives 'are influenced
profoundly by forces which have nothing to do with gentility,
decency, or politeness'. Instead the poet may be faced with the so-
called advancement of the twentieth-century 'forces of disintegra-
tion . . . their public faces are those of the two world wars, of the
concentration camps, of genocide, and the threat of nuclear war'
(p. 26). Poets appearing in the first edition included Ted Hughes,
Geoffrey Hill, Robert Lowell and John Berryman; the revised
edition published in 1966 included Sylvia Plath and Anne Sexton.
Lowell, Berryman, Sexton and Plath would later be grouped
together under the somewhat disparaging moniker of 'confessionalism' or 'confessional poetry'. Alvarez's introduction also makes a
link between the evolution of psychoanalysis and history, or what
he acknowledges as 'the forceable recognition of mass evil outside
us has developed precisely in parallel with psychoanalysis' (p. 27).

As a general tendency, confessional poetry presented psychoan-
alytical concerns in addition to dramatising extreme states of being
and violence. The word 'dramatising' here is key; an early critical
trend had been to examine the work of these poets through their
biography, rather than view the extreme voices as a series of per-
sonae. One might consider, for example, the intrusion of popular
culture into the construction of selfhood exhibited in Plath's
poems such as 'Lady Lazarus' and 'The Applicant'. Or, there is
the teasing playfulness of Berryman's *The Dream Songs* with its
evolving multi-persona Henry. 'Dream Song 14' comes to mind
with its statement: 'Life, friends, is boring' and the engaging retort
to his mother's admonition ' "Ever to confess you're bored / means
you have no / Inner Resources." ' Henry replies 'I conclude now I

have no / inner resources'.[19] To an extent the psychoanalytic turn can be viewed as a belated identification in poetry, corresponding to Alvarez's more recent essays on poetry, in which he notes that:

When during the celebration of his seventieth birthday, one of his disciples hailed Freud as 'the discoverer of the unconscious', he answered 'the poets and philosophers before me discovered the unconscious. What I discovered was the scientific method by which the unconscious can be studied.'[20]

Similarly, psychoanalysis in the confessional school acts as a framing device rather than a stylistic determinant. Alvarez's anthology presented a post-World War II poetic that was urgently attempting to address new subject matter for poetry, as well as responding to the more constraining elements of The Movement, in a desire to find articulation, or what commonly became referred to as 'finding one's voice'.

In the USA the emergence of Donald Allen's collection of American poets *The New American Poetry* (1960) collected three general tendencies in American poetry. The first was an experimental grouping, collectively known as the Black Mountain School, primarily identified with the tutelage of Charles Olson (Olson, Robert Creeley, Robert Duncan, Denise Levertov). The anthology also included poets from the San Francisco Bay Area whose work probed the social aftermath of World War II, as well as a general examination of new social collectives. Poets such as Kenneth Rexroth, Robert Duncan, Jack Spicer, Gary Snyder, Jack Kerouac, Allen Ginsberg, Lawrence Ferlinghetti and Levertov were collectively linked to the San Francisco Renaissance. Finally, the New York School provided a collective naming to artists whose work was loosely affiliated to the representational enquiry enacted by abstract expressionism (Frank O'Hara, John Ashbery, Kenneth Koch, Amiri Baraka (formerly LeRoi Jones), Helen Adam and Levertov). In a retrospective note to the new edition of the volume, operating under the title *The Postmoderns: The New American Poetry Revised* (1982), Allen is keen to stress that the identification of his anthology with the purely experimental runs a risk of marginalising the work of the poets included:

Increasingly literary and cultural historians have come to
recognize that these are among the most truly authentic,
indigenous American writers following in the mainstream of
Emerson and Whitman Pound and Williams.[21]

Allen is keen to characterise the poems he selected under the rubric
of immediacy and spontaneity. Here we are far from the logical
restraints of retrospective reflection and control through craft
that dominate the methodology of Conquest's *New Lines*. Allen
suggests that the poets in *The New American Poetry*:

> Respond to the limits of industrialisms, and high technol-
> ogy often by a marked spiritual advance or deference, an
> embracing of the primal energies of the tribal or communal
> spirit, side by side with the most stubborn sort of American
> individualism. Their influence on English speaking poetry
> at large has reversed the longstanding obeisance to academi-
> cally sanctioned formalism. Their most common bond is a
> spontaneous utilization of subject and technique, a prevailing
> 'instantism' that nevertheless does not preclude discursive
> ponderings and large canvassed reflections. (p. 9)

Turning to the essays of this anthology, compiled as *The Poetics of
The New American Poetry*, there is an immediate sense of poetry
as a plurality of responses to differing communities.[22] Central to
many of the discussions is the perception of poetry itself as performance. Frank O'Hara's mock manifesto 'Personism' (1959),
which is often read as an antidote to confessional poetry, challenges that 'Personism, a movement which I recently founded and
which nobody knows about . . . has nothing to do with philosophy,
it's all art', adding 'It puts the poem squarely between the poet
and the person' (p. 354). In a spirit of playfulness, O'Hara poses 'I
don't even like rhythm, assonance, all that stuff. You just have to
go on your nerve' (p. 353). Gary Snyder's interests in Buddhism,
the environment and anthropology would later inform ecocritical
movements and studies in ethnopoetics. Amiri Baraka's explo-
sive 'State/meant' (1965) written as a radical gesture during the
emergence of Black Power and Black pride in the mid-sixties,

forces us to consider poetry as militant action. Moreover, Baraka's 'Expressive Language' (1963) introduces ideas of colonialism and slavery to a discussion of the wresting of power in poetic language. He articulates the need for poetry to assert racial difference through forms that challenge tradition. Baraka chillingly asserts that 'being told to "speak proper"' means that 'you become fluent with the jargon of power' (p. 377). We could add to these Allen Ginsberg's visionary poetics, his meditations on sexuality and a queering of poetic expectation in 'Prose Contribution to Cuban Revolution' (1961):

> Meanwhile for a sense of the rightness of life I trusted people most, that is Friendship & the recognition of the light in people's eyes; and from then on I pursued & idealized friendship especially in Poesy which was the manifestation of this light of friendship secret in all man, open in some few. (p. 336)

Allen's anthology presents a compendium of influential approaches to configuring the poetics of a new American poetry. Reading the anthology half a century later, one is aware how the poetic essay and manifesto raise crucial ideas regarding the responsiveness of poetry to configurations of race, performance, sexuality and gender.

BLOOD, BREAD AND POETRY: GENDER AND POETICS

In her cornerstone essay on gender and poetry 'Blood, Bread and Poetry' (1979) Adrienne Rich reflects upon the momentum of the 1960s as releasing a revolutionary ambition:

> The idea of freedom – so much invoked during World War II – had become pretty abstract politically in the fifties. Freedom – then as now – was supposed to be what Western democracies believe in, and the Iron Curtain Soviet bloc was deprived of. The Existentialist philosophers who were beginning to be read and discussed among young intellectuals spoke of freedom as something connected with revolt.[23]

The search for the direct representation of women's experiences through literary production was a key motivation to Rich's poetic evolution. In this context a new poetic was the immediate address of the drive towards political, financial and social equality for women. Rich comments that 'To write directly and overtly as a woman, out of a woman's body and experience, to take women's existence seriously as a theme and source for art, was something I had been hungering to do . . . all my writing life' (p. 535). But this acknowledgement of a poetic programme was not an easy encounter since she admits: 'It placed me nakedly face-to-face with both terror and anger; it did indeed imply the breakdown of the world as I had always known it, the end of safety' (p. 535). We witness this evolutionary movement in Rich's own poetry which abandons the earlier, more constraining formality of tone, to a direct address of women's daily experience. The brutal admonitions of Rich's poem from *Leaflets* (1969) entitled '5:30 A.M.' are evident. In this poem the speaker describes 'Birds and periodic blood' and a pharmaceutical industry which manipulates a collective 'us' with 'pills for bleeding, pills for panic', to which she urges 'wash them down the sink'.[24] Rich's slightly later volume *The Will to Change* (1971) includes similar poems of protest against war, and the abuse of human and women's rights. Her poetry also brings to light women's histories, which can be seen as a part of a recuperative project of affirming and celebrating women's narratives within history. 'Planetarium' is dedicated to Caroline Herschel (the sister of the astronomer William Herschel), who was credited with the discovery of eight comets. In this poem Rich makes a direct comparison between the representation of constellations as mythic monsters – 'a monster in the shape of a woman / the skies are full of them' (p. 114) – and the figure of the female astrologer as a medium for receiving 'heartbeat of the pulsar' as well as 'encountering the NOVA' (p. 115). In effect Catherine is presented as the receptor of transmissions, she is 'an instrument in the shape / of a woman trying to translate pulsations' (p. 116). Rich's recuperative project would be followed by diverse poets such as American Susan Howe's excavations of literary texts and documents, Irish poet Eavan Boland's exploration of politics and violence, and Jamaican Jean 'Binta' Breeze's combination of orality and performance to represent women's everyday experiences in dub poetics. As Rich reflects in 'Blood, Bread and Poetry', 'Women have understood that we needed an art of our own: to remind us of our history' (p. 536).

MULTIFORMALISMS: FORM AND CONTEMPORARY POETRY

Charles Olson in his celebrated essay 'Projective Verse' (1950) claimed that 'FORM IS NEVER MORE THAN AN EXTENSION OF CONTENT'. Olson argued for an open poetics, what he famously termed as 'composition by field', as a challenge to predetermined form and composition. Reading recent poetry, Olson's essay has a surprising resonance, particularly his insistence upon musicality and what he termed *kinetics* (or a form of poetic energy) as a guiding principle to poetic form. While contemporary poets might engage with open propositions of form guided by the liberties of free verse, it would be a mistake to consider contemporary poetry as 'formless'. The frequent analogies between poetry and musicality made over the past decades by poets such as Bernstein, Linton Kwesi Johnson, Baraka and Kate Fagan suggest that the alliterative, onomatopoeic and material possibilities of language remain central to contemporary composition. Although far from the 'call to order' through craft, measure and rhyme exhibited in Conquest's *New Lines*, numerous contemporary poets find formal constraints as a way of exploration and paradoxically enabling variation in their writing. An evident example in this study is Hejinian's use of numerical rules for her evolving poetic prose autobiography *My Life* (1980). Written at age thirty-seven, the autobiography included thirty-seven sections each with thirty-seven sentences. On its republishing at age forty-five, eight new sections were added and eight sentences added in each of the existing sections, as Hejinian considered it a generative and ongoing work. Many of the poets I examine in this book are engaged in an exploration of the longer poetic work (or sequence), which depends upon anaphoric structures for development and structure – poets as diverse as Michael Palmer, Gwyneth Lewis, John Kinsella, Geoffrey Hill and Juliana Spahr.

It is important to note, however, that contemporary poets use established forms as a guide, such as the villanelle, epic poem with its terza rima and sonnet structures. Annie Finch and Susan M. Schultz's edited collection of essays *Multiformalisms: Postmodern Poetics of Form* revises any alignment of formalism with a return to didactic structures.[25] According to Finch, 'poetic formalism is now much more widely recognized as an infinitely complex set of poetic possibilities than it was ten years ago, and younger critics and scholars are increasingly realizing the numerous theoretical possibilities for addressing poetry in form' (p. 11). Finch's aim is to redeem the idea of that formalism no longer perceived as anachronistic, or hopelessly out of touch with contemporary life. She hopes that 'Another truism this book may shake up is the idea that formal poetry has an inherent connection with rational or discursive kinds of discourse' (p. 12). Finch questions whether 'the subversion of syntax is the only way to foreground and complicate poetic language? Recent work . . . shows that metrical poetry can easily coexist along with the subversion of grammatical and syntactical conventions' (pp. 12–13). In contrast, Schultz's focus is on the relationship between form and politics and race. Pertinently she poses: 'How must considerations of form in contemporary poetry be adjusted to look at the work by minority writers, whose relationship with the tradition [aka the Western tradition], is more fraught with peril than that of majority writers?' (p. 15).

The most stunning example of a contemporary poet's engagement with formal structure must be Caribbean poet Derek Walcott's epic *Omeros* (1990). Michael Schmidt has declared that for Walcott:

Herrick and Herbert belong to him as much as they belong to Larkin . . . To hear Walcott (on the page) can make it possible for a poet in St Lucia, Auckland, Delhi or Vancouver to hear his or her language more precisely.[26]

Divided into seven books, the epic adventure of Homer's *Iliad* and *Odyssey* was refigured by Walcott by also drawing on Renaissance poetry and setting the volume in modern St Lucia. The title itself is the Greek for Homer. However, Walcott retains the epic format of terza rima, a three-lined interlinked stanza sequence where the second line of each stanza rhymes with the first and third of the next. This refiguration of form is central to what Schmidt considers to be the dispersal of an English tradition and its adaption on a global level: 'Unboundaried experiences of this kind are part of the vigour of a literature which in despite of geography, remains English. To insist on continuity is not to suggest identity: on the contrary, it is to discover the *value* in difference.'[27]

An early section of *Omeros* illustrates how Walcott refigures the epic structure into a Caribbean context. In Book 1, Chapter IV the third section grants us the perspective of the poet/narrator on St Lucia as he encounters the young woman Helen whose attentions become the focus of a rivalry between two men, Achille and Hector. The poet sits waiting for 'a cheque / Our waiter, in a black bow-tie, plunged through the sand / between the full deck-chairs, bouncing to discotheque'.[28] Deftly Walcott places the contemporary scene of a nightclub into the seemingly incongruous restraint of three-lined verse. Playfully he draws attention to the waiter as 'Lawrence of St Lucia' who is 'Like any born loser' (p. 23). Crucially, Walcott superimposes the contemporary scene upon a landscape which evokes the Greek narrative of Helen of Troy, describing the emergence of 'a beauty / that left, like a ship, widening eyes in its wake' (p. 24). When questioned the waitress responds '"She? She too proud!"' adding with a sneer '"Helen"' and all the rest followed (p. 24). Even this brief excursion into *Omeros* illustrates how Walcott strategically uses terza rima to frame his epic narrative. In turn this formal device enables a degree of tension between the modern and the classical, creating a work of considerable hybridity. Unsurprisingly, in an early interview Walcott described conflicts and contradictions as central to his biography: 'I was a knot of paradoxes: hating the Church and loving her rituals, learning to hate England as I worshipped her language . . . a Methodist-lecher, a near Catholic-ascetic, loving the island, and wishing I could get the hell out of it.'[29]

A further example of the engagement in contemporary poetry with established forms is made evident in *The Reality Book of Sonnets*.[30] The anthology showcases a range of eighty-three contemporary poets' experimental engagement with the sonnet from the USA, UK, New Zealand, Ireland, Canada and Australia. When one considers that 'stanza' can also mean room, Beverly Dahlen's admission that the sonnet is 'a kind of padded cell in which I go mad' (p. 12) seems particularly apt. This anthology is not promoting neo-formalism but rather the rupturing and interrogation of the sonnet's form. Various engagements with an 'opening' of the sonnet include found work, excerpts from extended sequences, the breaking down of lyric enunciation, concrete poetry, visual punning, collage, homophonic translation, process writing and the arrangement of what could be called 'baggy' quotidian sonnets.

One of the major poets renowned for the rewriting of the sonnet was Ted Berrigan. Part collage, part process writing and lyrical evocation, Berrigan's *Sonnets* (1964) show how lines of apparent non sequiturs can be constantly rearranged to alter a context of interpretation. Berrigan's emphasis on the line as a unit of composition creates some surprisingly charged adaptations. Take for example an excerpt from Sonnet XV: 'The black heart beside the fifteen pieces / Monroe died. So I went to a matinee B-Movie' (p. 43), which becomes in Sonnet LIX 'Today / I am truly horribly upset because Marilyn / Monroe died, so I went to a matinee B movie and Ate King Kong popcorn' (p. 43). Berrigan is playfully emphatic on the rights of the sonnet. In Sonnet XV he adds 'Doctor but they say "I LOVE YOU" / and the sonnet is not dead' (p. 43). Similarly, Juliana Spahr's *Power Sonnets* (2000) arrange 'found' web material, such as 'After Bill Clinton: Press Briefing and Press Release, White House Website April 2000', which examines the relationship between education, web access and race. Maurice Scully's delightful 'Sonnet' from *Sonata* (2006) performs writing in the space of 'my little pop-up book of knowledge' (p. 205).

Geraldine Monk's *Ghost & Other Sonnets* (2008) are lyrically dense, sonorous and often captivating; there is a sense of condensation in her final rhyming couplets, which are sustained throughout the volume.[31] Take, for example, the following: 'All at sea once more / Maroon will never be the new black' (p. 47), 'Barnacle Geese reclassified as fish or fruit / Eaten under the subterfuge of natural language' (p. 57) and 'Aside from this we kiss the / Doldrums upping entropy to bliss' (p. 31). American poet Laynie Browne revisits the potential of the sonnet to inscribe the mundanity of daily life in her collection *Daily Sonnets* (2007).[32] In Browne's words, her 150 poems approach 'all mental states, traps, games and assemblages . . . My sonnets are an approachable unruly gathering. What the poems have in common is that they practice permeability' (p. 158). As a busy mother of two, the warping of the fourteen-lined cell provides liberation in the mapping out of duration and the everyday. Her titles alone suggest this fracturing of the sonnet form: 'Half Sonnet +1', 'Two fourteenths Sonnet', and 'After-Shower Sonnet'. The world of the kindergarten humorously informs the making of the poetry, as with the mode of questioning in Sonnet 25: 'Why do I require these sudden / Tablets of concentration / She made poetry sound like a playdate / Squeezing her wrought hands' (p. 25). Brown offers a comic translation of Shakespeare's Sonnet 116, in which 'Let me not to the marriage of true minds' becomes a refracted and sonorous equivocation: 'Let me not to the marrow of truant minds / Admit the impenetrable. Lozenge is no lounge / Which alternates when it altercation finds' (p. 119). Browne adds in her afterward to the book that 'I think of the modern sonnet as an increment of time within a frame. Something that often physically fits into a little rectangle (but not in thought) . . . this book is an invitation' (p. 159). Far from extolling the sonnet form as a display of technical virtuosity, Browne emphasises the responsiveness of form to the pressures of daily life. Her volume illustrates how contemporary versions of the sonnet enable surprising freedoms of expression and performance.

STRUCTURE OF THE BOOK

Jahan Ramazani highlights 'The spread of English worldwide to its use by nearly a third of the world's population' and he crucially reminds his readers that this dissemination is 'rooted in the might of the British Empire and has been perpetuated by the military and economic power of the United States'.[33] Considering the future of English literary studies, Ramazani proposes:

> Literary criticism on English and other imperial-language literatures must co-exist with studies of writing in local and

regional languages of the global South. Even so, one way to complicate an imperial 'Anglophony' from within criticism of English-language poetry is to explore the multiplicity of Englishes in which poetry is written, some of which, such as the Jamaican Creole of Claude McKay, Louise Bennett and Linton Kwesi Johnson, was once seen as unworthy of poetry. Another is to widen the geographic scope of Anglophone poetry studies so that poems from the United States, Britain and Ireland are read alongside poetries from English-speaking dominions, territories and ex-colonies. (p. 19)

Ramazani's study moves the contemporary critic away from tightly defined and contained definitions of national literatures and promotes instead the adaptation of English across countries and cultures. This book in turn attempts to illustrate how the dissemination of English has produced an expansive practice of Anglophone poetries. A decision was made early in the project to divide the range of poetries thematically, as opposed to discrete national identifications. To this aim, the *Edinburgh Critical Guide to Contemporary Poetry* seeks to enact conversations between poetries which would not customarily be read in tandem, and to dismantle too often rigid dichotomies between so-called 'mainstream' and 'experimental' poetries.

While I do not hold completely with Ramazani's opening position in his *Transnational Poetries* that 'Poetry is more often seen as local, regional or stubbornly national' (p. 3), I do find myself receptive to his description of cross-fertilisation between different poetries as creating an energising force field:

Because poetic compression demands that discrepant idioms and soundscapes, tropes and subgenres be forces together with intensity, poetry – pressured and fractured by this convergence – allows us to examine at close hand how global modernity's cross-cultural vectors sometimes fuse, sometimes vertiginously counterpoint one another. (p. 4)

Yet I am far from suggesting that contemporary poets have taken one global aesthetic path into pluralism. Bruce Robbins pertinently reminds us that identifying oneself as part of a 'global feeling' is not necessarily at the expense of national identifications.[34] He proposes that 'forms of global feeling are continuous with forms of national feeling', adding that although:

Potential for a conflict of loyalties is always present, cosmopolitanism or internationalism does not take its primary meaning or desirability from an absolute and intrinsic opposition to nationalism. Rather it is an extension outward of the same sorts of potent and dangerous solidarity. (p. 15)

Opening with 'Subjectivities', the first chapter considers the representation of the personal in the work of recent poets and how the everyday can become part of a poetic composition. I consider initially a theory of lyric expression in the elegies of Andrew Motion and Lee Harwood. The representation of women's biography is fundamental to the work of Grace Nichols and Cathy Song, which develops to an analysis of 'self-reflexive' lyricism in the portraiture poetry of John Ashbery, Sujata Bhatt and Jorie Graham. Concentrating on the poetry of Michael Palmer and Jennifer Moxley, the discussion considers what happens to the individual speaking voice or lyric 'I' when the self is displaced from a centre stage and an experience of language takes its place.

Tackling the tricky proposition of poetry and politics, Chapter 2 investigates poetry's relationship to commentary on war and terrorism through the poetry of Northern Ireland (Seamus Heaney, Derek Mahon and Paul Muldoon). The chapter also consider the reports of the Iraq war by Eliot Weinberger and Charles Bernstein, as well as Choman Hardi's account of the Iraqi genocide or *Anfal* in Kurdistan, and Yusef Komunyakaa's experience as a Vietnam veteran. Central to this chapter is a worry about creating poetry which may read as rhetoric. A section is given to the presidential inauguration poetry of Maya Angelou and Elizabeth Alexander. The chapter also considers how politics can be examined through a certain textuality, a process which could be thought of as no longer writing 'about' politics but 'with' them. This proposition is of particular relevance to my comparative reading of M. NourbeSe Philip's account of slave trading, which is compared to historical excavation by Rita Dove of accounts of mass murder in the Dominican Republic.

Much critical attention of late has been given to the relationship between poetry and theories of performance. Chapter 3 initially considers the proposition of a 'projective' poetry – as a performance both on and off the page – in the work of Amiri Baraka's jazz poetic, Lawrence Ferlinghetti's declamatory style and Mutabaruka, Linton Kwesi Johnson and Benjamin Zephaniah's versions of a 'dub' poetic. Paul Durcan and Don Paterson's poetry offers the proposition of the poet as performer. Theoretically the chapter engages with a proposition of 'performativity' in Hejinian's poetry as well as a phenomenological performance in Kate Fagan's work. Closing with Caroline Bergvall, the chapter examines the definition of multimedia work often referred to as 'performance writing'.

Ideas of space and environment form the basis for the fourth chapter, which examines how poetry represents the environment. Propositions of environmental thinking – such as ecocriticism, ecological writing and ecopoetics – guide in different ways Gary Snyder, Juliana Spahr and John Kinsella's poetry. Through an interrogation of ideas of place, the chapter analyses the poetry of Robert Hass, Anne Szumigalski and Geoffrey Hill. While place and environment might initially trigger reflections upon regional landscapes, the discussion also provides readings of the cityscape in the poetry of Edwin Morgan, Kathleen Jamie and Paula Meehan. The relationship of the regional to the global is central in Robert Minhinnick and Lorna Goodison's poetry, while the disorienting psychogeographical spaces of Iain Sinclair's work provide an alternative way of mapping the modern metropolis.

My final chapter 'Dialects, Idiolects and Multilingual Poetries' explores how contemporary poetry addresses the development of English as a global language. Beginning with the more immediate use of dialect in Tony Harrison's poetry, the discussion examines linguistic hierarchies and regional and national identification, and how these are confronted in Tom Leonard and Jackie Kay's poems. Introducing ideas of an 'ethnopoetics', Simon Ortiz and Joy Harjo's native poetries provide a further perspective on the imperial dissemination of English. Bilingualism, translation and interlingualism form key considerations in Gwyneth Lewis, Li-Young Lee and Lorna Dee Cervantes's poetry. In closing, Tusiata Avia and Daljit Nagra's poetry shows how the poetic text can become a space for linguistic cross-fertilization and the exploration of idiomatic texture. Poet-practitioners greeted the emergence of the Internet with considerable optimism, and my conclusion offers a reading of the impact of multimedia and web technologies upon poetic language and form. For poets such as John Cayley, the possibilities of technology are celebrated as a site for visual and textual experimentation, otherwise known as 'electronic writing'. Other poets consider the Internet as tool of poetic composition and chance operations such as 'Flarf' poetry. Evidently the Internet offers a role in the dissemination of poetic material as well as the awareness of breaking news material instantly, which proves crucial to the work of labour activist and poet Mark Nowak. I close on a consideration of what this may mean for the potency of a poetry that aims towards political activism and communal engagement.

Invariably there are omissions in this project; the field of Anglophone poetics is a vast one, yet I would hope that the book grants a cross-section of recent developments, practices and future concerns. To this end this volume provides a snapshot of what Schmidt gestures to as: 'the enabling continuities, the elements both of specific difference and of commonality, the "vulgar tongue" which individuals refine according to their light, but also according to its own blazing lights'.[35]

NOTES

1. Juliana Spahr, *American Poets in the 21st Century*, ed. Claudia Rankine and Lisa Sewell (Middletown, CT: Wesleyan University Press, 2007), p. 131.
2. Lyn Hejinian, 'If Written is Writing', *The L=A=N=G=U=A=G=E Book*, ed. Bruce Andrews and Charles Bernstein (Carbondale: Southern Illinois Press, 1984), p. 29.
3. Ezra Pound, *Make it New: Essays* (New Haven, CT: Yale University Press, 1935).

4. Viktor Schklovsky, 'Art as Technique', *Russian Formalist Criticism: Four Essays*, trans. Lee T. Lemon and Marion J. Reis (Lincoln, NE and London: University of Nebraska Press, 1965), pp. 3–24.

5. Robert Conquest, *New Lines* (London: Macmillan, 1956), Al Alvarez, *The New Poetry* (Harmondsworth: Penguin, 1962), Donald Allen, *The New American Poetry* (New York: Grove Press, 1960), Michael Schmidt, *New Poetries* (Manchester: Carcanet, 1992), Michael Hulse, David Kennedy and David Morley's *The New Poetry* (Newcastle: Bloodaxe, 1993) and Claudia Rankine and Lisa Sewell's *American Poets in the 21st Century: The New Poetics* (Middletown, CT: Wesleyan University Press, 2007).

6. Gertrude Stein, 'Composition as Explanation', *A Stein Reader*, ed. Ulla E. Dydo (Evanston, IL: Northwestern University Press, 1993), p. 501.

7. Stein, 'Composition as Explanation', p. 501.

8. Ron Silliman, 'Of Theory to Practice', in *The New Sentence* (New York: Roof Books, 2003), pp. 58–62 (p. 60).

9. Silliman, 'Of Theory to Practice', p. 60.

10. Jerome McGann, *The Point is to Change It* (Tuscaloosa: University of Alabama Press, 2007), p. xi.

11. Alex Preminger and T. V. F. Brogan (eds), *The New Princeton Encyclopedia of Poetry and Poetics* (Princeton, NJ: Princeton University Press, 1993), p. 930.

12. Ibid.

13. Lyn Hejinian, *The Language of Inquiry* (Berkeley: University of California Press, 2000), p. 356.

14. Juliana Spahr and Joshua Clover, 'Leave the Manifesto Alone: A Manifesto', *Poetry*, 193.5 (2009), 452.

15. Romana Huk, 'A New Global Poetics', *Literature Compass*, 6.3 (2009), 758–84 (p. 760).

16. Rey Chow, 'The Old/New Question of Comparison in Literary Studies: A Post European Perspective', *English Literary History*, 71.2 (2004), 289–311 (p. 290).

17. Peter Finch, 'British Poetry Since 1945: A View from 2001' in *The Continuum Encyclopaedia of British Literature*. Available online at www.peterfinch.co.uk/enc.htm.

18. Alvarez, *The New Poetry*, p. 25.
19. John Berryman, 'Dream Song 14', in *Selected Poems 1938–1968* (London: Faber & Faber, 1977), p. 73.
20. Al Alvarez, *The Writer's Voice* (London: Bloomsbury, 2005), p. 17.
21. Donald Allen (ed.), *The New American Poetry Revised* (New York: Grove Press, 1982), p. 9.
22. Donald Allen and Warren Tallman (eds), *The Poetics of the New American Poetry* (New York: Grove Press, 1973).
23. Adrienne Rich, 'Blood, Bread and Poetry: The Location of the Poet', *Massachusetts Review*, 24.3 (1983), 521–40 (p. 535). Originally given as a lecture in 1979.
24. Adrienne Rich, *The Fact of a Doorframe: Poems Selected and New 1950–1984* (New York: Norton & Norton, 1984), p. 91. All subsequent references to this edition are given in the text.
25. Annie Finch and Susan M. Schultz (eds), *Multiformalisms: Postmodern Poetics of Form* (Cincinnati: WordTech Communications, 2008).
26. Schmidt, *New Poetries*, p. 9.
27. Schmidt, *New Poetries*, pp. 9–10.
28. Derek Walcott, *Omeros* (London: Faber & Faber, 1990), p. 23. All subsequent references to this edition are given in the text.
29. Derek Walcott, 'Leaving School', in *Hinterland: Caribbean Poetry from the West Indies and Britain*, ed. E. A. Markham (Newcastle: Bloodaxe, 1989), p. 93.
30. Jeff Hilson (ed.), *The Reality Book of Sonnets* (Hastings: Reality Street Editions, 2008).
31. Geraldine Monk, *Ghost & Other Sonnets* (Cambridge: Salt, 2008).
32. Laynie Browne, *Daily Sonnets* (Denver, CO: Counterpath, 2008).
33. Jahan Ramazani, *A Transnational Poetics* (Chicago: Chicago University Press, 2009), p. 19.
34. Bruce Robbins, *Feeling Global: Internationalism in Distress* (New York: New York University Press, 1999), p. 15.
35. Schmidt, *New Poetries*, p. 11.

CHAPTER I

Lyric Subjects

In the essay 'Tradition and the Individual Talent' T. S. Eliot famously declares that 'Poetry is not a turning loose of emotion, but an escape from emotion; it is not the expression of personality, but an escape from personality.'[1] Eliot also adds playfully: 'But, of course, only those who have personality and emotions know what it means to want to escape from these things' (p. 21). It might seem curious to open this chapter with Eliot's essay of 1919, but his highlighting of poetry as work that is created and formed, as opposed to spontaneously expressed, draws important attention to how we think about poetry. Discussions of poetry often draw attention to the articulation of the poet's voice, poetry as an expression of personal sentiment or the poem as the recollection of events. While Eliot's claims for poetry are arguably based on an attempt to secure the legacy of his work, the distinctions between control, craft and the spontaneous expression of personality lead to some useful questions when approaching the work of contemporary poets. One might ask, how do recent poets approach the personal in their work? How can everyday experience make for poetic material? To what extent do contemporary forms offer a challenge to our perceived notions of voice in poetry? How does recent poetry negotiate ideas of memory and recollection? Moreover, what happens to the individual speaking voice, or lyric 'I', when the self is displaced from centre stage and an experience of language takes its place?

Al Alvarez in his retrospective account of post-war poetries
The Writer's Voice (2006) identifies a key moment in the history of
American poetry. He recalls a reading by Allen Ginsberg at SUNY
Buffalo in 1966. Ginsberg's notorious opening to his early poem
'Howl' – 'I saw the best minds of my generation destroyed by
madness, starving hysterical naked, / dragging themselves through
the negro streets at dawn looking for an angry fix' – generates
expectations of countercultural critique, musicality and performance.[2] However, Alvarez's comments on Ginsberg's reading indicate a discomfort regarding the poet as prophetic voice:

> I now understand what I was witnessing that evening in
> Buffalo was something new and strange: the transformation
> of poetry into showbiz . . . Poets were private people and
> reading their work was still a private pleasure . . . Ginsberg
> changed all that by sheer force of personality. Or rather by
> using verse as a vehicle of showmanship, he helped turn a
> minority art into a form of popular entertainment based on
> the cult of personality.[3]

Echoing Eliot's critique of personality, Alvarez points us towards a
central and basic conundrum of recent poetry: in order to address
its audience compellingly, does the contemporary poem always
necessitate extremity of emotion and personality? Writing over two
hundred years ago William Wordsworth and Samuel Coleridge
claimed in their introduction to *Lyrical Ballads* (1798) that:

> Poetry is the spontaneous overflow of powerful feelings: it
> takes its origin from emotion recollected in tranquillity: the
> emotion is contemplated till by a species of reaction the tran-
> quillity gradually disappears, and an emotion, kindred to that
> which was before the subject of contemplation, is gradually
> produced, and does itself actually exist in the mind.[4]

Following this Romantic precedent in considering the poets
from the United Kingdom, USA, Jamaica and India, we will contemplate how the personal lyric in contemporary poetry conveys
subjective states of mind and how the personal poem adapts its

address. It is important to consider what happens to the poem when subjectivity is no longer represented as a stable voice. This destabilising of voice and persona in the poem is what the American poet Lyn Hejinian proposes as subjectivity that is less a fixed entity than 'a mobile (and mobilized) reference point'.[5]

TOWARDS A THEORY OF LYRIC EXPRESSION

The lyric or personal poem is often considered as expressive, and the 'expressive' lyric posits the self as the primary organising principle of the work. Central to this model is the articulation of the subject's feelings and desires, and a strongly marked division between subjectivity and its articulation as expression. M. H. Abrams identifies an expressive theory of the lyric poem as the internal made external:

> A work of art is essentially the internal made external, resulting from a creative process operating under the impulse of feeling, and embodying a combined product of the poet's perceptions, thoughts, and feelings. The primary source and subject matter of a poem therefore, are the actions and attributes of the poet's own mind . . . The first test any poem must pass is no longer, 'Is it true to nature?' or 'Is it appropriate to the requirements either of the best judges or the generality of mankind?' but a criterion looking in a different direction; namely 'Is it sincere? Is it genuine?'[6]

Although Abrams has in mind primarily the poetry of the nineteenth century, this model resonates as a general impulse in poetry from the twentieth and twenty-first centuries, especially in its evocation of sincerity and authenticity. The symbolic use of the external world as a psychic landscape for the subject's state of mind is one we are familiar with, even in Eliot's proposal of the objective correlative: 'in other words, a set of objects, a situation, a chain of events which shall be the formula of that *particular* emotion; such that when the external facts, which must terminate in sensory experience, are given, the emotion is immediately evoked'.[7]

Critic Charles Altieri identifies the dominant model of the 1970s as the 'scenic mode', and suggests that this model of the lyric poem is firmly rooted in the extension of a romantic ideology.[8] The impetus of the work is towards an expression of an inchoate interiority and the poem in his words:

> Places a reticent, plain-speaking and self-reflective speaker within a narratively presented scene evoking a sense of loss. Then the poet tries to resolve the loss in a moment of emotional poignance, or wry acceptance, that renders the entire lyric event an evocative metaphor for some general sense of mystery about the human condition. (p. 10)

This impetus towards description and expression is characterised by the poet Robert Pinsky as 'discursive writing'.[9] Pinsky states that the discursive lyric presents 'the poet talking, predicating, moving directly and as systematically and unaffectedly as he would walk from one place to another' (p. 133). Broadly speaking, both these models of an 'expressive lyric' posit the self as the primary organising principle of the work. Central to this tendency is the articulation of the subject's feelings and desires, and a strongly marked division between subjectivity and its articulation as expression. This focus on expression is frequently evoked with reference to the speaker's voice and a suggestion of a certain 'sincerity' and 'authenticity'. What is most apparent in the expressive model of the lyric poem is the immanence of the self, its centrality within the composition as the subject of the writing, and the role of language as a transparent medium for communicating intense emotion.

ELEGY AND EPISTLE: ANDREW MOTION AND LEE HARWOOD

An early poem, 'Anniversaries' by Andrew Motion, written before he became Poet Laureate in 1999, illustrates how an expressive model of the lyric addresses and represents intense emotions of bereavement.[10] Motion's lyric sequence of tightly constructed four-lined stanzas in five sections acts as an elegy, a reminder and marker of loss, and also an attempt to recompose the past. The five sections that comprise the sequence mark time in a circuit: we start with the fourth anniversary, move to the first then the second and third to conclude with a fourth anniversary once more. Looking closely at 'Anniversaries', it becomes clear that the poem through these acts of reflection seeks to work through ideas of trauma and grief. Motion's poem points us significantly to his biography. 'Anniversaries' chronicles his mother's riding accident and subsequent years of being in a coma. But the opening stanzas do not point to this directly; instead what one is presented with is a sense of continuation and repetition set in a snowscape: 'I have it by heart now / on this day in each year' (p. 6). Words such as 'lost', 'waiting', 'setting' reinforce the sense of a ritual which accompanies the bedside vigil.

The five sections enact a conversation with the absent mother. In this way the poem functions similarly to Pinsky's suggestion of a discursive lyric, the speaker's voice in its personal reflection indicates private meditations overheard. Motion's emphatic repetition of the lyric 'I' in the second section – 'What I remember', 'I watched', 'I am still there' (p. 7) – indicates not only the attempts of recollection, but also an implication of solitude, as though the subjective is literally rooted to the spot. Motion also makes use of nature as a psychic landscape where sentiment is superimposed upon his surroundings. We are told that while waiting for his mother's return the tap 'thaws' (p. 7) then hardens to ice. These small observations also bear witness to the marking of time. The impression of a solitary individual alone in a hostile environment is enforced when the horse returns to the farm. The reins trailing behind mark a pattern, 'a trail across the plough / a blurred riddle of scars' (p. 7). This image of premonition superimposes the trails in the snow and a cosmic sky as Motion plays on 'the plough' as constellation and the sonic suggestion of 'scars' as possible stars. As the sequence unfolds the speaker attempts to deconstruct the loss of a parent. The second, third and fourth anniversaries commit themselves to understanding the 'blurred riddle' (p. 7) of amnesia and stillness. He witnesses his father's attempt to engage with his mother: 'If you can hear me now squeeze my hand' (p. 8). Empathetically Motion sets the bedside rituals in correspondence with the natural world since in the third anniversary his mother is described as having a 'shadow of clouds' (p. 8) upon her face. More terrifying for the speaker is the moment when the mother momentarily awakens and speaks, only to retreat to an imposed stillness with a look that refuses 'to recognise my own' (p. 9). Motion's poem can be read as a form of arrested elegy, it marks the attempts of a plain-speaking voice to understand the death-like trance and suspension of his mother's life. Moreover, the form of the poem, its division into neat four-lined stanzas and sections denoting each year, attempts to grant form and order to experience through narrative. Throughout Motion's poem personal events are communicated and expressed through the intimacy of a single speaking voice.

English poet Lee Harwood offers a further response to expressing bereavement through the poetic elegy. Unlike Motion, Harwood's poem is less assured of the viability of its task. Harwood's work questions whether poetry can mediate his experience and recollections. The poem enacts a form of 'doubting' elegy as he searches for a discursive form which can enact a conversation with the person lost. Harwood is moreover suspicious of committing immediate experience into poetic form, and alert to the dangers of inscribing too much of his own persona at the expense of the person he is grieving. The title of Harwood's elegy is disarming and self-explanatory: 'African violets for Pansy Harwood my grandmother 1896–1989'.[11] But the opening lines disrupt any sense of static backdrop to the elegy; we are plunged into a world of motion and attempts to create shape and form. The poem describes the movement of flags on 'silver pyramids', purple flowers that 'present themselves to the air' and the straining of a composition as Chopin 'fights his way' into music (p. 432). This spatial disorientation is echoed by Harwood's attempt to organise his recollections around hospital visits, childhood memories and processes of making art. Threads of phrases and conversation intervene, such as snippets like 'A real heartbreaker' and ' "That was a bit unnecessary son" ' (p. 432). These intrusions succeed in demolishing any illusion of control that one may associate with the unitary voice. Rather than the distinct chronicle of time exhibited in Motion's 'Anniversaries', the speaker in Harwood's elegy admits that for him '(the tense continually shifts, past and present blur)' (p. 433). Moreover, Harwood's elegy is filled with anxious rhetorical questions based on ideas of reciprocity, exchange and legacy: 'What did I give you', 'And you gave me?'(p. 432).

At every point in the poem the knowledge of his grandmother's everyday life informs the tumbling array of recollections. The speaker's frustrations at his inability to commit these everyday experiences to the written page are also evident. With rage the speaker taunts his ambition to reduce 'this to yet another poem', savagely dismisses his elegy as 'pages of words creating old routines' that are 'easy with the "truth", turning facts to meet the story' (p. 432). In a tirade against the gentrification of experience and memory he acts by 'systematically' smashing 'all those pretty pictures' since 'they won't do anymore' (p. 432). Indeed the speaker refers to the legacy left by the grandmother as the 'other "stuff"' that 'continues' (p. 433). Whereas for Motion his poem is guided by the ritual of bedside vigils and calendar months, Harwood's poem dramatises the knowledge of ritualised tasks and gestures observed such as pickling onions, bottling fruit, mending shoes; in effect the daily working patterns of 'cooking, making, fixing' (p. 433). In 'African Violets' continuity is created across generations. The speaker notes that: 'I find myself moving as you would / not the same but similar' (p. 432). Harwood's poem jettisons any formal shape which will guide his elegy for fear that it will immobilise his reflections. Instead he attempts through free verse to inscribe the momentum and often unpredicted pattern of a conversation. In 'African Violets' the single speaking voice attempts to 'talk to you again and again / I see you again and again sat there' (p. 433).

SPEAKING (AUTO) BIOGRAPHICALLY: CATHY SONG AND GRACE NICHOLS

Since the late 1960s there has been considerable discussion of what indeed constitutes an author. Critical and continental theory has questioned the omnipotence of the author as one who orchestrates and controls the meaning of any writing produced. Most famously Roland Barthes's essay 'Death of the Author' (1967) and Michel

Foucault's 'What is an Author?' (1968) challenged any determinate meaning to any text. Barthes's later identification of what he termed a 'writerly text' can be understood as 'ourselves writing', whose goal he characterises as a desire 'to make the reader no longer a consumer, but a producer of the text'.[12] This momentum towards reconfiguring the concept of the author as the bastion of all meaning can be traced to a shift in literary criticism from the 1930s that increasingly focused on the literary work as an entity in its own right. Critics such as Jack Stillinger trace the emergence of these concerns from established philosophical debates:

> Literary theorists especially those writing under the influence of Barthes and Foucault (and of those earlier writers like Nietzsche and Freud who influenced Barthes and Foucault), have increasingly treated literary texts and frequently all writing together, as autonomous, separate from any idea of determinate meaning.[13]

The proposition of literary texts as having no final interpretation challenges New Criticism's valorisation of the literary work as the 'well-wrought urn', where meaning and structure coalesce.

What does this mean for the personal lyric? The single-speaking poetic voice is often linked to an impression of intimacy, the speaker in some essence articulating words that seem at once 'overheard' by the reader. The prominence of the personal lyric in the 1970s established an important relationship between intimacy and the examination of biography. For many poets the relationship between biography and cultural legacy and inheritance cannot be differentiated; in effect then the mapping of a life story can become an enquiry into unvoiced personal, family and national histories. Paradoxically perhaps, from the 1960s onward we witness a growth in the production and reception of autobiographical works. The critic Philippe Lejeune describes autobiography as a 'retrospective prose narrative written by a real person conveying his own existence where the focus is his individual life, in particular the story of his personality'.[14] For other critics autobiography is 'an affirmation of individual worth' (p. 140). The 1970s and 1980s mark an affirmation of the personal poem coupled with an examination of autobiography through considerations of race, cultural inheritance, ethnicity and gender. In the USA in particular, the rise to prominence of the personal lyric (often referred to as the 'workshop' lyric) during the 1970s and 1980s is connected to the proliferation of creative writing programmes in the academy. The increasing professionalisation of poetry had its roots in the post-war years, and in the flourishing of New Criticism we can trace the basic premise of the workshop poem as a well-crafted, self-sufficient composition. Moreover, during this time in the USA, identity politics – the categorisation of different groups often according to race, ethnicity, gender and sexual orientation – found a fertile and often recuperative role in contemporary poetry. Essentially identity politics focuses upon the experience of often marginalised communities as enabling possibility for political discussion and action.

Cathy Song is sometimes identified as a Hawaiian, Chinese-American or Korean-American poet. The immediate compendium of distinctive, yet coexisting identities is addressed in her work, as well as the history of the immigrant experience in the USA. Song's narratives are intensely personal, but her poetry also voices a collective immigrant cultural history. The entitling of her first volume *Picture Bride* (1983) emphasises this concern immediately.[15] Critic Gayle K. Fujita-Sato states that:

> Picture brides was a method of arranging marriages used by Japanese and Korean immigrants before the war. Usually a man would ask his parents or relatives to find a prospective bride, and the couple then exchanged photographs of themselves. When marriage was agreed upon, an official ceremony was held in the home country before the woman departed to join her husband. In many cases the picture bride's arrival was the couple's first face-to-face meeting.[16]

Picture Bride maps out spaces for often-unobserved women's activities, such as acts of applying make-up, cooking and sewing. In 'The Seamstress' this sense of invisible tasks or silent histories is made evident through the descriptions of the single-voiced narrator. The seamstress informs us that she works in 'difficult light' with her 'blind fingertips' next to 'an entire wall without windows' (p. 79). Throughout the poem Song pays particular attention to the artisanship and unacknowledged beauty of the seamstress's tools: 'Hands moist and white like lilies / The white-gloved hands of the magician' which move with 'miraculous flight' (p. 79). She also evokes elements from the Western fairy tale since her movement is described as the spider's slow-descending movement 'attached to an invisible thread / I let myself down off the chair' (p. 79). Her body establishes a horrifying verisimilitude with her work; the spine bent over her sewing machine creates the 'silhouette of a coat hanger' (p. 79).

Picture Bride also places a considered focus on mother-and-daughter relationships. In many of the poems this relationship is often framed in antagonistic terms as an older generation dictates the rules of filial practice. 'The Youngest Daughter' frames this relationship through the practised ritual of bathing and food preparation, the 'ritual of tea and rice' and gingered fish (p. 6). The fleshy mother of the poem appears far more visceral than the sickly daughter with her skin as 'damp and pale as rice paper' (p. 5) and the colour of aspirin. Song makes us acutely aware of the distance between the domestic carer duties and the world of outdoor work. Comparing their skin, she notices not only the difference in colour – her mother's is 'parched' in the 'drying sun' (p. 5) of the fields – but also the cartography of blue bruises from the medication of insulin. The speaker describes her mother as fecund with animal-like terminology. Her breasts are 'like two walruses / flaccid and whiskered around the nipples' (p . 5). This intimate portrait also suggests a suffocating distaste as she thinks 'six children and an old man / have sucked from these brown nipples' (p. 5). A sense of confinement generates the youngest daughter's desire to break free from domestic and filial responsibilities. The speaker admits that her mother knows she is 'not to be trusted' and is 'even now planning my escape' (p. 6). The final stanza's focus upon ideas of release, travel and even migration is echoed when the motif of a thousand cranes patterning the curtain 'fly up in a sudden breeze' (p. 6).

The five sections of *Picture Bride* are named after the American painter Georgia O'Keeffe's flower paintings: 'Black Iris', 'Sunflowers', 'Orchids', 'Red Poppy' and 'The White Trumpet

Flower'. Song's deliberate evocation of American art as a framing device for the book serves to make a sustained link with the USA. Importantly the volume interrogates the nation of the hyphenated identity 'Asian-American'. In this poem the identification of China as a cultural code which enables the female immigrant to establish a sense of selfhood and community, is juxtaposed with a legacy of Chinese history that rendered women without agency or power. In 'Lost Sister' the problem of identification becomes key: how does one retain a sense of cultural cohesiveness and sustain integration into a new country? Throughout the poem, cultural routines grant the female immigrant the necessary tools to create and affirm her identification. A litany of products and cultural references – from Mah-Jong tiles and firecrackers to jade and crickets – litter the poem. 'Lost Sister' parallels the historical lives of Chinese women who remain in China and those who migrate to the USA.

As with 'Youngest Daughter', 'Lost Sister' invariably presents the ideal of migration as a possibility of escape and rebellion. Divided into two sections, it presents us with women who are both subservient and resourceful. For them 'to move was a luxury / stolen from them at birth' (p. 52). Space and time are restricted into an image of painful and minute physical study as the women learn 'to walk in shoes / the size of teacups / without breaking / the arc of their movements' (p. 52). By contrast the lost sister rises 'with a tide of locusts' (p. 52) in the Chinese diaspora to the Pacific shore. Song deftly utilises the association of the grasshopper in the poem as a Chinese symbol of good luck and abundance, associated only with forward movement. Yet the poem keenly draws attention to the complexities and failures of cultural translation that are part of the experience of migration. Echoing images of miscegenation, the sister not only changes her name, but dilutes 'jade green with the blue of the Pacific' (p. 52). A sense of extreme cultural dislocation is emphasised in the second section which stresses the movement to a cityscape of 'dough-faced' (p. 52) landlords, cramped accommodation, laundry lines and restaurants. In this urban environment the necessity of cultural identification is represented also as a restrictive chain, China becomes the symbolic 'jade link handcuffed to your wrist' (p. 52). Like the other women of the opening section the poem indicates that the lost sister, as her mother, will leave 'no footprint' (p. 53), no major historical testimony of her life. But Song suggests that the extensive passage travelled over the Pacific is proof enough of 'the unremitting space of your rebellion' (p. 53). As a whole *Picture Bride* enables a space where biographies erased by the major narratives of history can be granted articulation and expression.

Grace Nichols's *The Fat Black Woman's Poems* (1984) also details an experience of migration.[17] Nichols states that the volume came initially 'out of a sheer sense of fun, of having the fat black woman doing exactly as she pleases . . . taking a satirical, tongue-in-cheek look at the world'.[18] Born originally in Guyana, Nichols immigrated to England in 1977, but her poetry is resolutely informed by her identity as a Guyanese-Caribbean. Yet Nichols warns that even this identification as a Caribbean poet must be read in terms of hybridity, influences upon her work come from 'the different immigrant groups who came out to the Caribbean: East Indians, Chinese and Portuguese. My voice as a writer has its source in that region' (p. 283). Nichols also states that 'Difference, diversity and unpredictability make me tick.'[19] *The Fat Black Woman's Poems* present a speaker who negotiates the problems of everyday living in London. Its discrete lyric mediations on family, sexual encounters and landscapes of Guyana frequently interrogate the legacies of slavery and colonialism. More recently Nichols has asserted that she does not specifically want to be read as a postcolonial poet but as a writer in a community of other immigrants:

> . . . living now in London, who had a past from which they have been uprooted and they were addressing an audience as uprooted as themselves, and not any one particular kind of audience. I suppose that in a way is a bit more appealing than postcolonial, because not just black writers have been uprooted.[20]

Nichols prefers instead to be identified as a 'trans-cultural writer', a term which embraces a range of immigrant experience.

The first section of the volume presents a larger-than-life character described in the first poem 'Beauty' as 'a fat black woman riding the waves' (p. 7). Nichols's fat black woman is adaptive, aphoristic and irreverent. She assumes a centralising focus in each of the small lyric poems of this section, sitting on 'the golden stool', refusing to move while 'white-robed chiefs / are resigned / in their postures of resignation' (p. 8). In making her central to the action of each poem, Nichols successfully creates a world where the black woman is neither marginal nor unheard. The sheer physicality of her presence in these poems adds spontaneity to the work. Some critics suggest that this tactic of corporeality can provide problems of recreating stereotypes. Mara Scanlon finds a difficulty in situating 'a reclamation of identity too resolutely in the body, that material presence which is invoked in literature philosophy and theory by feminists and non-feminists alike to counter the slippery identity constructions of poststructuralists'.[21] The danger, according to Scanlon, is that this focus on the physical body may just replicate the language of racist and sexist discourses. Nichols herself suggests that writing this way grants her 'some control over the world, however erroneous that might be. I do not have to accept a world that tries to deny not only black women but women on the whole.'[22]

'The Fat Black Woman Goes Shopping' draws attention to idealisations of beauty and the refusal of fashion products to cater to her own body. Shopping in London becomes 'a real drag' and 'de weather is so cold', with the shops displaying their 'frozen thin mannequins'. In response, the fat black woman 'curses in Swahili / Yoruba' and 'nation language' (p. 11). Apparent in these poems is nostalgia for warmth and community but Nichols is also at pains to point out the idealisation of Caribbean living. In 'Two Old Black Men on a Leicester Square Park Bench', in response to the men's memory of a 'sunfull woman you might have known', a voice chides 'It's easy / to rainbow the past' (p. 35). She acknowledges migration in fiscal and economic terms: 'the sun was traded long ago' (p. 35). Most compelling in this volume is Nichols's use of 'nation language', a challenge to the imperial 'correctness' of English that acknowledges the infusion of different languages, idioms and dialects into spoken Caribbean-English. Importantly, Kamau Brathwaite – in his cornerstone examination of the development of nation language in Anglophone Caribbean poetry – states that:

> We in the Caribbean have a kind of plurality: we have English,
> which is the imposed language on much of the archipelago. It
> is an imperial language, as are French, Dutch and Spanish.
> We also have what we call Creole English, which is a mixture
> of English and an adaptation that English took in the new
> environment of the Caribbean when it became mixed with the
> other imported languages. We have also what is called *nation
> language*, which is the kind of English spoken by the people
> who were brought to the Caribbean, not the official English
> now, but the language of slaves and labourers, the servants
> who were brought in.[23]

Nichols suggests that the use of Creole is a way of 'reclaiming our
language heritage and exploring it. It is an act of spiritual survival
on our part.'[24] Her commitment to Creole in poetry aims not only
to preserve culture, but to energise her writing: 'I do not think the
only reason I use Creole in my poetry is to preserve it, however. I
find using it genuinely exciting. Some Creole expressions are very
vivid and concise and have no equivalent in English' (p. 284). In
'Skanking Englishman Between Trains', she playfully focuses on
the appropriation of Jamaican Creole and culture by a 'small yellow
hair Englishman' (p. 33) with a ghetto blaster perched on his shoulder 'skanking', or pacing in time, to reggae at Birmingham Station.
The pose of the Englishman is comic, especially when he asserts
his abhorrence of English food 'I like mih drops / me johnny cakes
/ me peas and rice' (p. 33). Punctuating each of his statements with
a 'Man', the Englishman is truly a convert, but one also senses the
underlying critique that there is more to knowledge of another's
culture than an appetite for cornbread. Nichols's ironic turn of
phrase is apparent, she comments at the close 'he was full-o-jive /
said he had a lovely Jamaican wife' (p. 33). Here the ventriloquised
language of hipster-talk is placed into a sharp critical focus.

The final sections of the volume reinforce the complexities of
Caribbean history and culture and challenge its accessibility as
mere lifestyle choice. Nichols returns us to the language of economics, stating that 'Poverty is the price / we pay / for the sun girl'
(p. 42). Memories of childhood and the sayings of elders haunt the
images of returning home. Nichols inserts the rhetorical language

of the preacher in 'Be a Butterfly'. His cadence of the saying 'Don't be a kyatta-pilla / Be a Butterfly' (p. 49) informs the momentum of the poem as the refrain becomes equally a statement of ambition, self-belief and assertion. This shaping of nation language as a presence of dynamism asserts Nichols's desire that Creole is not read as a secondary language, as mere dialect, or at worst incorrect English. Through her negotiation of biography and life story Nichols revisits the complexities of Caribbean culture and historical violence, while ensuring that the linguistic inventiveness of Creole remains central to her narrative.

SELF-REFLEXIVE LYRICS: PORTRAITURE IN JOHN ASHBERY, SUJATA BHATT AND JORIE GRAHAM

I have already examined the concept of an 'expressive lyric' in reference to poetic forms such as the elegy, epistle and life story – as well as the representation of race and cultural inheritance. It is also essential that we acknowledge how contemporary poets depict the representation of selfhood through 'self-reflexive' techniques. Self-referential writing is not, of course, new terrain for poetry. Poetry has, across the centuries, displayed awareness of the act of its own making. Yet it can be proposed that for contemporary poets meditation on other media, particularly self-portraiture, enables a detailed examination of the construction of selfhood as a textual entity. Certainly contemporary poets John Ashbery, Sujata Bhatt and Jorie Graham share a general fascination for how self-portraits are created and what they tell us about the artist. Ashbery, Bhatt and Graham use their meditations upon portrait painting as a way of exposing and examining poetic techniques, what I will call a 'self-reflexive' lyric. Commenting on the works of others in this way draws useful attention to how poetry addresses not only the idea of selfhood, subjectivity and the role of the artist, but also poetry's engagement with everyday experience.

Susan M. Schultz writes of Ashbery that 'No poet since Whitman has tapped into so many distinctly American voices and, at the same time, so preserved his utterance against the jangle of influences.'[25] Ashbery in an interview comments upon the need to distil a voice from a cacophony of different voices available to a poet. He states his aim is to 'reproduce from the polyphony that goes on inside me, which I don't think is radically different from that of other people'.[26] Readers may initially find Ashbery's poetry bewildering, not least because of the expansive linkages between different subjects his work constructs. The clauses and sub-clauses of Ashbery's poetic line are often periphrastic – that is, refuting direct statement through digressive techniques. His poetry displays a self-awareness of its own creation; the reader is encouraged to consider the poem as action in process. Ashbery comments 'as far as my own poetry goes, while there's a lot of my unconscious mind in it, there's a lot of the conscious mind too, which is only normal, since we do sometimes think consciously – not very often, but sometimes.'[27] Occasionally this extreme self-awareness asserts itself as a criticism of the poem being written. In 'The One Thing That Can Save America' the speaker comments self-critically 'I know that I braid too much of my own / Snapped-off perceptions of things as they come to me'.[28] In later poems such as 'Novelty Love Trot' the poet is unusually disarming but tongue-in-cheek when he states 'I enjoy biographies and bibliographies / and cultural studies'.[29]

A brief reference to French philosopher Maurice Merleau-Ponty's *Phenomenology of Perception* (1945) helps us to understand the self-reflexive impulse in Ashbery's lyric.[30] Merleau-Ponty states that phenomenology is a philosophy 'for which the world is already there' and it is an attempt to achieve 'a direct and primitive contact with the world' (p. vii). Usefully he maintains that phenomenology is a 'rigorous science' (p. vii), but an investigation which has at its core 'a matter of describing and not analysing' (p. viii). Understood in this light a phenomenological impulse has as its aim not the objectification of the world into reducible knowledge, but 'an account of space–time and the world as we live them' (p. vii). Ashbery comments that 'Most of my poems are about the experience of experience . . . and the particular experience is of lesser interest to me than the way it filters through me.'[31]

'Self-Portrait in a Convex Mirror' takes as its starting point and subject matter sixteenth-century Italian Mannerist painter Francesco Parmigianino's self-portrait, 'the first mirror portrait'.[32]

The opening of the poem is almost ekphrastic, in that it describes in detail Parmigianino's painting, rendering visual art into poetry. The unusual scale of objects is emphasised in the poem: 'the right hand / Bigger than the head, thrust at the viewer / and swerving easily away' (p. 188). Ashbery's details of art history remind us that the portrait is a thing made; emphasised by his reference to Giorgio Vasari, a contemporary of Parmigianino's and author of the first Italian art history book *Lives of the Most Excellent Painters, Sculptors, and Architects* (1550). Already Ashbery's poem points to the self-reflexive intricacies of self-portraiture, art history, biography and their poetic interpretation. The momentum of his writing repossesses this sense of process and creation. We are told 'Vasari says' that the artist arranged 'a convex mirror, such as is used by barbers' (p. 188). The globed ball is used ' "with great art to copy all that he saw in the glass" ' (p. 188). Ashbery clearly delights in the fact that the verisimilitude that we see in Parmigianino's portrait results from 'his reflection, of which the portrait / Is the reflection once removed' (p. 188). The poem not only conveys the detail of the painting, but the effect of seeing the portrait and the impression that is formed by the viewer through a technique of near repetition. In this way it can be stated that Ashbery's poem performs phenomenologically, it grants us the perception of perception. What the portrait 'says', according to Ashbery, is a naked gaze that is 'a combination / Of tenderness, amusement and regret, so powerful / In its restraint that one cannot look for long' (p. 189).

Meditating upon his own craft, the speaker admits that his attempt to give form to the impression that the painting creates is conjecture: 'The words are only speculation / (From the Latin *speculum*, mirror)' (p. 189). Delighting in etymology, the poet paradoxically makes a link between portraiture and writing. Ashbery has commented that he sees the work of the poet as 'somehow elucidating a lot of almost invisible currents and knocking them into some sort of shape'.[33] The poem as a consequence results in the configuring of 'a life englobed' (p. 189). Processes of creating and the act of painting are seen as a moment of incipience:

> A peculiar slant
> Of memory that intrudes on the dreaming model
> In the silence of the studio as he considers
> Lifting the pencil to the self-portrait (p. 191)

Successfully, Ashbery in this poem removes over four centuries of distance between the portrait and the present. Moreover, these lines suggest that a key role of writing and painting is to activate memory; the memory referenced can be the impact of the transcribing of the world (as in the self-portrait), or in Ashbery's more duplicitous world the procedure of recreating a memory of the painter in the act of painting. In effect Ashbery attempts to reinstall into his poem the dailiness of Parmigianino's world, what he terms 'the strewn evidence . . . The small accidents and pleasures / Of the day as it moved gracelessly on' (p. 192). Pronouns in Ashbery's work generate considerable instability, and the poet comments upon the 'person' in his work as an emerging force, not a pre-existent entity before writing:

> A person is someone given an embodiment out of these proliferating reflections that are occurring in a generalized mind which eventually run together into the image of a specific person 'he' or 'me' who was not there when the poem began.[34]

Far from establishing stable relations between perceiver and perceived, or speaker and subject, Ashbery's poem constantly negotiates the relationship between the 'I' and 'you'. This highly self-aware approach can result in a blurring of the identities of artist and poet. The speaker's commentary on Parmigianino's technique results in describing actions that become embedded in the speaker's own world. Take for example the section of the poem where we are told that 'The picture is almost finished':

> The surprise almost over, as when one looks out,
> Startled by a snowfall which even now is
> Ending in specks and sparkles of snow.
> It happened while you were inside, asleep,
> And there is no reason why you should have

Been awake for it, except that the day
Is ending and it will be hard for you
To get to sleep tonight, at least until late. (p. 195)

Periphrasis in this section creates an extensive reflection which
challenges any definitive sense of space and time. The depiction of
the snow focuses on the impossibility of underscoring an event as
finished or complete. Moreover, the instability of 'you' and 'one'
suggests that both speaker and artist perform interchangeable roles.
At each stage the poet attempts to inscribe into the painting a narrative of movement, process and creation. Daringly, in this poem
he suggests that the creating of art is not dissimilar to the errors,
misunderstandings and misinterpretations which are central to
the game 'Chinese whispers'. Ashbery points to the intrusion,
which twists 'the end result / Into a caricature of itself' (p. 201).
Commenting on artistic intention and agency he suggests that a
similar principle 'makes works of art so unlike / What the artist
intended' (p. 201). Ashbery's highly self-reflexive writing, with
its digressive techniques, aims to energise the texture of the poem,
enacting processes of creation and perception. Daring to circum-
navigate the subject of his poems, Ashbery's periphrastic progress
challenges our idea of poetic expression. The poet remarks that
the challenges in the artistic avant-garde could equally apply to
his own work: 'Most reckless things are beautiful in some way,
and recklessness is what makes experimental art beautiful, just as
religions are beautiful because of the strong possibility that they are
founded on nothing.'[35]

Indian poet Sujata Bhatt approaches painting and in particular
self-portraiture as an important framing device for her volumes
The Stinking Rose (1995) and *A Colour for Solitude* (2002).[36]
The Stinking Rose places a focus on the self-portraiture of early
twentieth-century Mexican artist Frida Kahlo. Her paintings are
renowned for their painful autobiographical subject matter and her
groundbreaking use of the indigenous cultures of Mexico. Kahlo's
self-portraits do not flinch from depicting her own shattered spinal
column, miscarriages, intense physical pain or representations of
explicit sexuality. Bhatt considers *The Stinking Rose* as movement
away from early work, stating 'I consciously avoided writing about

my childhood.'[37] A native speaker of Gujarati, she usefully makes a comparison between her multilingual background and painting:

> I have never been monolingual, so I don't know what that feels like. I think sometimes I experience my languages like a concrete medium: like different colours of paint, for example. I'm intrigued by the way various languages coexist in one mind, the way they might clash and interfere with each other – but also the way they can enhance one another. It may well be that knowing all these languages and having had to live in different languages makes me more conscious of 'the right word' and of feeling that any given language is almost like a separate being.

Bhatt's gesture here to a certain viscosity of language, or language as a painter's palette, is made evident in her poem 'Nothing is Black, Really Nothing'. The title comes as a translation from Kahlo's diary 'nada es negro, realmente nada' and the speaker performs a homage to the lifework of Kahlo while framing a narrative with her own daughter. Bhatt's poem attempts to give an analytic accuracy to her knowledge of 'black' through a series of intersecting narratives through art history, anecdotal information, pedagogy and self-knowledge. Using Kahlo's quotation as the basis for her investigation and as a continual reprise throughout the poem, she questions: 'But Frida, how black you could paint' (p. 30). Placing her focus in one of Kahlo's famous self-portraits 'Fulang Chang and I' (1937), Bhatt comments how black 'the little dark hairs above your lips' and 'how black the hairs of your monkey' (p. 30). In an attempt to quantify what constitutes true blackness, the speaker adds that 'true' black 'breathes' (p. 30) also blue and red. This meditation leads to a consideration of the early black paint named elephantinum, noted in early Rome by the writer and chronicler Pliny. Not unlike Ashbery, Bhatt takes a detour to examine how the darkest black was made from elephants' tusks by Apelles, Alexander the Great's court painter.

Bhatt's speaker states that she must resist the temptation to create a compendium of alternative readings of black, descriptors such as 'black heart', 'black mood' (p. 31), since her quest is far less

existential. In a comic interlude the poet comments on her daughter's love of black – her insistence that her hair 'is black, black – /
not brown' (p. 31). At the close of the poem, Bhatt returns to the
opening image of Kahlo and places black in a context of female
creativity and self-knowledge. She emphasises how Kahlo found
so 'many different black strokes' in order to 'pull out every shade
/ of blackness / from your hair, your self' (p. 32). Using the figure
of the female painter, Bhatt is able to draw an extensive cartography of cultural references and global artistic practices. In this way
she creates a sense of connectivity between generations of women.
Bhatt admits:

> Part of the reason I have poems about women's experiences
> . . . is because I tend to write out of my own life – it is my life
> that I am trying to understand. In many poems I've changed
> things or put in a lot of fiction: often I have a female character
> who is not me, but an imagined woman in a different time
> and a different place. Of course, in some way these imaginary
> women are connected to me.[38]

Bhatt's focus upon women's experience, particularly in this case a
female painter's reputation and life, enables a process of aesthetic
self-interrogation.

   Similarly, Jorie Graham's early poetry depicts a fascination with
representing paintings, including icons and frescoes. A sampling
of poetry titles from her first volume *Erosion* (1983) illustrates this
preoccupation: 'Still life with Window and Fish', 'The Lady and
the Unicorn and other Tapestries', 'Two Paintings by Gustav
Klimt' and 'Massacio's Expulsion'.[39] The publication of *The End
of the Beauty* (1987) marked a notable rupture of the single-voiced
lyric in her work.[40] Critical accounts of Graham's poetry register
the shift in her poetry during this period, as a movement from
ekphrasis to iconoclasm. Moreover, the scrupulous 'painterly'
representations of her early work are forcefully broken down to
focus on the scrutiny of perception, and its mediation through a
certain linguistic textuality. The rupturing in the text is often seen
through gaps, spaces and questions. In 'Self-Portrait as Hurry and
Delay (*Penelope at her Loom*)' from *The End of Beauty*, Graham

references the classical narrative of Penelope's wait for her husband Odysseus. Traditionally associated with faithfulness and patience, Penelope in order to deflect her suitors devises a delaying tactic. Penelope uses as an excuse the need to complete a burial shroud for her elderly father-in-law, Laertes, before she can contemplate her suitors' advances. She weaves by day and unpicks her work at night. Split into twenty-three separate sections, many of which comprise only a single line of verse or a couple of words, Graham's self-portrait uses the motif of weaving and unthreading as a textual game of survival which emerges as the poem progresses. Graham describes in her opening: 'the flitting shadows the postponement / working her fingers into the secret place, the place of what is coming undone' (p. 48). The self-portrait enables three intersecting and synchronous narratives to coexist. On one level we are given Penelope's story but at points Odysseus's actions enter the frame, 'the here and the there, in which he wanders searching' (p. 49), as well as the self-portraiture of the artist and poet at work. Using the analogy of Penelope's loom Graham sees comparatives of detail in the weaving and unthreading which takes place in her own writing, what she refers to as 'the story and its undoing' (p. 48).

A fascination with lacunae, gaps and unthreading is also mirrored by other poems in *The End of Beauty*. In 'Pollock and Canvas' Graham places her focus on Jackson Pollock's abstract expressionism and action paintings; a process which she describes as 'choosing to no longer let the brushtip touch / at any point / the still ground' (p. 81). This movement is described moreover as retaining action, creating a 'hovering – keeping the hands off – the gap alive' (p. 83). In an interview Graham has suggested how acts of failure, even the failure of language to match the world, are a necessary part of creativity:

> I need to feel the places where the language fails as much as one can. Silence which is awe or astonishment the speech ripped out of you . . . I'd like to think you can feel by its accurate failures, the forces pressing against the sentence, the time order . . . From the labyrinthine ritual cave paintings of the Stone Age, through every period of human time, when we

have sought to enter, to break the surface, one of the ways it
has been crooked – the blindness that one may see. And in the
poets that go that way, twisted syntax, breaks against smooth
sequence or sense, line breaks of queer kinds, white spaces,
interruptions, dashes, overpunctuation, delays, clotted rich
diction, obscurity, disorder, ellipses, sentence fragments,
digressive strategies – every modulation in certainty – are all
tools for storming the walls.[41]

One can read into Graham's self-portraiture an evocation of the
phrase 'Penelope's web'. The phrase is associated with a task
that is perpetually in process but never done or completed. This
act of weaving in the poem is also associated with the patterning and evocation of memory. Graham's 'Self-Portrait as Hurry
and Delay' points to the loom as trapping Odysseus, 'her hands
tacking his quickness down as if soothing it to sleep' (p. 50).
Not unlike the evocation of 'keeping the gap alive' in Pollock's
action painting, Penelope's action of unthreading, snipping and
weaving enables what the speaker refers to as 'his wanting in the
threads she has to keep alive for him / scissoring and spinning and
pulling the long minutes free' (p. 51). Eventually creation and its
destruction are seen as a continual undistinguishable cycle, what
Graham points to as 'beginning always beginning the ending'
(p. 52). The title's reference to self-portraiture enables Graham to
meditate upon the motivations of poetic writing, its relationship to
memory and actions that have not yet occurred. Like Ashbery and
Bhatt, Graham places poignant reflections on artistic intention and
how self-portraiture generates questions regarding the writing of
poetry. She asks us to consider poetry's relation to absence, omis-
sion, creation and destruction.

NOBODY'S VOICE: MICHAEL PALMER

A key final question needs to be addressed: what happens to the
individual speaking voice, or lyric 'I', when the self is displaced
from centre stage and an experience of language takes its place?
American poet Michael Palmer suggests that the two apparently

conflicting possibilities of poetry – as an act of recovery and an act of unthreading – are, in effect, mutually dependent strategies:

> To recover the telling, the human, we must unwind the tale, unbind the tale, the present seems to say. And to recover meaning, we must resist its simulacra, cajolings and screens. We must allow the voice – the work – its plurality, its silences, its infinite, pleated body.[42]

Palmer proposes that compositional techniques must always be given an alert, if not sceptical eye. His perspective on the writing and reception of poetry considers the poem as a site of enquiry, an enfolding of infinite variations and a constellation of voices. The poet's role in Palmer's matrix is to scrutinise the mechanics of language, to reaffirm the importance of the personal utterance. At its most basic this 'unthreading' of the tale told forces us to reflect upon how meaning may be constituted and recovered. Since meaning is almost always a battleground for establishing authority, we could add that this attention to the structures of language has an implicit political and cultural angle. Voice and linguistic indeterminacy intersect in contemporary poetry to generate what Palmer refers to as 'nobody's voice'.

Palmer has often stated that his ambition is to create a composition that has 'nothing at its center'.[43] Indeed, Palmer's essays and poetry gesture to the lyric as the articulation of 'nobody's voice'. But 'nobody's voice' is not just the voice of 'no one'. In explaining what this phrase suggests, Palmer places us directly within a context of European lyricism and a tradition that he identifies as 'the analytic lyric'. The poet Paul Celan becomes for Palmer a key figure in this examination of the lyric self in language:

> His response to the discourse of totalitarianism is to create out of the German Expressionist tradition a body of intensely concentrated lyric poetry which addresses the reconstruction of human speech. I was . . . very much moved by the sense of the dispersal of the subject, but also the reaffirmation, the fact that it was *nobody's voice* and yet it was, also, something – again and again and again.[44]

The 'analytic lyric' in Palmer's words addresses 'the problematics of purely private utterance' by 'taking over the condensation of lyric emotion, and focusing it then on the mechanics of language' (p. 238). This approach produces in turn 'a critique of the discourse of power, to renew the function of poetry' (p. 238). In an early essay 'Memory, Autobiography and Mechanisms of Concealment' (1981), Palmer reverses our preconception of the act of recovery in poetry (be it biographical or historical). He proposes that 'what is taken as a sign of openness – conventional narrative order – may stand for concealment, and what is understood generally as signs of withholding or evasion – ellipsis, periphrasis etc. – may from another point of view stand for disclosure.'[45] In this light we can begin to read the resistances in contemporary poetry, even the gaps and lacunae we have experienced in Graham's poetry, as attempts to practise more authentic methods of representation.

There is no better place to start than with Palmer's more explicit examination of memory and the lyric voice in his 'rewriting' of Rainer Maria Rilke's 'Orpheus and Eurydice' (1904).[46] The poem from 'The Baudelaire Series' works both as a cogent unravelling of a story *and* the recovery of memory, since Palmer situates the reworking of the Orpheus and Eurydice myth within the context of reminiscence. We are given indications in both Rilke and Palmer's poems that the narrative centres on a state of amnesia. Rilke portrays Eurydice as 'deep within herself. Being dead / filled her beyond fulfilment'.[47] Palmer's poem gives us these statements: 'I'm not here when I walk / followed by a messenger confused / (He's forgotten his name)' (p. 24). His treatment of Rilke's poem enacts the three intersecting perspectives of Orpheus, Eurydice and the messenger god Hermes. These three points finally fuse at the poem's close. Eurydice in the opening stutters through an elliptical narrative and the poem enacts a sustained examination of 'how song broke apart' (p. 24) by focusing on the separate modalities that comprise the lyric. The fragmentary statements in the work create junctures in the poem that seem to indicate a recalling of events. But this process of recall disrupts the narrative even more. Palmer's poem, although it relies heavily on anaphoric constructions, shows hostility to naming and representative accuracy: 'Don't say things / You can't say things', 'Don't say his name for him / Don't listen to things' (p. 25). This poem can be read as an intersection of discourses, a kind of 'unthreading' of the lyric 'I'. The complexity of subjectivity for Palmer is prevalent in the final lines: 'Don't look through an eye / thinking to be seen / Take nothing as yours' (p. 25). These lines read as a commentary on the Orpheus and Eurydice myth; Orpheus of course does look back desiring recognition. But perhaps most alluring is reading the poem as an active process of negotiating memories as opposed to directly expressing them. The poem's linguistic instability foregrounds the complex balancing act between recovery and enquiry which the poem depends upon.

Palmer's volume *The Promises of Glass* (2000) features a series of eighteen autobiographical 'portraits'.[48] The earlier quest for a narrative is orchestrated strategically in this opening sequence as a theatricalisation of carnivalesque and philosophical figures. On one level we can read this volume in tandem with the prose journal *The Danish Notebook* (1999), which was written from a request 'to connect the dots' in his work.[49] Initially the poem reads as a stand-up routine commenting on a body of work, even twisting the rhetoric of the journal interview. The speaker prepares for the performance: 'as I was putting on my face: / base, blusher, mascara, ultra high-gloss lip enamel' (p. 17). In a mock confessional we are also told 'Dear Phil, What a hellish season it's been. For a time I thought I was another' (p. 18). Read as a ludic chronology of Palmer's work, the opening presents the poet as celebrity, the modulation of the extract is camp but not darkly ironic.

In 'If Not, Not', one of the more intensely 'lyrical' poems in *The Promises of Glass*, an anxious dialogue is enacted and rewritten within other possible stories, intentions and sensations. The poem circles its subject, a departure or romantic loss, in order to recreate the idealised narrative which perhaps never existed: 'They tell each other stories, / lies composed of dreams' (p. 61). In attempting to recover a past that was never present intervening sensations – an inflection of colour or lighting – 'rust, chrome, yellow, coral / chemical green' (p. 61) become compositional methods that momentarily frame and even divert the reminiscence. 'If Not, Not' is wonderfully self-cancelling, erasing an emergent conversation through a further unravelling of the story at each temporal plateau in the text. Hesitant, disorienting and painful statements are made and then discarded, such as: 'The music of moths, the small lamps', 'What we called the hour in those days' and 'I was there / cut in half, only to survive' (p. 61). As in Palmer's earlier rewriting of Orpheus and Eurydice, this poem balances a process of recovery with a threat of amnesia or immobilising silence: 'He means to say' (p. 61). The French theorist Maurice Blanchot understands this tension between memory and forgetting as an implicit drive in the writing of poetry. He notes that 'the poet speaks as though he were remembering, but if he remembers it is through forgetting'.[50]

CONCLUSION: JENNIFER MOXLEY'S DECEITFUL SUBJECTIVE

Jennifer Moxley somewhat playfully recognises that she has been identified as a lyric 'poster child' for her generation. And yet her initial impressions of contemporary American lyricism in the mid-1980s were far from auspicious:

> This was the mid-eighties, a time when if you opened a main-stream literary magazine all of the so-called lyric poems were little stories from an individual's perspective broken into lines and ending in an epiphany usually with a sense of either moral or political superiority, directed toward an absent interlocutor.[51]

As a younger poet, her work contemplates the experimental legacy of American poetry and the reception of lyric forms in the twenty-first century. Notoriously, Moxley's preface to her first major volume *Imagination Verses* champions the rights of the 'universal lyric "I"'.[52] In 'The Open Letter' series Moxley reiterates her belief in a community of readership; that the solitary reader of poetry is, in fact, interrelated to a network of other readers, a presupposition which is not so far from William Wordsworth's ideal of a 'common' language and Shelley's ideation of the imagination as the 'great instrument of moral good'. Moxley's own conditions for the lyric draw striking parallels for the consideration of the slipperiness of subjectivity and the configuration of memory:

> The lyric can provide a literary approximation of those fleeting moments of experience through which the present comes into being. In the lyric, where syntactically digressive devices work against narrative, the word both is and is not temporally fixed, and thus through lyricism, the past and the future along with the affective frames proper to each, namely longing and regret become presentized.[53]

The emphasis on the simultaneity of past and present indicates that lyric memory becomes the traditional complex of a present-tense evocation of the past. Moxley's reference to what she calls 'digressive' strategies points us to interruptions in the text, resonances that hamper poetry's assimilation into an immediate narrative. She questions emphatically the nostalgia and amnesia of experiential recounting, or what she lineates eloquently in 'The Cover Up' from her volume *The Line* (2004) as an experience gone 'except in the deceitful subjective'.[54] Her poetry is densely musical, incorporating citation, digression, meditation and a provisional self-reflexive testing of the personal poem.

The poems from *Imagination Verses* are highly charged and emotive in a way that challenges the more immediate revelations of confessional verse. A key characteristic of this volume is Moxley's ability to suture intense personal perception and political observation. Situating these poems in time can also be a difficult prospect. 'Ode on the Son' appears to place us in a quest for epic and romance with the questioning: 'Where is my field of wheat, / my flock, my ocean / my arsenal, my knight errant' (p. 17); while one of the longer poems from this volume, 'Ten Prolegomena to Heartbreak', makes reference to acts of duelling in conjunction with 'the Avant-Garde lover / of hope' (p. 85) and a protagonist who dreams of 'filmic meetings with big scores' (p. 88). Moxley's language is moreover one of constant detour and transgression; she states 'I am such an inept navigator / of woe betide, a miserable egomaniac' (p. 85).

In *Imagination Verses* lyricism can appear to be a doubtful strategy for political change, and feelings of hesitation and self-interrogation dominate the poems. At points there is also a search for patterns of interconnection and responsibility. She urges in 'Ode on the Particle', 'so forget the time you dwelt in insolence pretending to be unique' (p. 71), and seeks instead 'the unseen connection of any specific body' (p. 72). In a later poem from *The Sense Record* (2003), 'Grain of the Cutaway Insight', there is the berating of lyric form as a compulsion for order pitted against the desire to commit thought as momentum and investigation: 'My thoughts are too awkward, too erratic to rest / at ease in the beautiful iamb'.[55] The engagement of Moxley's poetry in the world seeks to counter what Charles Olson called the 'lyrical interference of the individual as ego'.[56] She states 'the lyric "I" is not a political universal, nor the guardian of the rights of men, but neither is it the flaccid marker of an outdated bourgeois egotism' (p. 57). As deceitful as Moxley's speaking subject may be, her work raises broader aesthetic questions to show us how linguistic instabilities can lead one to question the nature of selfhood and its relation to the larger social sphere.

SUMMARY OF KEY POINTS

- Expressive lyric poetry raises questions about poetic voice and articulation.
- In contemporary poetry differences exist between poets' approaches to the personal, illustrated, for example, in the elegy.
- The examination of autobiography in the 1980s is used by some poets to engage with questions of race and identity and ethnicity.
- Self-portraiture presents poets with opportunities to dissect processes of writing and composition, particularly in the poetry of John Ashbery and Sujata Bhatt.
- Many poets challenge the idea of the subject as a pre-existent entity. Some poets attempt to show an evolving subjectivity in their work, such as Jorie Graham.
- For others the expression of a self through language is displaced by an attention to the construction of language, for example Michael Palmer and Jennifer Moxley.

NOTES

1. T. S. Eliot, 'Tradition and the Individual Talent', in *Selected Essays* (London: Faber & Faber, 1920), pp. 13–22 (p. 21).
2. Allen Ginsberg, *Howl and Other Poems* (San Francisco: City Lights, 2001), p. 9.
3. Al Alvarez, *The Poet's Voice* (London: Bloomsbury, 2005), pp. 104–5.
4. William Wordsworth, *Lyrical Ballads*, in *The Poetic Works of William Wordsworth*, ed. Ernest De Sélincourt (London: Oxford University Press, 1953), p. 740.
5. Lyn Hejinian, 'The Person and Description', *Poetics Journal*, 9 (1991), p. 167.
6. M. H. Abrams, *The Mirror and the Lamp: Romantic Theory and the Critical Tradition* (Oxford: Oxford University Press, 1977), pp. 22–3.
7. T. S. Eliot, '*Selected Essays* (London: Faber & Faber, 1972), p. 145.
8. Charles Altieri, *Self and Sensibility in Contemporary American Poetry* (Cambridge: Cambridge University Press, 1984), p. 10.
9. Robert Pinsky, *The Situation of Poetry* (Princeton, NJ: Princeton University Press, 1976), p. 133.
10. Andrew Motion, *Selected Poems 1976–1997* (London: Faber & Faber, 1998), pp. 6–10. All subsequent references to this edition are given in the text.
11. Lee Harwood, *Collected Poems* (Exeter: Shearsman, 2004), pp. 432–3. All subsequent references to this edition are given in the text.
12. Roland Barthes, *S/Z*, trans. Richard Miller (Oxford: Blackwell, 2000), pp. 4–5.
13. Jack Stillinger, *Multiple Authorship and the Myth of the Solitary Genius* (New York: Oxford University Press, 1991), p. 3.
14. Philippe Lejeune, cited in Juliana Spahr, 'Resignifying Autobiography: Lyn Hejinian's *My Life*', *American Literature*, 68.1 (1996), 139–59 (p. 139).
15. Cathy Song, *Picture Bride* (New Haven, CT: Yale University Press, 1983). All subsequent references to this edition are given in the text.

16. Gayle K. Fujita-Sato, 'Third World as Place and Paradigm in Cathy Song's *Picture Bride*', *Melus*, 15.1 (1988), 49–72 (p. 50).

17. Grace Nichols, *The Fat Black Woman's Poems* (London: Virago, 1984). All subsequent references to this edition are given in the text.

18. Grace Nichols, 'The Battle with Language', *Caribbean Women Writers: Essays from the First International Conference*, ed. Selwyn R. Cudjoe (Wellesley, MA: Calaloux, 1990), pp. 283–9 (p. 287).

19. Grace Nichols, cited in Dennis Walder, *Post Colonial Literatures in English* (London: Blackwell, 1998), p. 147.

20. Grace Nichols, cited in *Talk Yuh Talk Interviews with Anglophone Caribbean Poets*, ed. Kwame Dawes (Charlottesville: University of Virginia Press, 2000), pp. 140–1.

21. Mara Scanlon, 'The Divine Body in Grace Nichols's *The Fat Black Woman's Poems*', *World Literature Today*, 72.1 (1998), 59–66 (p. 62).

22. Nichols, 'The Battle with Language', p. 289.

23. Kamau Brathwaite, 'Nation Language', in *History of the Voice: The Development of Nation Language in Anglophone Caribbean Poetry* (London: New Beacon, 1984), pp. 5-6.

24. Nichols, 'The Battle with Language', p. 284.

25. Susan M. Schultz (ed.), *The Tribe of John Ashbery and Contemporary Poetry* (Tuscaloosa: University of Alabama Press, 1995), p. 1.

26. John Ashbery, in Thomas Gardner *Regions of Unlikeness: Explaining Contemporary Poetry* (Lincoln: University of Nebraska Press, 1999), p. 74.

27. John Ashbery, 'In conversation with John Tranter New York City, 20 April 1985', *Jacket*, 2 (1985). Available online at http://jacketmagazine.com/02/jaiv1985.html.

28. John Ashbery, in *Postmodern American Poetry: A Norton Anthology*, ed. Paul Hoover (New York: Norton & Norton, 1994), p. 179. Originally published in *Self-Portrait in a Convex Mirror* (New York: Viking, 1975).

29. John Ashbery, 'Novelty Love Trot', in *The American Poetry Review*, 33.6 (2004), p. 6.

30. Maurice Merleau-Ponty, *The Phenomenology of Perception*, trans. Colin Smith (London: Routledge, 1999).

31. John Ashbery, cited in Richard Gray, *American Poetry of the 20th Century* (Harlow: Longman, 1990), p. 324.

32. John Ashbery, *Selected Poems* (London: Penguin, 1986). All subsequent references to this edition are given in the text.

33. Ashbery, cited in Gardner, *Regions of Unlikeness*, p. 74.

34. John Shoptaw, *On the Outside Looking Out: John Ashbery's Poetry* (Cambridge, MA: Harvard University Press, 1994), p. 135.

35. John Ashbery, 'The Invisible Avant-Garde', in T. B. Hess and John Ashbery (eds), *The Avant-Garde* (New York: Macmillan, 1968), p. 149.

36. Sujata Bhatt, *The Stinking Rose* (Manchester: Carcanet, 1995); *A Colour for Solitude* (Manchester: Carcanet, 2002). All subsequent references to this edition are given in the text.

37. Sujata Bhatt, 'Interview with Vicki Bertram'. Available online at www.carcanet.co.uk/cgi-bin/scribe?showdoc=4;doctype=interview.

38. Bhatt, 'Interview with Vicki Bertram'.

39. Jorie Graham, *Erosion* (New York: Ecco Press, 1983).

40. Jorie Graham, *The End of Beauty* (New York: Ecco, 1987). All subsequent references to this edition are given in the text.

41. Jorie Graham, 'Some Notes on Silence', in Philip Dow (ed.), *19 New American Poets of the Golden Gate* (New York: Harcourt, 1984), pp. 409–10.

42. Michael Palmer, cover note for Norma Cole, *Moira* (Berkeley: O Books, 1995).

43. Michael Palmer, 'From the Notebooks', *19 New American Poets of the Golden Gate*, p. 343.

44. Michael Palmer, 'Interview', in Gardner, *Regions of Unlikeness*, p. 239.

45. Michael Palmer, 'Autobiography and Mechanisms of Concealment', in Bob Perelman (ed.), *Writing Talks* (Carbondale: Southern Illinois University Press, 1985), pp. 207–29 (p. 227).

46. Michael Palmer, *Sun* (San Francisco: North Point, 1988), pp.

23–5. All subsequent references to this edition are given in the text.

47. Rainer Maria Rilke, *The Selected Poetry of Rainer Maria Rilke*, trans. Stephen Mitchell (New York: Vintage Press, 1989), pp. 49–53.

48. Michael Palmer, *The Promises of Glass* (New York: New Directions, 2000).

49. Michael Palmer, *The Danish Notebook* (Penngrove, CA: Avec Books, 1999), p. 9.

50. Maurice Blanchot, 'Forgetful Memory', in *The Infinite Conversation*, trans. Susan Hanson (Minneapolis: University of Minnesota Press, 1993), pp. 314–17 (p. 317).

51. Jennifer Moxley, 'Lyric Poetry and the Inassimilable Life', in *The Poker*, 6 (2005), 49–58 (p. 53).

52. Jennifer Moxley, *Imagination Verses* (New York: Tender Buttons, 1996), p. x. All subsequent references to this edition are given in the text.

53. Jennifer Moxley 'Lyric Poetry and the Inassimilable Life', p. 53.

54. Jennifer Moxley, *The Line* (Sausalito, CA: Post-Apollo Press, 2004), p. 36.

55. Jennifer Moxley, *The Sense Record* (Cambridge: Salt, 2003), p. 6.

56. Charles Olson, 'Projective Verse', in Donald Allen and Warren Tallman (eds), *Poetics of the New American Poetry* (New York: Grove Press, 1973), pp. 147–58 (p. 156).

CHAPTER 2

Politics and Poetics

In May 2009 Carol Ann Duffy became the first woman poet laureate in UK history. In recent decades the role of laureate became subject to increasing pressures of 'marking' royal events. Such were the demands placed upon Andrew Motion, Duffy's predecessor, that after some resistance, he began to write 'occasional' public verse. Provocatively, Duffy has eschewed the more ceremonial function of laureate and is intent upon raising awareness of poetry in the public sphere. The new laureate's first work was a pointed and topical criticism of the abuse of allowances by a number of British MPs. Responding to the published poem, Mark Brown comments:

> She could have chosen to write on Prince Philip's 88th birthday, or the sombre commemorations of the D-day landings in Normandy. Instead Carol Ann Duffy has chosen a far more meaty subject for her first poem as poet laureate: politics. And she's angry – more Duffy Furiosa in the words of one expert . . . It is a powerful, passionate commentary on the corrosiveness of politics on politicians and the ruinous effect of idealism.[1]

Through an insistent echoing of former Prime Minister Tony Blair's rallying cry 'Education, Education, Education', Duffy's poem articulates an absolute disaffection with the failure of politicians' promises.[2] Her poem entitled 'Politics' asserts the failure of ideals, since politics turn the face to 'stone', the right hand to 'a gauntlet', the left 'a glove puppet'.[3] Duffy allies political rhetoric to gambling and the fiscal, a politician's speech becomes 'your lips dice' and a kiss is a 'dropped pound coin'. While knowledge of the abuse of expenses forms the bedrock to understanding 'Politics', Duffy's disgust is levied at the manipulation of language and its perversion to 'Latin, gibberish, feedback static'. 'Politics' investigates the pact made between members of parliament and their role of representing the public good. In a bid to reinsert an ethics of representation and higher linguistic code, the speaker states that politics must roar to 'your conscience, moral compass truth'. Paradoxically, Duffy's closing cry of 'POLITICS, POLITICS, POLITICS' is not as an absolute dismissal, nor a rallying cry, but as an attempt to reclaim the word to a fundamental element of good upon which all action must be based.

FOUNDING PROPOSITIONS: POLITICS AND POST-WORLD WAR II POETRY

From these opening observations it may seem that the relationship between poetry and politics must always be one of competing claims for the rights to truth and representing the public good. The often cited and misunderstood quotation from W. H. Auden, 'poetry makes nothing happen', can be read as a central nexus of our discussion.[4] Following World War II there was a necessary and, at times, passionate questioning of the role of poetry in the public sphere. Indeed it might appear that the writing of poetry during times of political crisis equates to Nero fiddling as Rome burns. One may well question whether Shelley's nineteenth-century treatise on poets as 'the unacknowledged legislators of the world' in his 'A Defence of Poetry' (1821) retains any resonance.[5] Poetry, Shelley argued, is central to human life because it is the creator of culture; the poet creates a broad vision that transcends his time and place, to create a dialogue with past and future generations. While Auden might initially appear to be dismissive of poetry's power, his poem is an admission that poetry 'survives a way of happening, a mouth' (p. 242). Auden proposes that poetry is an enduring art form, a dynamic method of articulation.

Theodor Adorno's infamous statement that 'to write poetry after Auschwitz is barbaric' appears at the end of his 1949 essay 'Cultural Criticism and Society'.[6] Critics originally took it as a judgement upon the impossibility of writing lyric poetry following the Holocaust. Mechanised mass murder at Auschwitz obliterated the concept of individual suffering; as a result the idea of the viability of the single expressive voice in poetry is called into the question. However, Adorno later reflected upon the original statement and insisted upon the necessity of continuing to write poetry:

> I once said that after Auschwitz one could no longer write poetry, and that gave rise to a discussion I did not anticipate ... I would readily concede that, just as I said that after Auschwitz one could not write poems – by which I meant to point to the hollowness of the resurrected culture of that time – it could equally well be said, on the other hand, that one must write poems.[7]

Adorno's original statement takes us through a dialectical pronouncement: to write a poetry that infers the Holocaust, risks diminishing the catastrophe to a complicit artistic representation; equally a poetry that refuses to acknowledge the Holocaust serves only to silence history. His later reflection indicates that poetry needed to change and expresses the desire for poetry to serve as ethical witness.

When interviewed in the 1980s during the height of 'The Troubles' in Northern Ireland, Seamus Heaney reflects upon the question whether poetry can respond to barbarism:

> Can you write a poem in the post-nuclear age? Can you write a poem that gazes at death, or the western front, or Auschwitz – a poem that gives peace and tells horror? It gives true peace only if horror is satisfactorily rendered. If the eyes are not averted from it. If its overmastering power is acknowledged and unconcerned, so the human spirit holds its own against

its affront and immensity. To me that's what the 'end of art is peace' means.[8]

Heaney also calls upon the poet to bear witness to atrocity – the poet's responsibility is to render the horror of barbarism in the poetic work without complicity. His pronouncement can be allied to Jerome Rothenberg's insistence that poetry after the Holocaust must be human. Rothenberg suggests that a new form of lyricism creates a poetry not necessarily 'about the Holocaust, but a poetry that characterizes what it means to be human, to be a maker of poems (even lyric poems) after Auschwitz'.[9] We might add to this meditation Charles Bernstein's comment that 'In contrast to – or is it an extension of – Adorno's famous remarks about the impossibility of (lyric) poetry after Auschwitz, I would say poetry is a necessary way to register the unrepresentable loss of the Second War.'[10]

An appeal to politics in poetry is made evident in the mid-1980s and early 1990s with the growth of interest in a poetry of witness. Carolyn Forché's groundbreaking anthology *Against Forgetting: Twentieth Century Poetry of Witness* itemises the wars and turmoil of the twentieth century.[11] Her catalogue includes poets of the First and Second World Wars as well as poetry from the Holocaust; repression in Eastern and Central Europe, war and dictatorship in the Mediterranean; Indo-Pakistani wars; wars in the Middle East; repression and revolution in Latin America; the struggle for civil rights and liberties in the USA; wars in Korea and Vietnam; repression in Africa; and the struggles against apartheid in South Africa and for democracy in China. Working often with twentieth-century poetry in translation, Forché's introduction gives a compelling insight to the term 'witness':

We are accustomed to rather easy categories: we distinguish between 'personal' and 'political' poems – the former calling into mind lyrics of love and emotional loss, the latter indicating a public partisanship that is considered divisive even when necessary. The distinction between the personal and the political gives the political realm too much and too little scope; at the same time it renders the personal too important and not important enough. If we give up the dimension of the personal, we risk relinquishing one of the most powerful sites of resistance. The celebration of the personal however can indicate a myopia, an inability to see how larger structures of the economy and the state circumscribe, if not determine, the fragile realm of individuality. (p. 31)

Forché calls for a third term to be distinguished between 'the state' and 'the personal' which she names 'the social'. She adds that the social 'is a place of resistance and struggle where books are published, poems read and protest disseminated' (p. 31). Poetry, far from not making anything happen politically, can be read as what poet Michael Palmer refers to as 'something happening among other things happening'.[12] Cast in this light, poetry has political agency played out in the social realm. Palmer urges the poem to bear witness to the atrocities of the twentieth and twenty-first centuries. He comments upon the network of associations and configurations that make the poem. His reading of poetry's response to 'a moment of Barbarism' establishes the relevance of the contemporary poet's ongoing engagement with society:

> The poem is altered by events that it cannot possibly foresee . . . The point is not simply how work responds to current events, but how previous work is altered by and alters, them . . . Poetry as something happening among other things happening. As something happening in language, and to language under siege. Poetry as memory, sometimes memory of the future. Poetry as both fixed and in process, ever a paradox.[13]

As Palmer points out, poetry of the twentieth and twenty-first centuries has had to learn how to ethically address and represent brutality and war, from inter-ethnic conflict to global warfare. Theories of deconstruction and poststructuralist thought can persuade readers and students that the politics of a poem lies in an interrogation of linguistic structures. Given these differences, we will need to address the distinctions between a poetry which writes *about* politics, and a poetry which performs *politically*. World War II veteran and pacifist Lawrence Ferlinghetti's manifesto poem *Insurgent Art* (2007) offers a belief that poetry has political agency.

Ferlinghetti responds: 'What are poets for, in such an age? / What is the use of poetry? / The state of the world calls out for poetry to save it'.[14] He adds, with considerable optimism, that 'Words can save you where guns can't'.[15] As such, this chapter considers the extent to which contemporary poets are prepared to rest their belief for political change and critique, in the power of language.

A DAY IN POLITICS: INAUGURATION POETS MAYA ANGELOU AND ELIZABETH ALEXANDER

Arguably, no more direct intervention between poetry and politics exists than the presence of a poet's recitation during presidential inauguration day in the USA. Four American presidential inaugurations (John F. Kennedy, Bill Clinton (twice) and Barack Obama) have included a poet reading as part of the ceremony. The poets were Robert Frost (1961), Maya Angelou (1993), Miller Williams (1997) and Elizabeth Alexander (2009). Zofia Burr proposes that 'the occasion of the inaugural poem resurrects an ideology about the role of poetry in the public sphere that is as influential now as it was in the early 1960s'.[16] Burr proposes that in this ceremonial function the poet serves as an explicit 'outsider'. Both poet and poem's role is to question, from a position of integrity, the state of the political sphere:

> The function of the poet as a check on power is both analogous to that of the press of the Fourth Estate (understood as having a responsibility to scrutinize the actions of the government from the perspectives of the people) and also absolutely unlike that of the press . . . the very things that poetry is designed to check and counter in the name of integrity defined in the terms of the private, the personal the individual. Thus if poetry has a public role to perform, it is only by virtue of its ability to remain apart from all public discourses of society. (pp. 430–1)

Poetry and politics make odd bedfellows given poetry's association with privacy and politicians' perpetual search for an audience.

An estimated 38 million viewers watched Obama's inauguration ceremony around the world, but the tensions are evident in John F. Kennedy's proposal that 'politicians are the men who create power' and artists are 'the men who question power'.[17] Maya Angelou and Elizabeth Alexander's poems illustrate how poets attempt to avoid the rhetorical flourishes associated with public address while retaining a direct appeal to their audiences' expectations. Their poems create a dialogue with previous inaugural poems; Alexander's poem especially enters into a direct conversation with Angelou's earlier 'On the Pulse of Morning' (1993).

Angelou's poem problematises the ideal of an accomplished programme of nationhood. 'On the Pulse of Morning' is not a citizen's address to America, but includes three unexpected voices: a rock, a river and a tree. Borrowing from Native American animism, Angelou alerts us to a landscape that existed prior to the voyages to the New World of Columbus and other European adventurers. The America of Maya Angelou's poem is not a pre-existent space but an ambition to be made through exertion, care and community. The rock urges the people to 'face your distant destiny' and challenges a human predilection to remain 'face down in ignorance / your mouths spilling words. / Armed for slaughter'.[18] Building upon an ecological imperative, the voice of the river retells how the denominations of people create 'a bordered country' whose 'armed struggles for profit / Have left collars of waste upon / My shore, currents of debris upon my breast' (pp. 270–1). Borrowing from Walt Whitman's evocation of American citizenship as a body containing multitudes in *Song of Myself* (1855) Angelou uses a listing of identities evoking the complexity of America:

> The Asian, the Hispanic, the Jew,
> The African, the Native American, the Sioux,
> The Catholic, the Muslim, the French, the Greek,
> The Irish, the Rabbi, the Priest, the Sheik,
> The Gay, the Straight, the Preacher,
> The privileged, the homeless, the Teacher. (p. 271)

The intervention of the tree as a final speaking voice builds upon the diversity outlined by the river with a parallel gesture towards inclusion. Angelou dramatises how America exists as an intersection of individual narratives creating a tissue of connective narrative threads. These narratives convene to create an experience of migration, wanderlust, and in many instances exploitation and a bloody history, to include Pawnee, Apache, Seneca, Cherokee, Turk, Arab, Swede, German, Eskimo, Scot, Ashanti, Yoruba and Kru. Angelou opens the history of America with the violent annihilation of Native American cultures and includes the violence of slavery against African peoples: 'Sold, stolen, arriving on the nightmare. Praying for a dream' (p. 272). 'On the Pulse of Morning' urges a reconsideration of the ways in which a nation performs its politics. Echoing the refrain of the Civil Rights Movement, Angelou's poem states that the peoples of America 'will not be moved' (p. 272) and urges its audience to 'give birth again to the dream' (p. 272). Encouraging dynamics of community and shared agency, the poem proposes that this is a new day and wishes for

> the grace to look up and out
> And into your sister's eyes, into
> Your brother's face, your country
> And say simply
> Very simply
> With hope –
> Good morning. (p. 273)

This appeal to a communal ritual based in the everyday offers an explicit challenge to the rhetoric of ceremony.

Interviewed by the *New York Times* prior to the occasion of Obama's inauguration, Elizabeth Alexander stated that as preparation to her writing, she 'read the previous inaugural poems, as well as many others' – adding that 'the ones that appeal to me have a sense of focus and a kind of gravitas, an ability to appeal to larger issues without getting corny.'[19] Crucially Alexander admitted that her aim was to create a poem that did not 'talk down to some imagined audience'. Alexander's 'Praise Song for the Day' establishes a conversation with Angelou's poem.[20] Building on ideas of working life, her poem marks the inaugural day with the action of America's citizens. The poem echoes the momentum of work songs; its focus is upon acts of mending broken communities. Alexander's opening poses a caustic critique upon the failure of the Bush administration, the breakdown of an American polity and its dependence upon a language of mistrust, a failure to act in the spirit of a central 'good': 'Each day we go about our business / walking past each other, catching each other's / eyes or not, about to speak or speaking'.

In her essay on June Jordan, Alexander states that Jordan's emphasis on linguistic innovation poses an instructive example to her own work.[21] Alexander suggests that 'For time immemorial across geographies and peoples, poetry has taken as its subject politics, that is, the affairs of the polis, the community and its people' (p. 116). Commenting on the interrelationship between poetic form and politics she proposes that:

> Poets do have responsibility to make images that compel, to distil language, to write with model precision and specificity, that is what poetry has to offer to other genres. It makes something happen with language that takes the breath away or shifts the mind. For the poem, which is after all not the newspaper, must move beyond the information it contains while simultaneously imparting the information it contains.[22]

In Alexander's estimation the political poem refuses becoming reportage. Images of mending, regrouping, artistic creation and daily schedules become the loci of the poem. We are presented with a 'someone' who is darning as well as people making music, teaching, waiting for a bus and watching the weather. Far from being a praise song of America, the poem focuses on the elements within American society which fail to function – what Alexander refers to as the 'things in need of repair'. Importantly, the poem frames the relationship between citizens as a linguistic bond giving reference to the constitution as an 'encounter' in words. Whereas Angelou's poem stresses the importance of inclusion and multiplicity, Alexander's poem stresses the importance of encountering others through travel, and the curiosity to know what is beyond one's own community.

Alexander maps America through its highways, dirt tracks and rail lines as well as its buildings. Inscribed in their making is a history of incredible sacrifice, many that 'have died for this day', and the poet asks to 'sing the names of the dead who brought us here'. For Alexander and Angelou, America remains in a state of possibility and the role of the inaugural poem is not to glorify political achievements. Instead their poems display a need to find connections between citizens and act as a reminder of the failures, as well as the possibilities, inherent in political rhetoric. In this way, both are following Jordan's premise of the relationship between poetry and politics: 'I am saying that the ultimate connection cannot be the enemy. The ultimate connection must be the need that we find between us. It is not only who you are, in other words, but what we can do for each other that will determine the connection.'[23]

PASTORAL AND LUDIC: SEAMUS HEANEY AND PAUL MULDOON

On 8 May 2007 the opening of the Northern Irish Assembly at Stormont presented an unlikely coupling of First Minister Ian Paisley, the Democratic Unionist Party leader, and deputy First Minister Martin McGuinness, a former IRA commander. *The Guardian* commented that it was an 'extraordinary display of cross-community unity' marking 'a symbolic end to the Troubles'.[24] Eventually nicknamed the 'chuckle brothers', at the close of their shared ministerial office McGuinness gave a parting gift to Paisley. *The Times* noted that the gift was a pair of framed poems composed by McGuinness himself.[25] The paper added that 'Just in case Mr Paisley was not too keen on his poetic efforts, Mr McGuinness had also asked Seamus Heaney, the Nobel laureate, to write out in long-hand some lines from Heaney's *The Cure at Troy*.'

McGuinness's action illustrates how poetry is associated with ideas of intimacy and ceremony. The uneasy alliance between poetry and politics often conjures the fear of performing work that is mere rhetoric or polemic in verse. A snapshot of the poetry of Northern Ireland written between 1975 and 1983, from Heaney's *North* (1975), Derek Mahon's *The Snow Party* (1975) and Paul Muldoon's *Quoof* (1983), articulates an inherent scepticism towards the poet as polemicist, but a respect for the ethical questions poetry raises.[26] Heaney asserts that during The Troubles poetry served a marginal but important countercultural role whose language was an antidote to sectarian rhetoric:

> The fact that a literary action was afoot was itself a new political condition, and the poets did not feel the need to address themselves to the specifics of politics because they assumed that the tolerances and subtleties of their art were precisely what they had to set against the repetitive intolerance of public life. When Derek Mahon, Michael Longley, James Simmons and myself were having our first book published, Paisley was already in full sectarian cry and Northern Ireland's cabinet ministers regularly massaged the atavisms of Orangemen on the twelfth of July.[27]

The archaeologist P. V. Glob's *The Bog People* (1965) provided Heaney with accounts of bodies dug up accidentally by Scandinavian turf cutters, as well as evidence of ritualistic murder and burial in the Iron Age. In *Wintering Out* (1972) this exposure to Glob's book became the basis for a poem regarding sacrificial murder, 'Tollund Man'. However, in *North* the exhumation of the bodies serves as an acute political allegory for the sectarian violence of Northern Ireland. Heaney is explicit about the political analogy:

> Taken in relation to the tradition of Irish political martyrdom, for that cause whose icon is Kathleen Ni Houlihan, this is more than an archaic barbarous rite; it is an archetypal pattern. And the unforgettable photographs of these victims blended in my mind with photographs of atrocities, past and present in the long rites of Irish political and religious struggles.[28]

This element of simultaneity is evident in 'The Grauballe Man'. Found in Jutland, Denmark the man had had his throat slashed. As Heaney depicts: 'The head lifts / the chin is a visor raised above the vent' (p. 28). Grauballe Man looks as if he had 'been poured in tar' (p. 28) and gently removed as 'a forceps baby' (p. 29). Moving us to the twentieth century, Heaney closes with a reference to his shield which chronicles the weight 'of each hooded victim / slashed and dumped' (p. 29). In 'Punishment' the allegorical model is taken further in the poetic dissection of the body of a woman found in the bog with a noose around her neck, as punishment for sexual betrayal. Heaney attempts to sexually reanimate the body with her nipples 'as amber beads' and the wind 'on her naked front' (p. 30). Acutely attuned to this act of voyeurism, the confessional tone of the poem creates an unsettling intimacy with the preserved body. The speaker confesses that 'I almost love you' (p. 31). The poem moves introspectively to reflect upon modern Northern Ireland, as the speaker interrogates his own lack of agency, regarding the women tarred as punishment for their relationships with British soldiers. He questions his own position watching the bog woman's sisters weeping by railings. Invariably he recognises his own situation within the atavism of sectarian conflict by admitting to understanding, 'the exact / and tribal intimate revenge' (p. 31).

North divided critics; for some it glorified violence and ritualised murder. Poet Ciaran Carson wrote that Heaney was in danger of becoming a 'laureate of violence – a mythmaker, an anthropologist of ritual killing, an apologist for "the situation" in the last resort, a mystifier'.[29] Heaney's *North* could be interpreted as celebrating what politician Conor Cruise O'Brien has pointed to in his attack on the IRA and Sinn Fein as autocratic and fascist organisations, mired in the 'language of sacred soil and the cult of the dead'.[30] Heaney suggests that 'poetry and politics are in different ways, an articulation, an ordering, a giving to form to inchoate pieties, prejudices world-views.'[31] In 'Whatever You Say Say Nothing' the poet interrogates the language which represents Northern Ireland in the public domain. He draws our attention to overused terms that are in danger of becoming empty signifiers: 'Backlash' and 'crack down', 'Polarization', 'long standing hate' and 'the voice of sanity' (p. 52). Heaney also comments upon his own possible compliance towards encoding politics in 'all this art and sedentary trade' (p. 54). The poem's title is a warning, and the work gives a close analysis of differences between the religious communities. Names and schools signify affiliations, encrypted politics which infiltrate everyday life drawing attention to 'land of password, handgrip, wink and nod / of open minds as open as a trap' (p. 55). To this effect Heaney has seen his role less as claiming political leadership than as remaining witness to:

> Poetry's solidarity with the doomed, the deprived, the victimized, and the under-privileged. The witness is any figure in whom the truth-telling urge and the compulsion to identify with the oppressed becomes necessarily integral with the act of writing itself.[32]

The final poem in *North*, 'Exposure', displays the poet's position as a marginal spectator. He comments ruefully upon 'My responsible *tristia*' (p. 67), notoriously describing the poet as 'neither internee nor informer' but as 'an inner émigré' who has 'escaped from the massacre' (p. 68).

Published in the same year, 'A Disused Shed in Co. Wexford' is one of the key poems from Derek Mahon's volume *The Snow Party*. Mahon's approach towards the political landscape in Ireland is deliberately circumspect. The poem interrogates suffering, violence and the premise of ethical representation through poetry. Starting from a global map of human suffering, the poem addresses the haunting of Peruvian mines and Indian compounds to settle upon a shed in County Wexford. Here a 'thousand mushrooms crowd to a keyhole' having learned 'patience and silence'.[33] The mushrooms in this foetid environment serve as an imagining of the imprisoned and censored. Their patient waiting is seen as out of sync with the march of history and political discussion since they wait 'for us' since 'civil war days' (p. 89). Edna Longley poses that Mahon's poem 'does more than translate a defeated community into the narrative of history or even a lost people into symbolic salvation . . . He receives a defenceless spirit into the protectorate of poetry.'[34] The mushrooms may function as reminders of prisoners of conscience, and certainly Mahon's poem places a dubious focus on the 'the flash-bulb firing-squad we wake them with' (p. 90). Mahon extends this community of suffering to a trans-historical one, identifying it with the holocaust victims of Treblinka and the 'lost people of Pompeii' (p. 90). Questions regarding an ethics of

representation are posed in the poem since voices beg for us 'To
do something, to speak on their behalf / or at least not to close the
door again' (p. 90). 'A Disused Shed in Co Wexford' frames the
necessity of writing as a response to and articulation of the suffering of others, but warns that the representation of that suffering is
of key concern in considering political responsiveness.

Interviewed in 1985, Paul Muldoon responded to a question
on the relationship between politics and his poetry with the retort
'It doesn't matter where I stand politically, with a small "p" in
terms of Irish politics. My opinion about what should happen
in Northern Ireland is no more valuable than yours.'[35] Quixotic
and ludic, Muldoon's 'Gathering Mushrooms' in *Quoof* refuses
to remain still. He creates a space where memories of cultivation
compete with drug taking, news headlines and the dirty protest
in the H Block. While these intersecting narratives refute a political positioning, the poem can be read intertextually. We can see
a useful continuity between Muldoon's work and Mahon's 'A
Disused Shed in Co Wexford'. Set in a loose five-sonnet sequence,
Muldoon revisions an agrarian idyll by situating the pastoral in
a hallucinatory psilocybin haze. There is also reference to para-
military violence with the recollection of the IRA firebombing of
Malone House, Belfast in 1976. 'Gathering Mushrooms' from
Quoof features recollections of his father cultivating mushrooms,
playfully depicting him as one of the mythic 'ancient warriors /
before the rising tide' (p. 8). However, the play of the poem shifts
in the closing sonnet where reverberating political images surface.
Ventriloquised through a hallucinating friend the speaker recalls
a voice which begs '*Come back to us*' (p. 9). Framed in a prison
where '*beyond this concrete wall is a wall of concrete and barbed wire*'
(p. 9) the poem graphically evokes images of the H Block republi-
can prisoners' dirty protests of the late 1970s and the hunger strik-
ers of the early 1980s. The voice urges the poet that his song must
be of '*treading your own dung*' (p. 9). A gradual fading of the scene
in a '*soiled grey blanket of Irish rain / that will one day, bleach itself
white*' (p. 9) paces the gradual emaciation of the prisoner to death.

Muldoon challenges any deliberate intention to respond to
Mahon's poem. When asked about the allusions common to both
poems he responds:

The similarity is really an accident. I think it's worth remembering that in England there's much more mobility, a much wider range of experience. I'm not saying that there aren't any class barriers or distinctions in Ireland, but basically it's a fairly homogenous country in which everybody's experience is pretty much the same, and the same images just tend to turn up. And the same images turn up in American poetry. What more can I say?[36]

Certainly, both share a preoccupation with ventriloquising the voices of the dispossessed and an equivocation concerning direct political positioning. Longley reflecting upon the recent changes created by processes of peace and reconciliation in Northern Ireland proposes: 'Just as the Good Friday agreement may allow poetry to be read more aesthetically, so its "strands" focus the finer print of Northern Ireland not as a bordered space but as itself internally and externally intertextual.'[37] The three poets through their different processes of early engagement – mythic ritual in Heaney, questions of ethical responsibility in Mahon and empathy in Muldoon – display a shared commitment to refuting atavism and easy political positioning.

THE POLITICS OF LANGUAGE: POETRY AND THE PUBLIC SPHERE – CHARLES BERNSTEIN

An early poem by Charles Bernstein states quixotically that 'I read somewhere that love of the / public good is the only passion that really / necessitates speaking to the public'.[38] Bernstein's name is affiliated to a loose collective known under the rubric of 'language poetry' or writing, which began to appear in the early 1970s. Language writing can be characterised as a poetry which frequently works in terms of diminished reference, questioning the 'transparency' of language, or language's unequivocal claim as a finite medium of representation. The disruption of syntax, narrative and the foregrounding of language's generative properties through its slippages, puns and word play serve to create a poetry of intense linguistic opacity. For language writing the rupturing of the text and divergence of poetic language from public discourse had a political agency. Bernstein suggests that language must be seen as 'not accompanying but constituting the world'.[39] The premises of the tendency create an overall focus upon the reader as a 'co-producer' of the text, which would appear to align the tenor of their poetics neatly with Roland Barthes's identification of the 'writerly text'.[40] Barthes suggests that the writerly text can be understood as 'ourselves writing' (p. 5), and characterises its goal as a desire 'to make the reader no longer a consumer, but a producer of the text' (p. 4).

Bernstein's essays refute language as a vehicle of direct mediation. His early poetics stress a suspicion of the language of public discourse, and suggest that there is a troubling relationship between the hierarchies of language's rule-governed conventions and authority. The relationship between convention and a rhetorical address, he suggests, can be located as an attempt to master language. This link between rhetoric, rule-governed conventions and public discourse has for Bernstein an explicitly political dimension. He stresses that once 'we consider the conventions of writing, we are entering into the politics of language . . . Convention is a central means by which authority is made credible.'[41] Before equating Bernstein's poetry with the refutation of all rule-governed principles in language, it is clear that the poet considers not all conventions and authorities as 'corrupt' (p. 222). Instead he proposes that 'It is essential to trace how some uses of convention and authority can hide the fact that both are historical constructions rather than sovereign principles. For convention and authority can, and ought, serve at the will of the polis' (pp. 222–3).

Bernstein's comments indicate that a critique of convention is a legitimate method for revealing an authority which perhaps does not serve the polis. But can we begin to link this ambition to the writing of poetry? In an early essay, he suggests that the disruption of established rules of grammar and syntax is linked with a political agency, in effect opening the text to an affirmation of language as a shared commonality:

Prescribed rules of grammar & spelling make language seem outside of our control. & a language, even only seemingly, wrested from our control is a world taken from us – a world in which language becomes a tool for the description of the world, words mere instrumentalities for representing this world.[42]

Bernstein links the 'artifice' of poetry, or what he calls 'writing centered on its wordness' (p. 32) with an ambitious political and social claim:

Language is commonness in being, through which we see & make sense of & value. Its exploration is the exploration of the human common ground. The move from a purely descriptive, outward directive, writing toward writing centered on its wordness, its physicality, its haecceity (thisness) is, in its impulse, an investigation of human self-sameness, of the place of our connection: in the world, in the word, in ourselves. (p. 32)

The section 'World on Fire' from Bernstein's volume *Girly Man* (2006) examines the role of poetic language in a culture of the political soundbite.[43] Bernstein interrogates ideas of poetic responsiveness and the relationship between rhetoric and political enquiry. The title, taken as Arnold Schwarzenegger's deprecation of Democrats in 2004 as 'girly men', is used as an affirmative chant dedicated to Bernstein's son, 'The Ballad of the Girly Man':

> So be a girly man
> & sing this gurly song
> Sissies & proud
> That we would never lie our way to war. (p. 181)

The eleven poems in 'World on Fire' can be read as a poetic sequence which tackles the repercussions of 9/11. Indeed, 'Some of these Daze' marks the publication of Bernstein's initial responses to 9/11 posted on the Internet, with titles such as 'It's 8:23 in New York', 'Aftershock', 'Report from Liberty Street' and 'Letter From New York'. Bernstein acts as a bewildered reporter attempting to understand 'skies unnaturally clear of airplanes' (p. 18) and the 'What I can't describe is the reality; the panic; the horror' (p. 19).

Bernstein's poetry includes a texture of nonsense rhyme, black humour, punning, and the rewriting of found citations and sayings. His humour is often reliant upon the reader's reciprocative awareness to mistakes, errors and linguistic slippage. Take for example the following from 'The Folks Who Live on the Hill', which begins with a deformed evocation of a scene from *Casablanca*: 'It's still the same old lorry' (p. 39). He questions in this same poem: 'What's the / Use in clothespin when you haven't got / Even the idea of a line?'(p. 40). Images of social disaffiliation and disconnection constantly emerge through the sequence as in 'Lost in Drowned Bliss':

> 'Things are
> solid; we stumble, unglue, recombine.'

> *   *   *

> forest: we splinter the void to catch
> the light, then hail the sparks as paradise. (p. 49)

These poems do not seem assured in using humour as a weapon of resistance; the evocation of a lyric sensibility at the close of 'Lost in Drowned Bliss' signals a nostalgia if not for moral certitude, then at least for an affirmation of poetry's role in the public sphere. Paradoxically, Bernstein's riposte to military authority becomes most cogent when he assumes a more dogmatic rhetorical refrain. This method creates an impression of call and response in 'Broken English' which constantly questions '*What are you fighting for?*' (p. 47). These interjections are interspersed with a sickening evocation of doctored media images and airbrushed photographs:

> Brushing up fate pixel by pixel, burnishing
> dusk: the sum of entropy and elevation.

> Tony takes it in his intestine, the sharp
> pain in the body like ripples
> in a sand dune, his face exquisitely detached

> from any sign of the sensation. (p. 47)

Bernstein candidly recognises that 'it is almost a joke to speak of poetry and national affairs'.[44] Evoking Rousseau's *The Social Contract* he affirms that 'Poetry is one of the few areas where the right of reconvening is exercised.'[45] We can begin to understand the relationship between poetry and politics in Bernstein's language, writing not as protest poetry, but as a poetry that wishes to transform patterns of reading and assessing the world. The poet refers to this impetus as:

> Poets don't have to be read, any more than trees have to be sat under, to transform poisonous societal emissions into something that can be breathed. As a poet, you affect the public sphere with each reader, with the fact of the poem, and by exercising our prerogative to choose what collective forms you will legitimate. The political power of poetry is not measured in numbers; it instructs us to count differently.[46]

Bernstein's claims for poetry as enacting change enforces that it is a revolution in reading and understanding.

REPORTING WAR: ELIOT WEINBERGER

In a column for *Poetry* in 2008 David Orr considers how a poem may perform politically. He questions whether the political in poetry must be subdivided into categories of responsiveness to ideas of social relations, world events, reportage, language – even the ability of the poem to incite action:

> Is a political poem simply a poem with 'political' words in it, like 'Congress' or 'Dachau' or 'egalitarianism'? Or is it a poem that discusses the way people relate (or might relate) to one another? If that's the case, are love poems political? What about poems in dialect? Should we draw a firm line, and say that a political poem has to have some actual political effect? Should it attempt to persuade us in the way most 'normal' political speech does? . . . One of the problems with political poetry, then, is that like all speech, it exists at the mercy of

time, history, and other people. But that doesn't mean poetry itself is passive.[47]

Eliot Weinberger's *What I Heard About Iraq* is constructed from a montage of facts, sound bites, interviews and testimony.[48] Weinberger's prose poem sequence combines statistical statements with the words of politicians, soldiers and Iraqi civilians. Russian theorist Mikhail Bakhtin's account of heteroglossia in the novel, and his evocation of the text as 'contaminated' by a plurality of discourses, helps to explain how Weinberger's volume performs as a political critique. Bakhtin notoriously privileged the language of the novel as a site of verbal interaction heteroglossia, in relation to what he indicates is the largely monologic language of poetry: 'The world of poetry, no matter how many contradictions and insoluble conflicts the poet develops within it, is always illumined by one unitary and indisputable discourse.'[49]

What I Heard About Iraq gives challenge to Bakhtin's anchoring of poetry as a monologic language. 'Found' material acts as a form of reportage; the text becomes impregnated with a plurality of voices. Chronicling the reaction to 9/11 and the USA's entry into the Iraq War, the poem displays how political information is disseminated and within time contradicted by the same sources. Building with the refrain 'I heard', the poem also uses graphic facts at intermittent points. The constant increase of Iraqi civilian deaths becomes a shocking mantra in the poem: starting off with an initial figure of 10,000, towards the close we are told 'I heard that 100,000 Iraqi civilians were dead' (p. 74). Through the juxtaposition of quotations Weinberger is able to display the tragic absurdity of political language and decision-making. One key incident is the Bush and Blair administrations' alerts regarding Saddam Hussein's 'weapons of mass destruction'. In the opening sections we read the words of Secretary of State Colin Powell, President George Bush and Vice President Dick Cheney:

> I heard Colin Powell say: 'I'm absolutely sure that there are weapons of mass destruction there and the evidence will be forthcoming. We're just getting it now.'

> I heard the president say: 'We'll find them. It'll be a matter of
> time to do so.'
> I heard Donald Rumsfeld say: 'We know where they are.
> They're in the area around Tikrit and Baghdad and east,
> west, south and north, somewhat.' (p. 27)

Later these claims are contradicted:

> I heard Donald Rumsfeld say: 'We never believed that we'd
> just tumble over weapons of mass destruction.' (p. 51)

> I heard Condoleezza Rice say: 'We never expected we were
> going to open garages and find them.' (p. 51)

> I heard Donald Rumsfeld say: 'They may have had time to
> destroy them, and I don't know the answer.' (pp. 51–2)

> I heard Richard Perle say: 'We don't know where to look for
> them and we never did know where to look for them. I
> hope this will take less than two hundred years.' (pp. 51–2)

> I heard Tony Blair say 'We know that Saddam Hussein
> had weapons of mass destruction, and we know that we
> haven't found them, that we may not find them. But what I
> wouldn't accept is that he was not a threat, and a threat in
> WMD terms.' (p. 68)

Weinberger's sequence uses rhetoric against its assumed premise of
legitimation and authority to create a political critique. The poet's
careful juxtaposition of information indicates how quickly political narrative contradicts itself. German émigré Hannah Arendt
focused our attention on how, in totalitarian regimes, mass propaganda wilfully plays with falsehood as a strategy for alienation,
inertia and subsequent reaffiliation:

> The totalitarian mass leaders based their propaganda on the
> correct assumption that, under such conditions, one could
> make people believe the most fantastic statements one day,

and trust that if the next day they were given irrefutable proof of their falsehood, they would take refuge in cynicism; instead of deserting the leaders who had lied to them, they would protest that they had known all along that the statement was a lie and would admire the leaders for their superior tactical cleverness.[50]

Along these lines, *What I Heard About Iraq* is Weinberger's attempt to hold politicians accountable for both warmongering and misinformation. Central to Weinberger's text are acronyms which are presented with a chilling sense of rationality. Weinberger reports that 'I heard a marine at Camp Whitehouse say: "The 50/10 technique was used to break down EPWs and make it easier for the HET member to get information from them"' (p. 42). It is later explained that the '50/10 technique' was 'to make prisoners stand for 50 minutes of the hour for ten hours with a hood over their heads in the heat' (p. 42). Moreover, EPWs are explained as 'enemy prisoners of war' and HETs are 'human exploitation teams' (p. 42). *What I Heard About Iraq* also reports that photographs of coffins are banned and that the Pentagon renamed body bags 'transfer tubes' (p. 38). Weinberger reminds us how political language shields its audience from uncomfortable truths and miscarriages of justice. Overused words such as 'freedom' and 'liberation' are also highlighted to indicate how they perform brutishly. On the 'fall' of Fallujah it is reported· 'I heard an American soldier say: "It's kind of bad we destroyed everything, but at least we gave them a chance for a new start"' (p. 65). Also, it is reported: 'I heard Muhammed Kubaissy, a shopkeeper, say: "I am still searching for what they have been calling democracy"' (p. 65). Tim Woods suggests that 'the questioning of the nature of language to inform one about reality results in a political conclusion about the manipulation of discourse to inform one about specific ideological truths.'[51] Weinberger's use of 'found' materials as a basis for his poem powerfully illustrates the mendacities of political discourse surrounding the Iraq war. His critique moreover is enacted without a need for the poet to perform a political rhetoric of his own.

POLITICS AND POETICS OF EXILE: CHOMAN HARDI

Attention to a traumatic political history is explored by Kurdish poet Choman Hardi's volume *Life for Us*.[52] Hardi was born in Iraqi Kurdistan. His family fled to Iran, to return when the poet was a young child. When the Kurds were attacked by Saddam Hussein's chemical weapons in 1988, Hardi's family returned to exile, this time settling in the UK. She has researched the testimony of widows of genocide in Iraqi Kurdistan, in association with the Uppsala Program for Holocaust and Genocide Studies. A search for a safe domestic space where family life can be nurtured and protected dominates Hardi's poetry. In 'There was . . .' we are told that: 'There is a house with four bedrooms / where a couple live with their three children' (p. 9). Yet even in this contained space where a 'young man used to play his flute until the women cried' the poem presents a father 'torn between politics and poetry' (p. 9). The poet's role is often one of fact-finder, gatherer of narratives and the speaker on behalf of those who have suffered. 'The Spoils, 1988' presents a passage of documentation and evidence, and is dedicated to the '182,000 victims of Anfal, Kurdistan, Iraq'. Hardi's own research focuses upon interviews recording the experiences of widows in Kurdish cities and Kurdish women's experience of diaspora. Explaining the term 'Anfal', Hardi states it means 'spoils of war' and is the name of 'the eighth chapter of the Qura'an which came to the prophet in the wake of his first jihad against the non-believers'.[53] 'Anfal' was used by the Iraqi government as a naming of their military operations against Kurdish Muslims in Northern Iraq between February to September 1988. Hardi outlines the political and religious impact of naming the military strategy:

By using this word the government intended to mobilise support from within the country and to legitimise the operations in the Muslim world, portraying the Kurds as non-Muslims. Anfal took place in eight stages, targeting six geographically identified areas. In this process over 2600 Kurdish villages were destroyed and an estimated number of 100,000 civilians ended up in mass graves. Many more died as a result of bombardment, gas attacks, exodus to Iran and Turkey and life in the camps (Topzawa, Dibis, Nugra Salman, Nizarka, Salamya). At the beginning of each Anfal stage chemical attacks were used to kill, terrify and destroy the morale of the people. After the air raids and alongside conventional bombing the ground attacks started. The attacks were designed to steer civilians towards certain collection points near main roads where they were awaited by the army and the *jash* forces (Kurdish mercenaries who worked for the Iraqi government).[54]

This role of the poet as a chronicler of testimonies is key to the poem 'Dropping Gas: 16th March 1988'. Amidst the confusion of war in Halabja, the poet listens to a neighbour who has lost his entire family 'he wants to show me' (p. 19), whereas others are 'journalists taking photos / some men robbing dead bodies' (p. 19). The poet serves as an ethical witness, questioning 'I stand detached from everything, / observing, believing and not believing' (p. 19).

Hardi's poetry presents the poet as exile, examining and dissecting the ravages of Kurdish diaspora. 'The Spoils 1988' negotiates how: 'Anfal came and some survived it' (p. 20). By contrast there are those who could not have 'left for unknown destinations / and started their lives in a new land' (p. 20). The imagined space of a home is equated with a return to a site of trauma. Even in 'What I want', the poet, in depicting 'humane soldiers', recreates a barbaric scene of counter-definition: 'soldiers who would never say: / "We will take you to a place / where you will eat your own flesh"' (p. 11). Memory and reminiscence are evoked through the mythmaking possibilities of Penelope's loom in 'The Penelopes of my homeland', dedicated to the '50,000 widows of Anfal'. In this poem the widows weave 'their own and their children's shrouds / without a sign of Odysseus returning' (p. 21). Hardi's evocation is strictly one of the anti-heroic. *Life for Us* presents the stark reality of women grieving after the 'disappeared', which in 'The 1983 riots in Suleimanya' is depicted as 'the mourning woman with unshaved legs / unshaped eyebrows and ashy lips' (p. 46). The liminal position of the exile is evident in Hardi's work. 'At the Border 1979' recounts the return to Kurdistan where the young sister plays with being present in two places simultaneously. She calls at the checkpoint, '"Look over here" she said to us, / "my right leg is in this country / and my left leg in the other"' (p. 30). One of the final poems, 'To Kurdistan', suggests a need for a cartography of place and home. Hardi recalls that once questioned on her destination, 'I will take the repeated advice / and will not say "to Kurdistan"' (p. 48). This need to map, locate and reorient the exile into a safe space is also echoed in the appeal towards creating safe domestic spaces.

Forché states that a poetry of witness 'reclaims the social from the political' and in doing so 'defends the individual against illegitimated forms of coercion'.[55] She adds that this poetic registers 'through indirection and intervention the ways in which the linguistic and moral universe have been disrupted by events' (p. 45). The genocide in Kurdistan is presented by Hardi as a history which is echoed in other political histories; a husband's retelling of world news stories becomes a site for revisiting trauma and the reinscription of a series of losses: 'Somewhere, people are fleeing again. / We hug and I cry. Somewhere / there is another war to be remembered by children' (p. 61). Hardi's poetry struggles to narrate this sequence of losses; from her research she stresses the therapeutic role of stories for women in exile:

> Narrative therapy is a way of empowering these women by enabling them to deconstruct the structures which oppress them as women and as ethnic minorities in the UK. Recounting histories in a group context enables them to give positive meanings to their experiences as well as establishing a support network. Coming together in groups also enables women to fight oppression and take on broader political aims for their community.[56]

Hardi's engagements with exiled Kurdish women in the UK reiterates the importance of discursive practices as a way of engaging with traumatic life histories, while also reconvening political communities.

VETERAN'S EXPERIENCE: YUSEF KOMUNYAKAA

Vietnam War veteran Yusef Komunyakaa began to write about his war experiences in 1984, almost fifteen years after his return from South-East Asia. These densely framed lyrics of testimony form the basis of the volume *Dien Cai Dau* (1984).[57] Komunyakaa describes the experience of writing the volume as cathartic, the poems surfaced with images that 'dredged up so much unpleasant psychic debris. All the guilt and anger coalesced into a confused stockpile of unresolved conflict . . . I hadn't forgotten a single thread of evidence against myself.'[58] In his essay on the relationship between poetry and music, Komunyakaa stresses that 'the poem is an action that attempts to defy structure as container or mould. However it does embrace control (an artist has to know and respect the instrument) in language.'[59] This element of control can be read in Komunyakaa's work as a detailed attempt to approach experience and history as a revisioning; poetry, the poet stresses, is not 'a gush but a felt and lived syncopation'.[60] He adds that 'revision means to re-see, and at times it seems more accurate to say re-live . . . How many ways can this tune be replayed?'[61]

In 'Camouflaging the Chimera' the inclusive pronoun 'we' is used to map out shared action and strategy. Komunyakaa describes the practicalities of jungle warfare as an attempt to weave 'ourselves into the terrain' (p. 3). Given that the mythic chimera is often pictured as a lion's head, goat's body and serpent's tail, Komunyakaa's title stresses the creation of one body out of a collection of disparate parts. The poem stresses that the manoeuvres of warfare are ultimately a political enforcing and claiming of land. 'Camouflaging the Chimera' illustrates the duration of waiting in war and the movement to an intense interiority. The soldiers wait for the enemy until 'something almost broke inside us' (p. 3). Komunyakaa's poem does not present an easily palpable anti-war message; instead the poem meditates upon the defamiliarisation of the landscape. Before the ambush the Viet Cong are depicted as 'black silk' (p. 3) and an intense subjectivity is framed in the arresting impression of the soldier's waiting 'as a world revolved / under each man's eyelid' (p. 4).

Komunyakaa's war poetry presents a politically complex testimony of the war. The poet questions the ideological and racial conflicts that arise from an African-American fighting in an Asian country for the USA at the close of the 1960s. As Kevin Stein observes, *Dien Cai Dau* questions the interrelationship between domestic and foreign policy which for many Americans 'remained well beyond the horizon of their attention, and equally beyond the periphery of their knowledge. Many of Komunyakaa's poems, to the contrary, address these larger ideological issues and their effects on black Americans.'[62] Nowhere is this problematic relationship between race and patriotism more evident than in 'Hanoi Hannah'. The poem evokes the voice of the female broadcaster who made English-language propaganda radio broadcasts for North Vietnam, directed towards American soldiers. Hannah queries not only the USA's involvement in Vietnam, but African-American participation in an army that tolerates latent racism ' "Soul brothers, what you dying for?" ' (p. 13). Psychological warfare raises confusion about action in war and the African-American participation in its credo. Komunyakaa displays an alert awareness of how his poems perform politically. In 'You and I are Disappearing', Komunyakaa recalls the horror inflicted upon small girl during a napalm attack, and in an attempt to represent the memory, Komunyakaa includes a string of similes. The girl burns 'like a piece of paper', 'like foxfire', 'like oil on water' and 'like a cattail torch' (p. 17). Komunyakaa is hesitant and reluctant to commit the child to one image or aestheticise her pain. The 'I' or eye of the poem is threatened by disappearance into the litany of descriptors: 'She rises like dragonsmoke to my nostrils / She burns like a burning bush / driven by a godawful wind' (p. 17).

Much critical attention has been given to the political space inhabited by the Vietnam Veterans Memorial in Washington, DC, completed in 1982. Its architect Maya Lin has stated that her ambition was to see the memorial not as an object, 'but as a cut in the earth that has then been polished, like a geode'.[63] The final poem in *Dien Cai Dau*, 'Facing It', confronts the polished surface of veterans' names on the memorial wall. Komunyakaa depicts the intense experience of his reflection entering the political monument of '58,022 names' and we are reminded that his 'black face fades, / hiding inside the black granite' (p. 63). Finding a position from which to read, both the inscriptions on the wall and the world around him become increasingly difficult. The mirroring of the mourners and visitors creates a simultaneous layering of reflections upon the wall, since Lin's memorial effectively breaks down the boundaries of monument and lived life. While Komunyakaa's speaker may touch the name of a Vietnam veteran, Andrew Johnson, and 'see the booby trap's white flash', the wall also reflects the scene of a 'brushstroke's flash' then 'a red bird's wings' and also a 'plane in the sky' (p. 63). Memorialising Vietnam in Komunyakaa's poetry means finding a space for a political present in the quotidian; a woman in this 'black mirror' may at first look like 'she is trying to erase names' but as the speaker stresses, 'No, she's brushing a boy's hair' (p. 63). In this way, Komunyakaa's intense lyricism chimes with Adorno's belief that voicing the subjective enables an important political resistance. In 'On Lyric Poetry and Society' (1957) the philosopher proposes:

> The unself-consciousness of the subject submitting itself to language as something objective, and the immediacy and spontaneity of that subject's expression as one and the same: thus language mediates lyric poetry and society in their innermost core. This is why the lyric reveals itself to be the most deeply grounded in society when it does not chime in with society, when it communicates nothing, when, instead, the subject whose expression is successful reaches an accord with language itself, with the inherent tendency of language.[64]

Far from seeing the lyric as a purely solipsistic enterprise or a voicing of estrangement, Adorno approaches the lyric voicing as simultaneous with social articulation. Cast in this light, Komunyakaa's withdrawal into subjectivity cannot be separated from the social realm, since it is an action, which implies political critique or opposition in itself.

RECLAIMING HISTORY: RITA DOVE'S 'PARSLEY'

Having considered how contemporary poetry addresses the political through public event and address, use of political reportage and first-hand experience of war, it is essential to consider how poetry can perform as witness to past events in history. In African-American Rita Dove's 'Parsley' (1983), attempts are made to interrogate history and reconstruct different narratives to those archived or in historical textbooks.[65] Dove's poem 'Parsley' shows the horrific and absurd logic of a tyrant while using a formal poetic pattern as a way of subverting hierarchy and authority. 'Parsley' approaches the horrific history of the Dominican Republic dictator Rafael Trujillo's command to massacre 20,000 Haitians for failing to roll the letter 'r' in 1937. This act of genocide later became known as the Parsley Massacre. To distinguish the Haitians, Trujillo's troops asked the inhabitants to pronounce *perejil* (the Spanish word for parsley). Dove examines the political brutality of Trujillo's dictatorship and the politics of language. Her exploration of poetic form raises important questions about the acquisition of traditions, and even their use as possible political subversion. Using the strict form of the villanelle, the opening of the poem presents the massacre from the Haitians' point of view. This traditional form with its governed metre and repetition of lines may seem counterintuitive, but the constant echoing of key words such as 'cane', 'imitating', 'parrot' and 'spring' (p. 133) reinforces a sense of claustrophobia and containment. Moreover, situating the Haitians' words within a lineage of poetic tradition highlights the barbarity of the incident, challenging Trujillo's perspective of Haitians as subaltern.

Controversially, 'Parsley' presents the absurd and perverted logic of the dictator's actions. Dove mentions: 'It was important to me to try to understand that arbitrary quality of his cruelty.'[66] The dictator's equating of linguistic control with the assertion of authority is clear, yet his voice in the poem is worked through in free verse. One perceives the desperate attempts of the Haitians to speak Spanish and save their lives – they sing 'without R's': '*mi madle, mi amol en muelte*' (p. 135). Dove has written that 'Parsley' was a response to her first encounter of the historical account of the Haitian massacre; she explains that there was no explanation of why Trujillo chose the word:

No mention of the French Creole spoken by the Haitians that rendered their 'R's' softly guttural, incapable of fluttering at the tip of the tongue. No description of the kind of execution, what instruments were used and how quickly the terror proceeded, no clue to the General's state of mind at the time. Just the bald facts: 20,000 dead over a word.[67]

The General's morbid fascination with the death of his mother becomes a way of entering his deluded psyche. While Dove's poem certainly does not aim to fill all the holes in the historical narrative, the perspectives enforce the portrait megalomaniac who surrounds himself with those who echo his words. In his palace is a parrot 'practicing spring' since even the parrot we are told 'can roll an R' (p. 135). Dove's narrative frames the horrifying ventriloquism that the General demands from his subjects and interrogates the barbarism of Trujillo's actions by performing the madness of his questioning 'Who can I kill today' for 'a single, beautiful word' (p. 135).

CONCLUSION: READING THE ARCHIVE – M. NOURBESE PHILIP'S *ZONG!*

For Caribbean-Canadian poet M. NourbeSe Philip, an ethical dilemma is created in how to form material, to perform what the poet describes as 'This story that must be told; that can only be told by not telling.'[68] This pressure upon authorial responsibility is echoed in the citation from German language poet Paul Celan in the fourth book of *Zong!* The citation states simply 'No one bears witness for the witness.'[69] As with Dove's 'Parsley', NourbeSe Philip's *Zong!* is based on a case of horrific historical cruelty. In 1781 a slave ship, the *Zong*, sailed from the coast of West Africa for Jamaica, captained by Luke Collingwood. Due to navigational errors the journey, which normally took six to nine weeks, lasted four months. The ship's cargo was fully insured, and in this case the 'cargo' consisted of 470 slaves. Collingwood's navigational blunder meant that water was scarce and the slaves began to die. NourbeSe Philip cites the documents in her account:

'Sixty negroes died for want of water . . . and forty others . . . through thirst and frenzy . . . threw themselves into the sea and were drowned; and the master and mariners . . . were obliged to throw overboard 150 other negroes.' Captain

Collingwood believed that if the African slaves died a natural death, the owners of the ship would have to bear the cost, but if they were 'thrown alive into the sea, it would be the loss of the underwriters.' In other words, murdering the African slaves would prove more financially advantageous to the owners of the ship and its cargo.

The owners, the Messrs Gregson, being fully insured, make an unsuccessful claim against the insurers for the destroyed cargo. The ship's owners are successful in their legal action against their insurers to recover their loss. The insurers appeal this judgment and a new trial ordered: *Gregson v. Gilbert* is the formal name of this reported decision which is more colloquially known as the *Zong* case.[70]

Zong! is an attempt to retrace the history but not in a chronological narrative. NourbeSe Philip uses the court case documentation as a loose framework for the work as a 'word-hoard' since the original text of the *Gregson v. Gilbert* case comes to a mere 500 words. The material is dispersed, scattered, fractured violently and assiduously mangled:

> Fragmenting and mutilating the text mirror the fragmenta-tion and mutilation that slavery perpetrated on Africans and African customs and life. In deliberately changing the story of the legal text, I engage in a similar duplicity that the actors in the *Zong* case engaged in to convince themselves that it was perfectly allowable to murder Africans in order to collect insurance monies.[71]

Rather than attempt to reconstruct the narrative into a coherent whole, NourbeSe Philip marks the range of competing voices in the text: lacunae, erasures and silences all constitute part of the narrative. The poet is suspicious of telling the stories 'in the traditional way, or the Western way of narrative – in terms of a beginning, a middle, and end'.[72] Importantly, NourbeSe Philip adds that 'I think part of the challenge, certainly for me, was to find a form that could bear this "not telling." I think this is what *Zong!* is attempting: to find a form to bear this story which can't

be told, which must be told, but through not telling.'[73] A glossary
at the close of *Zong!* points the reader towards the intervening
languages in the text which include Arabic, Dutch, Fon, French,
Greek, Hebrew, Italian, Latin, Portuguese, Spanish, Shona, Twi
and Yoruba. NourbeSe Philip comments that '*Zong!* bears witness
to the "resurfacing of the drowned and the oppressed"' and transforms the desiccated, legal report into a cacophony of voices: 'wails
cries, moans that had earlier been banned from the text'.[74]

The fugue's musical form provided an inspiration for the work,
providing a form of imitative counterpoint which helped the poet
approach her material. *Zong!* returns repeatedly to evocations of
the chained slaves being thrown overboard. One of the voices used
in the volume is that of a white European male, and the visual dis-
array and displacement of his perspective is made evident in the
following extract from the 'Sal' section of the book:

                                        there is
            creed there is
                            fate there is
                    oh   oh oracle
                                        there are
                    oh oh
                                            ashes
                        over
                                                            ifá
                                    ifá
                                                            ifá i
        fá
    fa
        fa   fall
                    ing over
                                                            &
                        over the crew
            touching there   is fate
                                            there is
                        creed
                                                there is
                                                    oh

oh
        the *oba* sobs
    again *ifá*   *ifá ifá i*
        fá over   and over
  the seven
seas   *ora*
    in this time   *ora*
  within   *ora ora*   time within
loss   (p. 60)

Different languages collide throughout the volume; here there is a non-hierarchical juxtaposition of English and Latin (*ora*) with Yoruba (*ifá*). Working from the original legal document, NourbeSe Philip incorporates silence into the text through gaps and omissions on the page. Visually the page re-enacts the momentum of the falling and drowning slaves, the rehearsal of prayer and a call for divination or *ifá*. The text performs an echo chamber as one language sonically intersects another, made clear in the visual and aural prompts created between *ifá* and the call to divination, as with the fractured 'falling' that haunts the entire volume. The sound of Yoruba rises in the text, and the poem performs as a score of lamenting voices. A desperate attempt at asserting control and authority is reinforced by the repeated mantra of 'there is fate', 'there is creed', as well as the recall of the comforting cliché 'seven seas'. Against this we have the tragic breaking down of the Yoruba king or ruler: 'the oba sobs'. The poet uses the Latin for bones, 'ora', as a musical marker or chant that forms a half echo with 'oba'. The musical counterpoints in the poem with their sonic and alliterative movements create suggestive liaisons, intersections and a review of history that are incremental within the volume.

From an archival report of two pages, NourbeSe Philip creates a poem spanning one hundred and eighty-two pages. In doing this she sees the poet's role as both magician and editor 'simultaneously censoring the activity of the reported text while conjuring the presence of excised Africans' (p. 199). Importantly, the poet stresses that experimentation is key in her approach to the material; that challenging the structures of language enacts a form of political critique. Her mentor is African-American writer Audre Lorde:

I think we've been using the master's tools (to use Audre Lorde's powerful metaphor) to dismantle the structures that hold us fast and that what is happening . . . We are beginning to fashion new tools to do the work, because the work cannot be done successfully using the master's tools. The master's tools were developed for us out of the master's relationship with us . . . I don't trust the archive, . . . the archive is much more unstable than we originally thought.[75]

NourbeSe Philip, through the disjunction and dislocation of the text, forces the reader to create meaning; she is asking the reader to 'make sense' of an event that can never be understood: 'What is it about? What is happening? This, I suggest, is the closest we will ever get, some two hundred years later, to what it must have been like for those Africans on board the *Zong*.'[76] She adds that in attempting to understand these events, the reader or audience 'shares the risk of the poet who herself risks contamination by using the prescribed language of the law'.[77]

SUMMARY OF KEY POINTS

- Following World War II, Theodor Adorno suggested that poetry needed to reconsider how it responded to the personal and the public.
- A key issue for poets after World War II was how to perform the role of witness and testimony.
- For many poets there is a problematic relationship between poetry and politics. A key suspicion would be a concern of creating work which is merely rhetorical, or dismissed as protest poetry.
- One way poets have found to address the public sphere is to use the personal and everyday as starting points for their reflections; others like Seamus Heaney and Rita Dove have used analogies with history and myth.
- Language use for poets like Charles Bernstein and M. NourbeSe Philip is a key medium for undermining prevailing authorities.

- Poetry serves an important role in its voicing against war as well as chronicling war experiences from the perspectives of both combat soldier and citizen.
- Poetry has a political role in excavating past histories and granting articulation to silenced voices.

NOTES

1. Mark Brown, 'Carol Ann Duffy Leaps into Expenses Row with First Official Poem as Laureate', *The Guardian*, 13 June 2009, p. 1. Available online at www.guardian.co.uk/books/2009/jun/12/carol-ann-duffy-politics-laureate.
2. Tony Blair's infamous declaration was made on New Labour's 1997 landslide victory in the United Kingdom, 1 May 1997.
3. Carol Ann Duffy, 'Politics', in *The Guardian*, 13 June 2009, p. 1. Available online at www.guardian.co.uk/books/2009/jun/12/politics-carol-ann-duffy-poem.
4. W. H. Auden, 'In Memory of W. B Yeats', in Edward Mendelson (ed.), *The English Auden: Poems Essay and Dramatic Writings, 1927–1939* (London: Faber & Faber, 1977), p. 242. All subsequent references to this edition are given in the text.
5. P. B. Shelley, 'A Defence Of Poetry' [1821], in David Lee Clark (ed.), *Shelley's Prose* (Albuquerque, NM: University of New Mexico Press, 1954), pp. 275–97 (p. 297).
6. Theodor Adorno, 'Cultural Criticism and Society', in *Prisms*, trans. Samuel Weber and Shierry Weber (Cambridge, MA: MIT Press, [1949] 1981), p. 34.
7. Theodor Adorno, 'Selections from Metaphysics: Concepts and Problems Lecture Fourteen', in Rolf Tiedemann (ed.), *Can One Live After Auschwitz?: A Philosophical Reader*, trans. Rodney Livingstone (Stanford, CT: Stanford University Press, 2003), p. 435.
8. Rand Brandes, 'Seamus Heaney: An Interview', *Salmagundi*, 80 (1988), 21.
9. Jerome Rothenberg, 'Khurbn and Holocaust: Poetry After Auschwitz', *Dialectical Anthropology*, 24.3–4 (1999), 279–91 (p. 287).

10. Charles Bernstein, 'Second War and Postmodern Memory', in *A Poetics* (Cambridge, MA: Harvard University Press, 1991), p. 217.

11. Carolyn Forché, *Against Forgetting: Twentieth Century Poetry of Witness* (New York: Norton & Norton, 1993).

12. Michael Palmer, 'Poetry and Contingency: Within a Timeless Moment of Barbaric Thought', *Chicago Review*, 49.2 (2003), 65–76 (p. 75).

13. Palmer, 'Poetry and Contingency', pp. 75–6.

14. Lawrence Ferlinghetti, *Poetry As Insurgent Art* (New York: New Directions, 2007), p. 3.

15. Ferlinghetti, *Poetry as Insurgent Art*, p. 9.

16. Zofia Burr, 'Of Poetry and Power: Maya Angelou', in Maria Damon and Ira Livingston (eds), *Poetry and Cultural Studies: A Reader* (Chicago: University of Illinois Press, 2009), p. 430.

17. John F. Kennedy, 'Dedication: *The Robert Frost Library* 1963', in Erwin A. Glikes and Paul Schwarber (eds), *Of Poetry and Power* (New York: Basic Books, 1964), pp. 135–7.

18. Maya Angelou, *The Complete Poems Collected Poems of Maya Angelou* (New York: Random House, 1994), p. 270. All subsequent references to this edition are given in the text.

19. Dwight Garner, 'Elizabeth Alexander: Inaugural Poet with an Outsize Audience', *The New York Times*, 26 December 2008. Available online at www.nytimes.com/2008/12/27/arts/27iht-poet.1.18936672.html.

20. Elizabeth Alexander, 'Praise Song for the Day', *The New York Times*, 20 January 2009. Available online at www.nytimes.com/2009/01/20/us/politics/20text-poem.html.

21. Elizabeth Alexander, 'Black Alive and Looking Straight at You: The Legacy of June Jordan', in *Power & Possibility: Essays Reviews and Interviews* (Ann Arbor, MI: University of Michigan Press, 2007), pp. 116–20.

22. Alexander, 'Black Alive and Looking Straight at You', pp. 116–17.

23. June Jordan, *Some of Us Did Not Die: New and Selected Essays* (New York: Basic Civitas Books, 2003), p. 219.

24. Owen Bowcott, 'Paisley and McGuinness Mark New Era', *The Guardian*, 8 May 2007. Available online at www.guardian.co.uk/uk/2007/may/08/northernireland.northernireland.

25. David Sharrock, 'Martin McGuinness Makes Parting Gift of Poetry to Ian Paisley', *The Times*, 6 June 2008. Available online at www.timesonline.co.uk/tol/news/uk/article4075640.ece.

26. Seamus Heaney, *North* (London: Faber & Faber, 1975); Derek Mahon, *The Snow Party* (Oxford: Oxford University Press, 1975); Paul Muldoon, *Quoof* (London: Faber & Faber, 1983). All subsequent references to these editions are given in the text.

27. Seamus Heaney, *The Government of the Tongue: Selected Prose, 1978–1987* (New York: Farrar, Strauss and Giroux, 1990), p. xxi.

28. Seamus Heaney, *Preoccupations: Selected Prose 1968–1978* (London: Faber & Faber, 1981), pp. 57–8.

29. Ciaran Carson, 'Escaped from the Massacre?' *The Honest Ulsterman*, 50 (1975), 183.

30. Conor Cruise O'Brien, *States of Ireland* (New York: Pantheon, 1972), p. 319.

31. Seamus Heaney, 'Unhappy and at Home: Interview with Seamus Heaney by Seamus Deane', *The Crane Bag*, 1:1 (1977), 61–7 (p. 62).

32. Heaney, *The Government of the Tongue*, p. xvi

33. Derek Mahon, *Collected Poems* (Oldcastle: Gallery Press, 1999), p. 89.

34. Edna Longley, 'Poetry and Politics in Northern Ireland', *The Crane Bag*, 9.1 (1985), 26–40 (p. 36).

35. Michael Donaghy, 'A Conversation with Paul Muldoon', *Chicago Review*, 35.1 (1985), 76–85 (p. 85).

36. Paul Muldoon, 'An Interview with Paul Muldoon by Claire Wills, Nick Jenkins and John Lanchester', *Oxford Poetry Online*. Available online at www.oxfordpoetry.co.uk/texts. php?int=iii1_paulmuldoon.

37. Edna Longley, 'Altering the Past: Northern Irish Poetry and Modern Canons', *The Yearbook of English Studies*, 35 (2005), 1–17 (p. 11).

38. Charles Bernstein, *Controlling Interests* (New York: Roof Books, 1980), p. 6.

39. Charles Bernstein, 'Thought's Measure', in *Content's Dream* (Los Angeles: Sun & Moon Press, 1986), pp. 61–86 (p. 62).

40. Roland Barthes, *S/Z*, trans. Richard Miller (Oxford: Blackwell, [1970] 2000).

41. Charles Bernstein, 'Comedy and the Poetics of Political Form', in *A Poetics*, pp. 218–28 (pp. 218, 220).

42. Charles Bernstein, 'Three or Four Things I Know About Him', in *Content's Dream*, pp. 13–33 (p. 26).

43. Charles Bernstein, *Girly Man* (Chicago: University of Chicago Press, 2006). All subsequent references to this edition are given in the text.

44. Bernstein, 'Comedy and the Poetics of Political Form', p. 225.

45. Bernstein, 'Comedy and the Poetics of Political Form', p. 225.

46. Bernstein, 'Comedy and the Politics of Poetic Form', p. 226.

47. David Orr, 'The Politics of Poetry', *Poetry*, 192.4 (2008), 409–18. Available online at www.poetryfoundation.org/journal/article.html?id=181746.

48. Eliot Weinberger, *What I Heard About Iraq* (London: Verso, 2005). All subsequent references to this edition are given in the text.

49. Mikhail Bakhtin, 'Discourse in Poetry and Discourse in the Novel', in Michael Hoquist (ed.), *The Dialogic Imagination* (Austin: University of Texas Press, 1981), p. 286.

50. Hannah Arendt, *The Origins of Totalitarianism* (New York: Schocken Books), p. 382.

51. Tim Woods, *The Politics of the Limit: Ethics and Politics in Modern and Contemporary American Poetry* (Basingstoke: Palgrave, 2002), pp. 249–50.

52. Choman Hardi, *Life for Us* (Newcastle: Bloodaxe, 2004). All subsequent references to this edition are given in the text.

53. Choman Hardi, 'Breaking the Circle of Silence about Anfal Women', available online at www.chomanhardi.com/research.html.

54. Ibid.

55. Forché, *Against Forgetting*, p. 45.

56. Choman Hardi, 'Kurdish Women Refugees: Obstacles and Opportunities', *Researching Asylum in London Database* (2005). Available online at www.researchasylum.org.uk/?lid=366.

57. Yusef Komunyakaa, *Dien Cai Dau* (Middletown, CT: Wesleyan

University Press, 1984). All subsequent references to this edition are given in the text.

58. Yusef Komunyakaa, *Blue Notes: Essays, Interviews, and Commentaries* (Ann Arbor, MI: University of Michigan Press, 2000), p. 14

59. Komunyakaa, *Blue Notes*, p. 36.

60. Ibid. p. 36.

61. Ibid. pp. 36–7.

62. Kevin Stein, 'Vietnam and the "Voice Within": Public and Private History in Yusef Komunyakaa's *Dien Cai Dau*', *The Massachusetts Review*, 36 (1995–6), 541–61 (p. 548).

63. Maya Lin, cited in Carol Becker, *Surpassing the Spectacle: Global Transformations and the Changing Politics* (Lanham: Rowman & Littlefield, 2002), p. 90.

64. Theodor Adorno, 'On Lyric Poetry and Society', in Rolf Tiedemann (ed.), *Notes to Literature, Volume One*, trans. Shierry Weber Nicholsen (New York: Columbia University Press, 1991), pp. 37–54 (p. 43).

65. Rita Dove, *Selected Poems* (New York: Pantheon, 1993), pp. 133–5. All subsequent references to this edition are given in the text.

66. Rita Dove, 'Stan Sanvel Rubin and Judith Kitchen: Interview with Rita Dove', *Black American Literature Forum*, 20.3 (1986), 227–40 (p. 232).

67. Rita Dove, 'Writing "Parsley" ', in Robert Pack and Jay Parini (eds), *Introspections: American Poets On One of Their Own Poems* (Middlebury, VT: Middlebury College Press, 1997), p. 79.

68. M. NourbeSe Philip, *Zong!* (Middletown, CT: Wesleyan University Press, 2008), p. 194. All subsequent references to this edition are given in the text.

69. NourbeSe Philip, *Zong!* p. 100.

70. M. NourbeSe Philip, *Zong!*. Available online at www.fascicle. com/issue01/Poets/philip1.htm.

71. Ibid.

72. M. NourbeSe Philip, 'Defending the Dead, Confronting the Archive: A Conversation with M. NourbeSe Philip by Patricia Saunders', *Small Axe: A Caribbean Journal of Criticism* (June 2008), 63–79 (p. 72).

73. Ibid.
74. NourbeSe Philip, *Zong!* p. 203.
75. NourbeSe Philip, 'Defending the Dead', pp.70–1.
76. NourbeSe Philip, http://www.fascicle.com/issue01/Poets/philip1.htm.
77. Ibid.

CHAPTER 3

Performance and the Poem

The term 'performance poetry' is now commonly used to describe a presentation that may never be transcribed into volume or a book. 'Performance' in this context indicates the interaction of poetry with its audience; the event may often be ephemeral and experiential, such as a slam poem or improvised talk. The focus of this chapter is to consider how contemporary poetry may 'perform' in a plurality of senses. Drawing from poetic manifestos, we can consider the poetry performance as a form of musicality: poetry, as Charles Olson suggested, becomes a score for the voice. Focusing on poets associated with cultural movements and protest writing, poetry can also perform the demands of appealing to an audience and inciting change. Performance poetry in this light allows for textures of call and response, humour, parody and polyphony. While performance may emphasise a dramatic component, in considering textual performance contemporary poetry also 'performs' visually on the page – through experimental typography. I consider the various ways that poetry may perform or can be considered in Judith Butler's formulation 'performative'. Approaching performance as the sonic or textual iteration of rhetorical gestures and personas enables a more nuanced consideration of how identities are performed as processes of mobility and change. Increasingly in both critical and poetic circles there has been attention to 'performance writing' that places its focus upon an investigation of the performance of language in different fields.

OPEN FIELD POETICS AND PROJECTIVE VERSE: ADAPTATIONS

Published in 1950, Charles Olson's groundbreaking manifesto essay 'Projective Verse' presents an important envisioning of the relationship between poetry and performance.[1] Olson describes projective verse as a form of open poetry. The essay centres around the energy, or what he calls the '*kinetics*', of writing, and also importantly links the relationship between writing and the body with its sustained reference to an ideation of breath. Central to Olson's essay is the proposition of an open or projective verse as 'COMPOSITION BY FIELD', which creates a space for the poem 'opposed to inherited line, stanza, overall form' (p. 148). The motivation for such writing is described aphoristically by the poet, as 'FORM IS NEVER MORE THAN AN EXTENSION OF CONTENT' (p. 148). Olson's emphasis upon the act of perceiving – 'ONE PERCEPTION MUST IMMEDIATELY AND DIRECTLY LEAD TO A FURTHER PERCEPTION' (p. 149) – suggests a degree of immediacy to the writing and the creation of an open form that resists preconceived structures. Key to our understanding of performance is Olson's emphasis on the relationship between the poem and musicality, the poem in effect as a score for the human voice. Discussing the importance of the typewriter in the process of composition Olson states:

> It is the advantage of the typewriter that, due to its rigidity and its space precisions, it can for a poet, indicate exactly the breath, the pauses, the suspensions even of syllables, the juxtapositions even of parts of phrases, which he intends. For the first time the poet has the stave and the bar, a musician has had. For the first time he can, without the convention of rime and meter, record the listening he has done to his own speech, and by that one act indicate how he would want any reader, silently or otherwise to voice his work. (p. 154)

Olson's acknowledgement of the intimate relationship between page, breath, voice and body animates an appreciation of both poetry as spoken word performance and the textual performance on the written page. The graphemic possibilities inscribed in Olson's work are developed by contemporary critic and poet Michael Davidson.[2] Davidson examines the modern poet's foregrounding of the materiality of language and suggests how the poetic text can be read as a site for phantasmagorical writings and the layering of previous inscriptions. In describing the multiple strata of writing, Davidson draws on the inflection of palimpsest which becomes in his own coining 'palimtext'. The palimtext in his account is an attempt at describing:

> Modern writing's intertextual and material character, its graphic rendering of multiple layers of signification. The term also suggests the need for a historicist perspective in which textual layers refer not only to previous texts but to the discursive frame of the present in which they are seen.[3]

We can interpret performance in poetry as dependent not only upon an audience, but upon the reader as a co-producer of meaning. This element of co-production is key for Lyn Hejinian as a utopian possibility:

> For a writer, it is language that carries thought, perception, and meaning. And it does so through a largely metonymic process, through the discovery and invention of associations and connections. Though it may seem merely technical, the notion of linkage – of forging connections – has in my mind, a concomitant political and social dimension. Communities of phrases spark the communities of ideas in which communities of persons live and work.[4]

As we will see, the challenges faced by the reader of contemporary poetry as co-producer of meaning become central to how a poem is performed and subsequently interpreted.

COUNTERCULTURAL PERFORMANCE: LAWRENCE FERLINGHETTI

In his essay 'Modern Poetry is Prose' (1978), Lawrence Ferlinghetti nostalgically looks back at a tradition of song in modern American poetry:

> Wallace Stevens with his 'harmonious fictive music'. And there was Langston Hughes. And Allen Ginsberg, chanting his mantras, singing Blake. There still are others elsewhere, jazz poets and poetic strummers and wailers in the streets of the world, making poetry out of the urgent, insurgent.[5]

Ferlinghetti's poetry is associated with the countercultural movements of 1950s America. The Beats' emphasis upon the importance of the spoken word meant poetry inhabited the public sphere, often as protest. The emergence of Ferlinghetti's poetry in the 1950s coincides with the movement of poetry from the confines of the academy to a more accessible and spontaneous form – or what Robert Lowell referred to as the difference between 'the raw and the cooked'.[6] In an early poem, 'Constantly Risking Absurdity' (1958), Ferlinghetti pinpoints this emphasis upon performance as a trademark of the poet's work.[7] The poet is both an acrobat performing 'above the heads / of his audience', balanced precariously on the 'high wire of his own making' (p. 45) and a comedian entertaining the audience as 'a little charleychaplin man' (p. 46). The 'acrobat' poet strives towards the 'high perch' where the figurative ideal of 'Beauty stands' (p. 46), whereas the 'comic' poet has the task of catching her 'spreadeagled in the empty air' (p. 46). In the poem the poet embraces two roles: one stuns with his daring feats and risks in the face of danger, while the other acts as a performing comic everyman. This is not unlike the description of poetry in Ferlinghetti's essay 'What is Poetry?' as 'a clown' who 'laughs' and 'a clown [who] weeps dropping his mask'.[8]

A powerful rhetorical appeal is performed by Ferlinghetti's 'I am Waiting' (1958), which addresses American policy-making, historical narratives, ideas of spiritual awakening and literary history. The performance of the poem relies upon the repeated phrase 'I am Waiting', which acts as a refrain. Paradoxically, this phrase's constant recontextualisation creates a dynamic movement, while also affirming that the poet is in a static position waiting for change. As a chorus, 'I am Waiting' adds a curious twist – inciting a desire for action and agency. This dynamic possibility is coupled with humour and irony, and the focus of Ferlinghetti's anger is directed at the Cold War USA. The speaker states: 'I am waiting for someone to really discover America / and wail' (p. 46) and 'I am waiting / for them to prove / that God is really American' (p. 47). Ferlinghetti's poem seeks to rewrite histories, his liberal anarchist sentiments are clear in his wait for 'the Last Supper to be served again / with a strange new appetizer' and 'for the meek to be blessed / and inherit the earth / without taxes' (p. 47) – as well as 'a reconstructed Mayflower / to reach America / with its picture story and TV rights' (p. 48). The speaker is painfully aware of the different media that compete against the performance of his poem, as well as a pressure to reanimate literary history. One section of the poem is dedicated towards what he terms as 'some strains of unpremeditated art / to shake my typewriter' as he waits to write 'the great indelible poem' (p. 49). Ferlinghetti's poem performs against a largely romantic literary backdrop, waiting for 'retribution for what America did to Tom Sawyer', for Alice in Wonderland to 'retransmit to me her total dream of innocence', as well as an evocation of William Wordsworth in the desire to 'get some intimations / of immortality' and a final reproach to the lovers in John Keats's 'Ode to a Grecian Urn' 'to catch each other up at last' (p. 49). The poet's closing pronouncement that he is waiting 'perpetually and forever' (p. 49), indicates that his desire for change has attained a status of perpetuity – if not immortality. Certainly the reprise creates the invocation of a litany within Ferlinghetti's poem, which he performs as a mock sacrament upon his audience.

PERFORMING RACE: AMIRI BARAKA'S JAZZ POETIC

If Ferlinghetti's awareness of an audience is apparent in his use of humour and a mock reverential pronouncement, Amiri Baraka's poetry also shares his intention to reach a public and incite political change. Originally named LeRoi Jones, Baraka assumed his Muslim name in 1967, which coincided with his focus upon Black Nationalism. Baraka's writing during this time placed an emphasis on poetry as a political vehicle generating action and cultural definition, and allied to radical social revolution. In an early poem Baraka addresses his own work as 'assassin poems' or poetry as weaponry.[9] This sentiment is emphasised in his militant and early manifesto that claims:

> The Black Artist's role in America is to aid the destruction of America as he knows it. His role is to report and reflect so precisely the nature of society, and of himself in that society, that other men will be moved by the exactness of his rendering and, if they are black men, grow strong through this moving.[10]

While Baraka's political emphasis shifted from Black Nationalism to Third World Marxism in 1974, he remained attuned to the sonic resonance of poetry as a performance. Baraka indicates that Olson's sense of an open form is integral to his own writing. In 'How do you Sound' the poet announces that poetic form must be free and not predetermined: '"All is permitted" . . . There cannot be anything I must fit the poem into. Everything must fit into the poem. There must not be any preconceived notion or design of what the poem ought to be.'[11] In our context of performance, it is important to note that Baraka also states that '"Who knows what a poem ought to sound like? Until it's thar" Says Charles Olson . . . & I follow closely with that' (p. 645). This early work debunks ideas of tradition by adding 'The only "recognizable tradition" a poet need follow is himself . . . & with that, say all those things out of tradition he can use, adapt, work over into something for himself. To broaden his own voice with' (p. 645).

The importance of voice *as* performance is crucial to an understanding of Baraka's poetry. In the essay 'Expressive Language' (1963) the poet emphasises the power of discourse and the importance of adopting different personas within the play of linguistic performance:

Know the words of the users, the semantic rituals of power
. . . Words' meanings, but also rhythm and syntax that frame
and propel their concatenation, seek the culture as the final
reference for what they are describing of the world.[12]

'Leadbelly Gives an Autograph' (1969) meditates upon the
intersection of poetry, music and racial heritage as evinced by the
framing of the poem's title with its reference to the blues singer.
The backdrop of the poem indicates initially decay and cultural
atrophy with 'the dying wood of the church', and the speaker
laments the fact that 'We thought / it possible to enter / the way of
the strongest'.[13] Later we are told that 'the delay of language' is 'A
strength to be handled by giants' (p. 262). Clearly the speaker associates linguistic control with political power. The poem also chronicles an attempt to find an alternative tradition that can perform
with immediacy in response to the violence and racial injustice.
Baraka calls for 'The possibilities of music' by affirming that it
'does exist.' and that 'we do, in that scripture of rhythms' (p. 262).
Moreover, the rhythm is presented as a component of the earth and
nature. Instead of offering us a spiritual enclave, the speaker insists
upon the 'scripture of rhythms' where soil is 'melody' (p. 262). The
visual presentation of the poem on the page moves us from brief
staccato with its opening 'pat your foot / and turn' to the counter-
punctual melodies of longer and digressive lines such as 'looking
thru trees / the wicker statues blowing softly / against the dusk'
(p. 262). In his pursuit of an open form Baraka does not sacrifice
the poem's melody and incantatory rhythm. Indeed, it could be
stated that he is searching for an alternative tradition, an antidote
to a history that is described in the terrifying image of 'An old deaf
lady / burned to death / in South Carolina' (p. 263).
    In the pursuit of alternative forms of performance, Baraka
engages with alternate traditions. The poem 'Ka'Ba' (1969) takes its
title from the central point of Muslim faith in Mecca. Written at the
height of Baraka's interest in Black Nationalism, the poem affirms
the beauty of blackness, of a people with 'African imaginations'
seeking to make 'our getaway into / the ancient image' (p. 263).
Jerome Rothenberg in his work on poetry performance and ethnopoetics in the 1970s suggests that there has been a shift from 'a great

tradition centred in a single stream of art and literature in the West
to a greater tradition that includes, sometimes as its central fact,
preliterate and oral cultures throughout the world'.[14] Rothenberg
adds that he views this adaptation as creating a sense of continuity
within human arts, and maintains that a 'drive toward performance
goes back to our pre-human biological inheritance – that performance and culture, even language, precede the actual emergence of
the species: hence an ethnological continuity as well'.[15] This call to
an earlier tradition is made evident in 'Ka'Ba' in the appeal made
to create 'sacred words' and a need for magic: 'we need the spells,
to raise up / return, destroy and create' (p. 263). Nowhere possibly
is the intersection of a preliterate oral culture of performance and
music made more evident in Baraka's poetry than his long poem
AM/TRAK (1979), written in memory of jazz musician John
Coltrane. Critic Meta DuEwa Jones contends that: 'through the
arena of performance, a dimension of Baraka's poetics emerges that
counters a one-dimensional interpretation of his poetry as appall-
ingly flattened by his political motivations.'[16] Baraka borrows from
the idioms of jazz performance and – as Jones contends – the poet's
use of anaphora and repetition indicates that 'a jazz aesthetic struc-
turally influences the poem's form.'[17] The ethnomusicologist Ingrid
Monson suggests that in a jazz performance 'an exchange will begin
with the repetition of a particular musical passage or a response
with a complimentary musical interjection'.[18] This sense of call
and response, constant syncopation and transition, is exhibited in
Baraka's poem as an ongoing imaginary dialogue with Coltrane –
poetic form is adapted to transcribe jazz sounds. The poet himself
states that 'the recent concern in the West for the found object and
chance composition is an attempt to get closer to the non-Western
concept of natural expression of an Art object.'[19]

The opening of *AM/TRAK* with its emphatic vocals 'Trane. /
Trane / History Love Scream, Oh / Trane, Oh' (p. 267) plays on
the title's use of the name for the US rail network, which it then
proceeds to phonically link with Coltrane. This implied linkage
creates a hurtling movement through the poem where syncopation,
or contradictions of rhythms in the lines, are asserted throughout
the work. Set against the Newark race riots of 1967 and Baraka's
own imprisonment for resisting arrest in possession of an illegal

firearm, the poem pays homage to Coltrane as '*black blower of the now* / The vectors from all sources – slavery renaissance / bop charlie parker' (p. 270). The poem moves quickly from short accumulative rhythms to the extended swoon of longer lines. In the following passage, jazz poetics and political protest conjoin:

> nigger absolute super-sane screams against reality
> course through him
> AS SOUND!
> "Yes, it says
> this is now in you screaming
> recognize the truth
> recognize reality
> & even check me (Trane)
> who blows it
> Yes it says
> Yes &
> Yes again Convulsive multi orgasmic
>   Art
>   Protest   (pp. 270–1)

The iterative momentum of these lines leads to a crescendo of sound; moreover, their visual layout on the page propels the dynamic of the narrative. Baraka's performance includes street language; changes in the typeface can create the implication of shouts and chorus. The poet incorporates the refrains of the saxophonist's music as part of his rhetorical appeal to create a radical work that not only has relevance, but political purpose as protest. Throughout *AM/TRAK* one is given a sense of an improvised performance and certainly the transcription of sounds such as 'blow, oh honk-scram (bahhhhhhh-wheeeeeeee)' (p. 271) reinforces this impression of immediacy. However, it should be noted that, as Gayl Jones reminds us, in jazz-inspired writing 'the concepts "improvisational" and "extemporaneity" are only a manner of speaking: jazz is mastery of technique, and a superb jazz text is as exciting a form as its musical counterpart.'[20] Baraka's adaptation of open form and performance are not a mere freefall of words and sound, but carefully accumulative. Importantly, the poet has noted that his own compulsion towards a jazz poetic is the inscription of history within the performance of the work. He states: 'Jazz incorporates blues – not just as a specific form, but as a cultural insistence, a feeling matrix, a tonal memory. Blues is the national consciousness of jazz – its truthfulness', and adds that 'Just as blues is, on one level, a verse form, so Black poetry begins as music running into words.'[21] Key to Baraka's collaboration of sound with form is the desire to represent cultural memory through anaphoric and iterative constructions.

DUB POETRY AND ITS DESCENDANTS: MUTABARUKA, LINTON KWESI JOHNSON AND BENJAMIN ZEPHANIAH

Baraka's interest in establishing a jazz poetic as the central tenet to his writing is mirrored by other contemporary poets' relationships to music, and its impact for the performance of poetry. Already we have considered how performance is inscribed in ideas of spoken word, and the rhetorical possibilities of addressing an audience. For Jamaican-born poets such as Mutabaruka and Linton Kwesi Johnson, reggae music in the seventies offered an alternative tradition to directly express and engage with an audience. Initially responding to the improvised commentary and narration by sound DJs speaking aloud over instrumental reggae records (an improvised rapping called 'toasting'), both Mutabaruka and Johnson's work is classified as dub poetry or dub lyricism. The term, coined by Johnson, appeared initially in two articles published by the poet: 'Jamaican Rebel Music' in *Race and Class* and a review in *New Musical Express* 1976. Dub poetry initially covered the performance of poetry over musical performance and a strong reggae beat. In an interview Johnson states that dub poetry arose from a need to find viable tradition in his Jamaican culture:

When I began to write, I had no poetic models to draw from because I wasn't much into poetry at school . . . From the moment I began to write in the Jamaican language music entered the poetry. There was always a beat, or a bass line going on in the back of my head with the words.[22]

Initially, he explains dub poetry as an attempt to find a way of addressing what DJs at the time were doing. They would 'get a piece of instrumental music . . . and improvise spontaneous lyricism describing everyday happenings and events' (p. 256). In responding to the application of the term to his own work, Johnson argues that he and poets such as Mutabaruka and other Black British poets perform poetry in its own right, creating 'poetry to be recited to a poetry-listening audiences, something separate from the sound system tradition' (p. 257). Critic Christian Habekost argues that dub poetry also emerges from 'the musical cross hybridization of African rhythms and North American sounds' which result in the formation of Ska music.[23] Habekost adds:

> One of dub poetry's crucial achievements is its artful fusion of different artistic expressions, its bridging of the gap between oral and text media, singing and talking, music and literature. In the wider context of cultural dynamics, dub poetry functions as a connecting link between the 'black' oral tradition and the white literary tradition. For a Caribbean culture it represents both the African presence and European influences.[24]

Dub poetry's inception in the 1970s enabled an important bridging of divergent and often antithetical traditions.

Key to dub poetry is its engagement with narratives of oppression, histories of economic exploitation, protests against racism and police brutality. The performance of the work illustrates what E. A. Markham considers as a play with the role of the poet through emergent and competing personas:

> The poet as performer is coming out of this side of not being quite the preacher/teacher/activist/comic/apologist/ bore, stripping off the sermon/lesson/protest/joke/cause of outside authority, thereby admitting to a degree of vulnerability, thereby working against structures (most of them oppressive) which, in order to deny/conceal that vulnerability, wear the face of authority. In this spirit performance is a continuous process of becoming.[25]

Although initially associated with poetic performance in front of an audience, the poets affiliated with dub poetry turned to the dissemination of their work through audio media and the printed page. Leading dub poets include Michael Smith, Jean 'Binta' Breeze, and Levi Tafari. Mutabaruka's famous work 'Dis Poem' questions the placing of his own work within a canon of literary endeavour; the poem becomes a site for the intersection of history, cultural upheaval, political unrest and insurrection.[26] The ongoing process of the poem is stressed, with an emphasis placed upon a poetics of spontaneity and responsiveness. Mutabaruka emphasises the poem's responsibility to respond to colonial history – 'the wretched sea / that washed ships to these shores' – as well as bear a chronicle and testament to names of black challenge and endeavour. The poem will 'call names' which include black radical activists, politicians and campaigners of the twentieth century: Jomo Kenyatta, Malcolm X, Marcus Garvey and the emperor of Ethiopia, Haile Selassie. The immediacy and intimacy that the poem establishes is evident from the way it performs as speaking and calling to its audience. Mutabaruka uses Jamaican English, often referred to as patois, which the critic Kamau Brathwaite addresses as an affirmation of Caribbean speech or 'nation language'. His description illustrates nation language as a potentially defiant force influenced strongly by:

The African model, the African aspect of our New World/ Caribbean heritage. English it may be in terms of some of its lexical features. But in its contours, its rhythm and timbre, its sound explosions, it is not English, even though the words, as you hear them, might be English to a greater or lesser degree.[27]

Rather than viewing Caribbean English as a variant of 'correct English', or as a dialect, Brathwaite asserts that Nation Language has its own status and sound modulations.

Anger is apparent in 'Dis Poem' with the speaker 'vexed / about apartheid / racism / fascism / the klu klux klan / riots in brixton'. As a vehicle of revolution and a verbal weapon, we are told, 'dis poem is revoltin against / first world / second world / third world / division'. Not unlike Baraka's early vindication of 'assassin poems', Mutabaruka's poem is both a call to arms – 'dis poem is knives . . . bombs . . . guns' – as well as a call for unification of African nations, becoming a drum uniting the languages of 'ashanti / mau mau / ibo / yoruba'. Mutabaruka also plays with paradoxes and contradictions in his work. Initially he delights in the poem's status as countercultural since 'dis poem will not be amongst great literary works', neither will it be 'recited by poetry enthusiasts', 'quoted by politicians / nor men of religion'. Later we are informed that 'dis poem' is a sampling from 'the bible / the prayer book / the new york times, reader's digest as well as the cia and kgb files'. The poet insists that 'dis poem' is not inscribed between the covers of a book; instead it is an ongoing conversation, a 'speakin' which will continue on the stage of world history. Mutabaruka's poem stresses an immediacy which will survive history and be disseminated to an audience to 'continue in your mind'.

Linton Kwesi Johnson takes the element of spontaneity inherent in dub poetry and combines it with a belligerent reportage in his 'Di Great Insohreckshan'.[28] Responding to the Brixton riots of 1981, Johnson's use of 'Insohreckshan' uses nation language as a way of offering a further perspective upon newspaper reports as well as a vehement critique of British hierarchies of power. Nation language enables Johnson to undermine the authority of English language's association with ideals of sovereignty. Brixton becomes a site of 'historical okayjan' whose unrest spreads 'ovah di naeshan' in the face of 'oppreshan' (p. 271). In this poem Johnson also inverts associations by juxtaposing the sovereign beliefs of nationhood and a British identity with the power and necessity of insurrection and revolt:

> dem a taak bout di powah an di glory
> dem a taak bout di burnin an di lootin
> dem a taak bout smashin an di grabbin
> dem a tell mi bout di vanquish an di victri (p. 271)

The poem offers a further and alternative perspective on the story of the Brixton's rioting. Johnson's emphasis upon the urban space as 'di ghetto grapevine' (p. 271), offers an imprint of the disenfranchised community. Moreover, the incorporation of terms and tactics associated with warfare and crowd control makes the poem not only a weapon of instruction and rebellion, but also an opportunity of reinvention and play. The text performs a struggle for power; the repeated use of 'di plastic bulit' and 'di waatah cannon' creates an unexpected rhythmic phrasing in the poem that culminates with a desire to 'bring a blam-blam' (p. 272). Also, the poem incorporates references to public officials such as Lord Scarman, who led the enquiry into the Brixton riots. Scarman becomes, in effect, a sonic resonance of both the dub beat and the action of 'mash up plenty police van' and 'mash up di wicked wan plan' (p. 272). The poem appeals to its audience: 'neva mine Scarman will bring a blam-blam' (p. 272).

To many readers and listeners, the British poet Benjamin Zephaniah has become the more accessible and possibly acceptable inheritor of dub poetry. Like both Mutabaruka and Johnson, his poetry works off the dub beat and also plays with contrapuntal rhythms. But it is possible to add that anger in Zephaniah's poetry is slightly more muted, or focused on the domestic. Echoing Mutabaruka's 'Dis Poem', an early poem by Zephaniah, 'Dis poetry' from *City Psalms* (1992), plays on its dependence on refrain as a way of moving the work through conjectures of literary history and politics in order to situate the poem in the public sphere where it can be heard and even imitated. Zephaniah chants that 'Dis poetry is Verbal Riddim, no big words involved / An if I hav a problem de riddim gets its solved'.[29] This ongoing commentary on the making of the poem creates two impressions. One is the implication of immediacy, even if, as the poet confesses, 'Dis poetry is not fraid of going ina book' (p. 12). But possibly more revealing of the drift away from the initial anger of dub poetics is Zephaniah's admission in this poem that 'Dis poetry is not Party Political / Not designed fe dose who are critical' (p. 12). Compared with the incitement to insurrection and anger available in Linton Kwesi Johnson's poetry, Zephaniah views the movement and performance of poetry as a healing gesture. According to 'Dis poetry', the melodies and movement of Zephaniah's poetry, although entitled as a form of 'Dub ranting', where 'de tongue plays a beat', are performed 'fe de good of de Nation', becoming a form of shared 'Chant / in de morning' (p. 12).

In another poem, 'Rapid Rapping', Zephaniah gives thanks to poet precursors, as well as emphasising the importance of poetry's history as an oral performance and viewing history as an oral narrative. Far from 'playing mystic', Zephaniah insists that poetry was oral and approachable, 'something dat people understood' (p. 39). As an ethnopoetics, 'Rapid Rapping' tells how 'Poetry was living in every neighbourhood / Story telling was compelling listening, an entertaining' (p. 39). He lists in his rapping poetic predecessors who include 'Linton Kwesi Johnson and de Brother Martin Glynn . . . Jean Binta Breeze speaks wid ease so don't feget de name' (p. 39). Moreover, he acknowledges a debt to 'Mutabaruka, Oku Onuora, John Agard an Grace Nichols / All people who are capable an dey hav principles' as presenting work which 'pave de way, yu see / Long time agu before de book existed' (p. 39). This suturing between a combative tradition and more mainstream assertion is evident in Zephaniah's gesture to performance as a site of restitution and reconciliation. The implications of this healing are evident in Zephaniah's desire to create poetry, as he puts it in 'Dis poetry', which 'goes to yu / WID LUV' (p. 13).

THE POET PERFORMER: DRAMA AND COMEDY IN PAUL DURCAN AND DON PATERSON

The perception of the poet as one who articulates through different masks or personas is intrinsic to an idea of performance and poetry. This sense of a dramatic narrative is key to understanding the poetry of Paul Durcan. As Kathleen McCracken Gahern suggests, Durcan acts as a mediator of characters and voices, fulfilling a traditional role for the poet as humourist and chronicler:

Durcan's poetry is essentially dramatic. It is comprised of monologues and duologues, brief or connected scenarios complete only when they are spoken, or 'performed.' Durcan is akin to the early Irish *fili* or bard in that he is a maker and an entertainer, a satirist and an historian. He acts as a communicator through which the thoughts and experiences of the personages he evokes are enacted and transmitted to the community that gave rise to them.[30]

In 'The Beckett at the Gate', Durcan's dramatic monologue is framed within the experience of another drama. The protagonist of Durcan's poem could also be read as an updated version of the socially awkward Prufrock in T. S. Eliot's 'The Love Song of J. Alfred Prufrock' (1915). In a slight but humorous swipe at the consumers of cultural zeitgeist, our character bemoans that he could not go anywhere that spring 'Without people barking at you, / Button-holing you in the street and barking at you'.[31] The key question posed is: 'Have you not seen Barry McGovern's Beckett / have you not been to the Beckett at the Gate?' (p. 131). Durcan uses this questioning as a constant refrain in his work which successfully builds up dramatic tension. Well known for his delivery and oral performances, Durcan has eschewed his categorisation as a 'performance poet' in the narrowest sense of the word, as a poet whose work is written only for oral performance.[32] Gahern proposes that Durcan's dramatic poems echo the patterns of dramatic monologue and duologue in Browning and Yeats to create 'an extremely effective method of poetic discourse, allowing the writer a highly desirable amalgamation of objectivity and subjectivity, it is a form which lends itself with great facility to performance'.[33]

The cultural 'groupies' have forced our speaker to attend and hilariously he comments:

> I got there in good time.
> I like to get to a thing in good time
> Whatever it is – the bus into town,
> or the bus back out of town –
> With at least quarter of an hour to spare,
> preferably half an hour, ample time
> In which to work up an adequate steam of anxiety. (p. 132)

Without even having begun to experience Beckett on stage, as readers we are already encountering a Beckettian performance. In a recent article Erik Martiny draws attention to the shadow of the dramatist upon the speaker's world as 'deeply oppressive'.[34] Technically Beckett exerts an influence in the key repeating of clauses and the macabre comedy of the time-obsessed speaker waiting for the bus. As Martiny poses, this element of repetitive performance in the poem conveys 'Beckettian unease and a sense of nightmarishly cyclical endlessness . . . The opening lines of "The Beckett at the Gate" represent Durcan's foray into an existentialist world where hell is most definitely other people.'[35] Guided by his seat number, the speaker is forced to sit next to a woman (she is later referred to as Michelle), in a near empty theatre. At this point both dramatised stage work and the audience's experience turn into vaudeville: 'Not since the Depression of the 1950s / And the clowns in Duffy's Circus / have I laughed myself so sorry' (p. 134). This sense of carnival is also heightened by the speaker's proximity to his neighbour who at each belly laugh kicks him 'in the backs of my legs' (p. 135) as well as gripping his arm, howling and leaning her head on his shoulder. As a storyteller, Durcan's narrative is frequently sidetracked by excursions into further analogies or related stories. His initial attempts at describing his companion become a distracted listing of theatrical and Biblical women:

> I mean talk about Susannah
> or Judith and Holofernes
> Or any of those females
> In the Old Testament
> Sarah or Rachel or even Eve;
> Not to mention the New Testament,
> Martha or Mary or Magdalen –
> Michelle was – well, Michelle. (p. 134)

These are all women of varying if not conflicting attributes. Susannah is associated with innocence and subsequent betrayal, while Judith famously seduced the warrior Holofernes and decapitated him. A fairly prescriptive perception of female role models is offered by the references to the moral failings of Eve, the beauty of Sarah or the purity of Rachel. Turning to examples from the New Testament, the speaker of 'The Beckett at the Gate' is torn between the domestic activity of Martha the task bearer, the virtue of Mary, and the tenacity and belief of Mary Magdalen. These characteristics become confused in the presence of the woman nearby who is 'all rouge and polythene' (p. 135). Invariably and humorously in Durcan's poem, the narrative comes to a romantic anti-climax with the disappearance of his chance companion once the curtain rises. A chance encounter with Michelle at a bus stop leads to no acknowledgement, only a serene scrutiny as 'if she had never seen me before' (p. 137). Building from the earlier use of refrain as a heightening device, the evocation of Beckett at the close becomes a desperate elegy to unrequited love: '*There's a beckett at the gate, there's a beckett / at the gate, Michelle*' (p. 138).

Scottish poet Don Paterson's 'The Last Waltz' presents two simultaneous narratives within a virtuoso display of poetic form.[36] Paterson's poem shows how rules of rhyme are not necessarily confining, but can create a form for elements of improvisation and experiment. 'The Last Waltz' is written in terza rima, a form traced to Dante's *Divine Comedy* and dependent upon a strict interlocking rhyming scheme of no determinate lineation. Within this framing, Paterson explores through a monologue a history of World War II combat in the Pacific interspersed with reflections on a musical tour by two jazz musicians in the late twentieth century. On one level the poem performs as a palimpsest, superimposed upon the latent histories in Borneo and Malaysia. As a counter against the reader's increasing sense of familiarity with rhyme, Paterson disrupts the modality of our expectations with the insertions of brand names, such as 'SilkAir 777', ghostly intertexts from songs such as 'And I feel fine', unfamiliar icons such as 'Padmasambhava' (p. 35), the sage guru of tantric Buddhism, as well as a synthetic alternative to quinine, 'chloroquine' (p. 36). Working within a traditional form, Paterson is keen to strategically emphasise a friction between the intoxicating global travels of the two musicians against the more restrictive yet also enabling closures of poetic form.

In sketching the history of British involvement in the Pacific, which is prefaced with references to 'Blighty' and 'Dunkirk' (p. 35), the speaker displays an alert awareness of nationalism, nationhood and the advance of English as a global language. He recalls their inability to play the correct anthemic song 'that we'd been assured / was their rallying, their *I belong to Glasgow* / their *Cwm Rhondda*' (p. 36). The performance of music is used as a vehicle to draw attention to distinctions of affiliation. This humiliating awareness draws the speaker to acknowledge that this mistake echoes historical cultural ignorance: 'I knew the shame the letter feels / when it makes its address but its stamps fall short' (p. 36). Paterson surreally uses the analogy of musical failure as a way of evoking an earlier bombing of the island 'that infrasonic boom / that verdant hush that spread like a bad word' (p. 36). Again Paterson plays with the constriction that formal structure grants as well its opportunities for expansiveness. In a sweeping pan, he suggests that the resultant error made every bat in Kota Kinabalu fly 'headlong into the nearest tree' while the street dogs went 'lulu' and grotesquely the 'audience bled appreciatively / from their ears' (p. 37). Although the closed form of the terza rima may be far from Olson's sense of a projective verse, Paterson examines ideas of performance within the interstices of structure. Terza rima becomes a score for a retrospective accounting of the jazz musician's failings and sense of colonial culpability.

PERFORMATIVITY: LYN HEJINIAN

Surveying elements of twentieth-century poetic practice, critic Charles Altieri proposes that:

> There is no distinctive knowledge of the self; there are only contingent moments of more or less charged awareness of the psyche focused on the self, rather than on other aspects of the world . . . Therefore there is no privileged knowledge distinctive to the first person. Knowledge of the self must be filtered through sensations produced by the performance of self.[37]

Altieri's commentary on subjectivity in contemporary poetic practice – as mediated and enacted through performance – resonates with theoretical propositions of the 1980s examining gender construction. Judith Butler argues that gender is neither a pre-existent nor an innate category, but reliant upon the imitative performance of socially accepted categories of behaviour. In 'Performative Acts and Gender Construction' (1988), Butler emphasises that:

> Gender reality is performative which means, quite simply, that it is real only to the extent that it is performed. It seems fair to say that certain kinds of acts are usually interpreted as expressive of gender core or identity and that these acts either conform to an expected gender identity or contest that expectation in some way.[38]

Butler's focus here on ideas of the 'performative' as opposed to performance indicates an action that is aware that it has no basis in origin, whereas performance assumes an object of imitation. 'Performance' in Butler's schema is linked to acts and gestures which are 'expressive of gender' and indicate that 'gender itself is something prior to the various acts, postures and gestures by which it is dramatized and known' (pp. 128–9). In this light, gender is perceived as something that is constructed through 'sustained social performances' that emphasise the conception of 'an essential sex, a true or abiding masculinity or femininity' (p. 129). Moreover, Butler views the construction of gender in terms of social power, dominance and hierarchies: 'As performance which is performative, gender is an "act"; broadly construed, which constructs the social fiction of its own psychological interiority' (p. 129).

Butler's work in the late 1980s and early 1990s opened the terms of debate regarding how a text may perform gendered positioning. Prevalent in elements of American experimental praxis at this time was the interrogation of the relationship between linguistic constructs and gender, or ideological positions. Lyn Hejinian's *My Life* (1987) interrogates the genre of autobiography by refuting any expectations for a linear or chronological narrative.[39] While *My Life* as a prose poem issues a challenge to any neat formal categorisation, as a procedural text the volume is premised on a strict numerical pattern. Originally composed when Hejinian was thirty-seven, the volume initially contained thirty-seven chapters each comprised of thirty-seven lines. When she was forty-five Hejinian republished *My Life* with an additional eight sections of forty-five lines and supplemented the original sections with eight lines. This process of inclusion is remarked upon in *My Life*: 'I could feed those extra words into the sentence already there, rather than make a new one for them, make place in the given space, and that would be the same thing, making more sense, which is all to the good' (p. 88). In her pivotal essay 'The Rejection of Closure' (1985), Hejinian remarks upon the evolving possibility of what she terms the 'open text':

> Language is productive of activity in another sense, with which anyone is familiar who experiences words as attractive, magnetic to meaning. This is one of the first thing one notices, for example, in works constructed from arbitrary vocabularies generated by random or chance operations.[40]

In this schema, subjectivity can be thought of as a process, or continual performance. Hejinian proposes subjectivity is less a fixed entity than 'a mobile (and mobilized) reference point'.[41]

My Life, while certainly not being a treatise to Butler's work, places into focus the performative element of gender construction. Iterative actions become a hallmark of performing motherhood. The speaker reflects upon the ritual of birthdays:

> At every birthday party that year, the mother of the birthday child served ice cream and 'surprise cake', into whose slices the 'favours' were baked. But nothing could interrupt those given days. I was sipping Shirley Temples wearing my Mary Janes. (p. 19)

In this extract Hejinian playfully demonstrates how names when used as nouns retain an element of their initial inscription. This element of repetition and iteration is evident in the text's construction: at one point we are told 'I quote my mother's mother's mother's mother: "I must everyday correct some fault in my morality of talents and remember how short a time I have to live"' (p. 37). Each of *My Life*'s section opens with a leitmotif, or aphoristic fragment, that is then recontextualised at various points throughout the volume. A key fragment, 'I wrote my name in every one of his books', demonstrates at one stage an entry into self-knowledge, and worry of being perceived as feminine. The key clause is followed by 'Was my handwriting dainty, or afraid? It was a pretty plaything. She trimmed first her nails and then the split ends of her hair' (p. 44). This awareness of the feminising of a young girl indicates an awareness that Butler ascribes to performativity. Hejinian's tactic of constantly recontextualising key clauses indicates the evolution of different performances of gendered conditions. For example, we have the admission of needing to inhabit a male space: 'But these words are meant to awaken in you such desire that . . . I wrote my name in every one of his books' (p. 93). Moreover, the emergence of selfhood through the act of writing is presented as a micro-narrative, claiming ownership amidst other narratives:

> One summer I worked as a babysitter and lived with a family and its babies at the beach, (this was the same summer that I read father's copy of *Anna Karenina* and thus made it my own, so that later that fall it was logical that I should write my name in every one of his books). (pp. 111–12)

My Life claims that 'As such a person on paper, I am androgynous' (p. 105). In her essays Hejinian remains sceptical of a so-called women's writing, or language as examined by French feminist theorists such as Hélène Cixous and Luce Irigaray. She responds that 'the narrow definition of desire, the identification of desire solely with sexuality and the literalness of the genital model for a woman's language that some of these writers insist on may be problematic'. Hejinian continues, asserting that 'The desire that is stirred by language is located most interestingly within language itself.'[42] A compulsion for change is made evident in *My Life* as a proposition of a 'new' composition. Midway in the volume a speaker comments that:

> I suppose I had always hoped that, through an act of will and the effort of practice, I might be someone else, might alter my personality and even my appearance, that I might create myself, but instead I found myself trapped in the very character which made such a thought possible and such a wish mine.

Any work dealing with questions of possibility must lead to new work. (pp. 47–8)

In her critique of an innate and stable subject, Hejinian dramatises in its place an evolving subjectivity that is situated in linguistic performance:

This becomes an addictive motion – but not incorrect, despite such distortion, concentration, condensation, deconstruction and digressions that association by, for example pun and ety-mology provide; an allusive psycho-linguism . . . The process is composition rather than writing.[43]

This interrelationship between performance and composition is key to Hejinian's poetry. She indicates that the suggestiveness of language generates a self-perpetuating linkage of associations.

Throughout *My Life* we witness a struggle between perceived gender expectations and the person or protagonist's attempt to divert and escape such codifying. We are told a received wisdom: 'If I was left unmarried after college, I would be single all my life and lonely in old age' (p. 53). Rather than offering us a chrono-logical narrative, elements of a life story emerge at strategic points, codified in terms of social gender expectations. Take for example the experience of pregnancy and motherhood in the following extracts:

I couldn't join the demonstration because I was pregnant, and so I had revolutionary experience without taking revolution-ary action. (p. 67)

The word 'version' is a comparative noun, which must imply its plural form – the one that includes many. Should a mother have more kids? (p. 68)

Far from seeing her text as offering only different versions of a life story, Hejinian's work is actively engaged in the continual develop-ment shifts and performances of the subject. This so-called inde-terminacy is a central concern of her work: she claims that she is constantly 'rewriting in an unstable text' (p. 113). Cast in this light, the ambitions of *My Life* bear a certain resonance with Butler's own inflection of performativity. Butler clarifies in an interview that 'It is important to distinguish performance from performativity: the former presumes a subject, but the latter contests the very notion of the subject'.[44] She adds also that 'what I'm trying to do is think about the performativity as *that aspect of discourse that has the capacity to produce what it names.*'[45] This deconstructive impulse features in *My Life* as 'such displacements alter illusions, which is all-to-the-good' (p. 88).

PERFORMANCE, THE VOICE AND THE WORLD: KATE FAGAN

One might ask the more general question of how the poem relates to the world around it, or, put another way, how does the poem perform in the world? A way of considering this inflection is to suggest how the poem may perform 'phenomenologically' or establishes a perception of perception in the poetry.[46] Australian poet Kate Fagan's volume *The Long Moment* (2002) details an encountering of the world into a form of perceptual rhythm. Her poems detail a self-conscious awareness of perception and how the poet's chronicle of the movement of perception may often be thwarted. Moreover, her interest in breath and musicality draws us in a full circle to Olson's 'Projective Verse'. There is evidently an awareness of the body in the world inscribed in her poetry. This pressure to chronicle a subjective performance in Fagan's poetry is described in 'Return to a New Physics' as: 'lyric interjects / demanding specific / impatient approval / quick like junk, / memorial about position / and meaning'.[47] In an interview Fagan focuses on the improvisatory element of her work, referring to her long poem 'The Waste of Tongues' as 'a long, serial work. I tend to work in series that are sort of "improvisations" of thinking and word, in a sense, not unlike musical improvisations. This one has, I suppose, a social and political impetus to it'.[48] David McCooey notes that Fagan's poetry performs a 'kind of metatextuality in which complex notions of text, identity, and form are integrated and interrogated . . . In this sense the lyric mode itself often makes strange and operates in an uncanny way'.[49] Fagan, in commenting upon the poetry of Hejinian, draws further attention to the sense of poetry as an encounter with the world. She comments that for Hejinian a sense of encounter can be read as a movement between 'abstract nomination (an encounter), and a process of acting or becoming (to encounter), between noun and verb'.[50] Importantly Fagan's understanding of 'encounter' places an emphasis upon ideas of movement and mobility: 'Emphasising flux, they remind us that encounter-discoveries such as those specified by Hejinian – aesthetic, political, ethical – are always mobile, and open to further meetings or happenings'.[51]

In 'The Waste of Tongues', Fagan declares that '*A writer cannot inherit an instance* / To dwell in the arrangement of things' (p. 105), suggesting that writing cannot merely be a commemorative act, but needs to respond, to perform in relation to the world around it. In this poem she writes of poetry as an accumulative act: 'news that absorbs news' (p. 105). Advancing on Ezra Pound's famous dictum that 'poetry is news that STAYS news', Fagan insists upon the poem's mobility and that its actions are dependent upon the world.[52] This responsiveness to the world as a breaking down of boundaries is described as wanting 'to touch the drifting matter' (p. 105). Following through from this phenomenological reading, the writing of the poem marks ideas of change. In writing 'relativity' on a blank page, the speaker notes how 'the way your *i* has changed over time, / a swift equation forming, *i* / time' (p. 89). This understanding of the relationship between poet and perceived world comes to the fore in another poem from this collection, 'Sentience'. Here Fagan performs an anatomy of description upon the act of enunciating: 'this sound breath makes' as it forms 'a lifting of bone to meet bone over the long reach of a sentence' (p. 85). The focus upon breath's mutability is clear in its division from the sentence as 'lust / emerging later as light' (p. 85). Fagan's 'Sentience' reads the situating of relations in the world, an erotic performance where 'a sense of sudden visibility drags / an eye from point to point' (p. 86), where the subject of the scene is attempting to 'interpret erotic scenery' (p. 86). In this schema, things become permeable and the impetus towards description is described by the poet as a form of 'leaning into attention' (p. 87). Moreover, in 'Sentience' a sense of needing to impart or express sentiment is given in painful terms: 'insides rendered outer' (p. 88).

Key to understanding the term 'performance' in Fagan's poetry is the interrelationship between text and music in her work, particularly in 'Sentience' where considerable attention is given to the articulation of a poetic voice. Fagan takes great pleasure in the sonic qualities of how her text performs linguistically. In this context Roland Barthes's essay 'The Grain of the Voice' (1972) offers a consideration of an understanding of music and its performance in poetry.[53] Barthes adopts Julia Kristeva's terms 'phenotext' and 'genotext' as part of this understanding of musical performance. The genotext, in Kristeva's account, lends itself to melodic devices. It is an ecstatic drive closely allied to the semiotic, while the phenotext suggests the communicative level of language – structures which underpin grammatical rules and conventions.[54] In 'The Grain of the Voice', Barthes transposes Kristeva's configuration to 'pheno-song' and the 'geno-song', the former becoming the impulse towards articulation, expression and performance and the latter delighting in the *jouissance* of linguistic materiality. As Barthes elucidates, the geno-song has 'nothing to do with communication'; instead it is:

That apex (or that depth) of production where the melody really works at the language – not at what it says, but the voluptuousness of its sound-signifiers, of its letters – where melody explores how the language works and identifies with that work. It is, in a very simple word but, which must be taken seriously, the *diction* of the language.[55]

Barthes places a particular emphasis on the display of the geno-song in the recital as a form of writing, and the recital through its heightened performance of the geno-song becomes in turn a text.

'The Waste of Tongues' impresses upon us the visceral and erotic relationship between words and the body. The speaker muses that 'A word-*balcony* – begins to curl / at my mind's tongue, tectorial seduction / of a lexeme, in licked syllable against another' (p. 95), and in 'Sentience' we are told of 'what seduction a tongue might exert' (p. 86). Fagan details the timing and enunciation of linguistic performance as 'brushing one syllable' up towards the lip, 'spilling' to gather more details 'revisited' (p. 86). In 'The Grain of the Voice' Barthes makes the distinction of the grain as a physical manifestation, the grain 'is in the throat, place where the phonic metal hardens and is segmented, in the mask that *significance* explodes, bringing not the soul but *jouissance*'.[56] The emphasis on the 'grain' forces us to reconsider how one applies the analogy of music to poetry; as an element of resistance in the recital, the grain raises a challenge to the idealisation of closure and perfection. Equally we can read this physical gesture of linguistic performance in Fagan's poetry as a 'horizon of intimate syllables' (p. 88). This appreciation of linguistic and sonic density becomes in 'Sentience' a 'horizon of intimate syllables', each word in effect as 'certain as teeth in eating space over and over' (p. 88).

CONCLUSION: PERFORMANCE WRITING AND EXPERIMENT – CAROLINE BERGVALL

In the past two decades there has been a steady expansion in the range of intradisciplinary writing which interrogates and addresses conceptualisations of performance. This is loosely referred to as 'performance writing'. Ric Allsopp suggests that the field of performance writing can be defined in its widest sense as 'the investigation of the performance of language'.[57] He proposes that 'performance writing' acknowledges that textual events are produced 'not only through a syntactical and semantic exploration of language but also through the impact of its material treatments' (p. 78). Read in this light, performance writing challenges our conceptions of the purely literary by emphasising multiplicity and interdisciplinarity. Allsopp comments that performance writing highlights 'the great diversity of artistic and writerly practices . . . which rely on the use of text and textual elements' (p. 78). He suggests that these may include elements of theatre, poetry, installation art, animation, soundworks and electronic art.

Caroline Bergvall's poetic practice may also be referred to as 'performance writing'. Bergvall poses that performance writing does indeed explore relationships 'text-based work entertains when developed in conjunction with other media and discourses'.[58] But she adds that the writing asks a question which is as much 'open to literary analysis, as one open to the broader investigation of the kinds of formal and ideological strategies which writers and artists develop textually in response or in reaction to their own time and their own fields'.[59] Bergvall asks a series of rhetorical questions in her early analysis of the term 'performance writing':

> So, what is Performance Writing not?
> Is Performance Writing not writing?
> Is it writing which performs not writes?
> Is it not performance which writes?
> But then does writing not perform?
> And when does writing not perform? And what kind of not performance are we talking about? Is it not performance to write or is it not writing to not perform?[60]

Clearly all writing, as Bergvall rather gnomically points out, can be taken at one level or another as a form of performance. Bergvall's own poetry wants to explode that false dichotomy between text and the articulation of voice itself as performance. As Nicky Marsh comments, Bergvall's poetry addresses:

> Not only the mutability of the realised performance but also the centrality of the body, mouth and tongue to the articulation of language. Such an approach questions the false distinction between a text and voice-based poetics and the assumed silence of the printed page.[61]

Goan Atom, an ongoing work by Bergvall, explores such distinctions between print and oral performance by emphasising the associative patterning of words, phonemic resonance, sonic implosions, resistances, fragments and aberrations within the text. At key points *Goan Atom* interrogates constructions of female sexuality and the performance of gender through an imploded and semantically unstable textuality:

Enters the EVERY HOST
dragging a badl Eg
Finally !
So that the inspiration for such thoughts
becomes visible through the navel in order
To take advantage of the interior mechanism
run through the thoughts retained of little girls
as a panorama deep in the belly
revealed by multicoloured electric
illumination[62]

The openness of Bergvall's text enables multiple interpretations, but one might suggest that references to the 'HOST' and 'inspiration' draw some strong kernel words from Catholic doctrine and practice. Against this we have the viscerality of the 'navel', possibly even a challenge to ideas of an immaculate conception. There are suggestions here of human reproduction: one has only to consider the 'little girls', 'badl' – possibly 'badly' – and 'eg' – maybe ovum. Another critic may find alternate readings, as Drew Milne states that Bergvall's poems work 'both as residues of performance poetics and as scripts for performative interpretation'. This in turn 'generates ambiguities for readers more used to studying texts in order to establish an ideal or finalised close reading'.[63] Certainly, if we follow through on our initial reading there is an equivocation here between the idea of spiritual inspiration and the synthesised rainbow colours of an 'electric illumination'.

To borrow from Barthes, Bergvall delights in the 'voluptuousness' in the soundings of languages. One section of *Goan Atom* orchestrates a multilingual play between verbs, as well as reintroducing deconstructions of gender and the intrusions of scientific cloning. Sonic association links this patterning of phonemes in the text:

Forte love
Forte loot
o found ConCubicles
Some Fav affemmée
an Ourite's Belle

y firms Con-Con
[. . .]
Her e commaes
such Air Errs Heir Hair

Enter DOLLY
Entered enters
Enters entered
Enter entre
en train en trail
en trav Ail Aïe
La bour La bour La bour
Wears god on a strap
Shares mickey with all your friends

The opening of this short extract posits importance on a gendered
and erotic language, which veers from English to a combination of
English and French and neologisms. One can hear the pleasure of
a strong or 'forte' love becoming 'found', and then transforming
to a field of possible concubine or 'ConCubiles'. A French tongue
intrudes into the word favourite. The associational phonic pat-
tering is heightened by the combination of 'Air', 'Errs', 'Heir',
'Hair'. These linguistic resistances in the text force the reader to
consider its performance both phonically and graphemically on
the page; how minute shifts of pronunciation can change a context
for understanding. 'DOLLY' can be read as a girly toy, but also as
the first cloned animal, a sheep, in 1996. This propels a grammatical exploration of 'cloned' sounds and words, as 'enter' 'mutates'
to 'entre', and points to the intrusion of new words 'en train' or
in the middle of a proposition. Bergvall then 'translates' homo-
phonically 'travaille' to 'labour', which is set out as 'La bour' or,
colloquially, the bourgeoisie in French. *Goan Atom*'s performance
writing invites and necessitates the reader's response to complete
a circuit of interpretation. The final line of this excerpt highlights
this gaming or 'mickey' that is shared between friends. Performing
not only in a participatory way, Bergvall's poetry also creates an
assemblage of political and gendered contexts for interpreting the

structures of language. Thriving on the contradictions between verbal and visual performance, Bergvall's poetry offers us a simultaneous examination of poetry on and off the page.

SUMMARY OF KEY POINTS

- Contemporary poetry has been viewed as a score for the voice. Modulations and pauses in the text can be represented spatially and graphically on the printed page.
- Poetry can often perform orally, especially in the context of dub poetry.
- The impression of spontaneity is often key to oral performance, particularly as a political or countercultural response.
- For some contemporary poets, performance can also be considered as the use of dramatic devices. The intervention of formal structures or self-imposed rules provides a framework for the poet to explore the act of composition.
- In considering the 'performative', contemporary poets such as Lyn Hejinian and Caroline Bergvall examine how gender is constructed and iterated.
- Intradisciplinary writing is often considered as 'performance writing', which often explores the dichotomy between performance on the page and oral performance.

NOTES

1. Charles Olson, 'Projective Verse', in Donald Allen and Warren Tallman (eds), *The Poetics of a New American Poetry* (New York: Grove, 1973), pp. 147–58.
2. Michael Davidson, *Ghostlier Demarcations: Modern Poetry and the Material Word* (Berkeley: University of California Press, 1997).
3. Davidson, *Ghostlier Demarcations*, p. 9.
4. Lyn Hejinian, 'Materials (for Dubravka Djuric)', in *The Language of Inquiry* (Berkeley: University of California Press, 2000), pp. 161–76 (p. 166).

5. Lawrence Ferlinghetti, 'Modern Poetry is Prose', in *Poetry as Insurgent Art* (New York: New Directions, 2007), p. 87.

6. Cited from Robert Lowell's acceptance speech at the National Book Awards for *Life Studies* in 1960. Available online at www. poets.org/viewmedia.php/prmMID/5903.

7. Lawrence Ferlinghetti, *Postmodern American Poetry: A Norton Anthology* (New York: Norton & Norton, 1994). All subsequent references to this edition of Ferlinghetti's poems are given in the text.

8. Ferlinghetti, *Poetry as Insurgent Art*, p. 36.

9. Amiri Baraka, ' Black Art', in *Selected Poetry of Amiri Baraka* (New York: Morrow, 1979), p. 106.

10. Amiri Baraka, 'State/Meant' [1965], in Donald Hall (ed.), *The Poetics of the New American Poetry* (New York: Grove Press, 1973), pp. 382–3, p. 382.

11. Baraka, *Postmodern American Poetry*, p. 645.

12. Amiri Baraka, 'Expressive Language' [1963], in *The Poetics of the New American Poetry*, pp. 373–7 (p. 375).

13. Amiri Baraka, *Postmodern American Poetry*, p. 262. All subsequent references to this edition of Baraka's poems are given in the text.

14. Jerome Rothenberg, 'New Models, New Visions: Some Notes Toward a Poetics of Performance', in *Postmodern American Poetry*, pp. 640–4 (p. 640).

15. Rothenberg, 'New Models, New Visions', p. 641.

16. Meta DuEwa Jones, 'Politics, Process & (Jazz) Performance: Amiri Baraka's "It's Nation Time"', *African American Review*, 37.2/3 (2003), 245–52 (p. 246).

17. Jones, 'Politics, Process & (Jazz) Performance', p. 248.

18. Jones, 'Politics, Process & (Jazz) Performance', p. 249.

19. Amiri Baraka, 'Hunting is Not Those Heads on the Wall', in *The Poetics of the New American Poetry*, pp. 378–82 (p. 380).

20. Gayl Jones, *Liberating Voices: Oral Tradition in African American Literature* (Cambridge, MA: Harvard University Press, 1991), p. 201.

21. Amiri Baraka, cited in Robert G. O'Malley (ed.), *The Jazz Cadence of American Culture* (New York: Columbia University Press, 1998), p. 538.

22. Linton Kwesi Johnson, in E. A. Markham (ed.), *Hinterland: Caribbean Poetry from the West Indies and Britain* (Newcastle: Bloodaxe, 1989), p. 253.
23. Christian Habekost, *Verbal Riddim: The Politics and Aesthetics of African-Caribbean Dub Poetry* (Amsterdam: Rodopi, 1993), p. 2.
24. Habekost, *Verbal Riddim*, p. 1.
25. Markham, *Hinterland*, p. 21.
26. Mutabaruka, 'Dis Poem'. Available online at http://aalbc. com/authors/mutabaru.htm. Originally recorded on *The Mystery Unfolds*, LP (Newton, NJ: Shanachie Records, 1986).
27. Kamwau Brathwaite, 'Nation Language', in *History of the Voice* (London: New Beacon Books, 1984), p. 13.
28. Linton Kwesi Johnson, *Hinterland*, pp. 271–2. All subsequent references to this edition are given in the text. Originally recorded LP *Making History* (1984).
29. Benjamin Zephaniah, *City Psalms* (Newcastle: Bloodaxe, 1992), p. 12. All subsequent references to this edition of Zephaniah's poems are given in the text.
30. Kathleen McCracken Gahern, 'Masks and Voices: Dramatic Personas in the Poetry of Paul Durcan', *Canadian Journal of Irish Studies*, 13.1 (1987), 107–20 (p. 108).
31. Paul Durcan, 'The Beckett at the Gate', in *A Snail in My Prime: Selected Poems* (London: Harvill Press, 1999), pp. 131–8 (p. 131). All subsequent references to this edition of Durcan's poems are given in the text.
32. Paul Durcan, 'It's All About Forgetting Yourself: Interview with Paul Durcan by John Knowles', *Fortnight*, 435 (2005), 20–2.
33. McCracken Gahern, 'Masks and Voices', pp. 111–12.
34. Erik Martiny, 'Demonic Forefather: Portraits of Samuel Beckett in the Poems of Paul Durcan', *Nordic Irish Studies*, 5 (2006), 149–56 (p. 150).
35. Martiny, 'Demonic Forefather', p. 150.
36. Don Paterson, *Landing Light* (London: Faber & Faber, 2003) pp. 35–8. All subsequent references to this edition of Paterson's poems are given in the text.
37. Charles Altieri, *The Art of Twentieth Century American Poetry: Modernism and After* (London: Blackwell, 2006), p. 163.

38. Judith Butler, 'Performative Acts and Gender Construction', in Michael Huxley and Noel Witts (eds), *The Twentieth Century Performance Reader* (London: Routledge, 1996), pp. 128–9.
39. Lyn Hejinian, *My Life* (Los Angeles: Sun & Moon, [1980] 1987). All subsequent references to this edition of Hejinian's poems are given in the text.
40. Lyn Hejinian, 'The Rejection of Closure' [1985], in *The Language of Inquiry* (Berkeley: University of California Press, 2000), pp. 40–58 (p. 51).
41. Lyn Hejinian, 'The Person and Description', *Poetics Journal*, 9 (1991), 167.
42. Hejinian, 'The Rejection of Closure', p. 55.
43. Lyn Hejinian, 'If Written is Writing', in *The Language of Inquiry*, pp. 25–9 (p. 28).
44. Judith Butler, 'Gender as Performance: An Interview with Judith Butler by Peter Osbourne and Lynne Segal for *Radical Philosophy*', in Kathryn Woodward (ed.) *Identity and Difference* (London: Sage, 1997), p. 235.
45. Butler, 'Gender as Performance', p. 235.
46. See the brief discussion in Chapter 1 of Maurice Merleau-Ponty, *The Phenomenology of Perception*, trans. Colin Smith (London: Routledge, 1999).
47. Kate Fagan, *The Long Moment* (Cambridge: Salt, 2002), p. 25. All subsequent references to this edition of Fagan's poems are given in the text.
48. Dom Romeo, 'Interview with Kate Fagan'. Available online at http://standanddeliver.blogs.com/dombo/2004/03/kate_fagan.html.
49. David McCooey, 'Surviving Australian Poetry: The New Lyricism', 1 May 2007. Available online at http://australia.poetryinternationalweb.org/piw_cms/cms/cms_module/index.php?obj_id=9031.
50. Kate Fagan, '"A Work of Acknowledgment," A Poetics of *Happily*', *How2*, 1.6 (2001). Available online at www.asu.edu/pipercwcenter/how2journal/archive/online_archive/v1_6_2001/current/readings/encounters/fagan.html.
51. Fagan, '"A Work of Acknowledgment"'.
52. Ezra Pound, *The ABC of Reading* (New York: New Directions,

1960), p. 29.

53. Roland Barthes, 'The Grain of the Voice', in *Music Image Text*, trans. Stephen Heath (New York: The Noonday Press, 1977), pp. 179–89 (p. 182).

54. Julia Kristeva, *Revolution in Poetic Language* (New York: Columbia University Press, 1984), p. 87.

55. Barthes, 'The Grain of the Voice', pp. 182–3.

56. Barthes, 'The Grain of the Voice', p. 183.

57. Ric Allsopp, 'Performance Writing', *A Journal of Performance and Art*, 21.1 (1999), 76–80 (p. 80).

58. Caroline Bergvall, 'What Do We Mean By Performance Writing?' Keynote paper for *1st Performance Writing Symposium* (Totnes: Dartington College of Arts, 1996). Available online at www.carolinebergvall.com.

59. Ibid.

60. Ibid.

61. Nicky Marsh, 'Review: *Goan Atom*', *How 2*, 2:2 (2004). Available online at www.asu.edu/pipercwcenter/how2journal/archive/online_archive/v2_2_2004/current/alerts/marsh.htm.

62. Caroline Bergvall, from 'Goan Atom', *Jacket*, 12 (2000). Available online at http://jacketmagazine.com/12/bergvall.html. Print version, *Goan Atom, 1. Jets-poupee* (Cambridge: rem press, 1999).

63. Drew Milne, 'A Veritable Dollmine', *Jacket*, 12 (2000). Available online at http://jacketmagazine.com/12/milne-bergvall.html.

CHAPTER 4

Environment and Space

READING SPACE AND THE ENVIRONMENT

Lawrence Buell in *The Future of Environmental Criticism* states that 'In one form or another the "idea of nature" has been a dominant or at least residual concern for literary scholars and intellectual historians ever since these fields came into being'.[1] Throughout literary history, poetry has always been attentive to the environment that surrounds the perceiving subject. More recently these ideas have been framed in terms of ecocritical thinking and theory. In considering ideas of environment and space, this chapter initially examines the term 'ecocriticism' and how poetry is responsive to the construction of identities through regional identifications – often referred to as a 'poetics of place'. During the twentieth and twenty-first centuries our ideas of 'nature' poetry have become more complex. Some poets exercise a taxonomist's eye for detailing the natural landscape and evoking a geographical history. Yet it should be stressed that contemporary poetry's relationship to 'nature' is being thought of as representing not only the immediate environment, but also its relationship to economic and cultural change, as well as physical threat. This difference between poetries is explicated succinctly by Jonathan Skinner: 'critics have made a useful distinction between nature poetry and ecopoetry – to paraphrase Juliana Spahr – one focuses (apolitically) only on the bird, the other considers as well the bulldozer about to destroy the bird's habitat.'[2] We will eventually consider how an understanding of ecopoetics might broaden our reading of poetry's relationship to the environment.

The publication of geographer-philosopher Henri Lefebvre's *The Production of Space* in 1974 introduced to a broader audience a spatial awareness to understanding the environment. According to experimental geographer Trevor Paglen, the more general idea of 'the production of space' which Lefebvre references proposes that 'humans create the world around them and that humans are, in turn, created by the world around them. In other words, the human condition is characterized by a feedback loop between human activity and our material surroundings.'[3] We will consider the impact of reading poetry 'spatially' specifically as the writer's response to urban landscape. Increasingly poets are subject and alert to a global mobility that undoubtedly challenges fixed ideas of region, cultural identity and geographic stability. Contemporary poets often introduce through their work a travelogue, or a narrative of cultural dislocation. Responding to the threat of environmental catastrophe, twenty-first-century poets attempt to assimilate scientific accounts, texts and news bulletins into their work to inform both the reader and themselves. The frequently apocalyptic scenes envisaged by such poetry are often counterbalanced by the possibility of imagined spaces. In this context contemporary poetry acts both as an elegy for a vanishing world and as an attempt at its reconstruction in a new ecological form.

ECOCRITICISM: LANDSCAPE AND ECOLOGY IN GARY SNYDER'S POETRY

According to Cheryll Glotfelty, ecocriticism is 'the study of the relationship between literature and the physical environment . . . ecocriticism takes an earth-centred approach to literary studies.'[4] Increasingly ecocriticism is seen as a multi-genre critical approach, linking disciplines such as ecology and environmental science with the plastic, digital and literary arts. One of the poets most associated with the ecocritical turn in the late twentieth century is Californian poet Gary Snyder. Snyder's body of work includes important volumes of essays such as *The Practice of the Wild* (1990) and *A Place in Space* (1995), which explore humanity's complex relationship to the environment and the need to remain aware of local communities.[5] Snyder writes that 'ecology' as a term 'derives etymologically from the Greek *oikos*, or household. Modern usage refers both to "the study of biological interrelationships and the flow of energy through organisms and inorganic matter;"' ecology can expand to other realms, from technology systems to – 'the ecology of thinking and composition'.[6] The interconnection between ecological thinking and writing is apparent in Snyder's most famous poem 'Riprap', where the poet instructs 'Lay down these words / Before your mind like rocks'.[7] Commenting on the recent academic interest in ecocriticism, Snyder states:

> Nature writing, environmental history, and ecological phi- losophy have become subjects of study in the humanities. There are, however, still a few otherwise humane historians and philosophers who unreflectingly assume that the natural world is primarily a building-supply yard for human projects. That is what the Occident has said and thought for a couple of thousand years.[8]

Snyder's cycle of lyrics 'Little Songs for Gaia' (2005) gestures emphatically to environmental scientist James Lovelock's pioneer- ing work on Gaia theory.[9] Gaia theory states that the Earth's bio- sphere behaves as if it were a single organism. As Lovelock explains in his latest book *The Vanishing Face of Gaia: A Final Warning* (2009), Gaia theory presents

> a view of the earth introduced in the 1980s that sees it as a self-regulating system made up from a totality of organisms, the ocean and the atmosphere tightly coupled as an evolving system. The theory sees this system as having a goal – the regulation of surface conditions so as to be as favourable for contemporary life as possible.[10]

Lovelock has been seeking over the decades to dispel the belief that humans are somehow the 'owners, managers, commissars or people in charge' (p. 6) of the earth. He emphasises that earth 'has not evolved solely for our benefit and any changes we make to it are at our own risk. This way of thinking makes clear that we have no special human rights; we are merely one of the partner species in the great enterprise of Gaia' (p. 6).

'Little Songs for Gaia' consists of twenty lyric sections and presents the ecology of Northern California, sounds from the immediate landscape, dream visions and the threat to the abundance of Gaia's biosphere. Snyder presents a panoptic vision of the landscape, often formed through the eye of a bird of prey. This position allows not only a cartographic reading of the landscape, but a comment upon the importance of humanity in the greater scheme of Gaia's ecosystem. The hawk 'dipping and circling' over the salt marshes of San Francisco elicits the reflection upon Gaia's 'slow-paced / systems of systems' (p. 49). Snyder comments that 5,000 years is all 'that a human can figure', and the human in question is framed as the absurd yet potentially destructive 'grasshopper man in his car driving through' (p. 49). In a later lyric the poet pictures earth's blue planet: 'Deep blue sea baby' (p. 54). Viewed from the 'Great Bird's' perspective, the earth presents a magnificent curve and momentum: 'Whirl of white clouds over blue-green land and seas / bluegreen of bios' (p. 54). Snyder also chides the impulse to chronicle and assume ownership over the environment:

> I'm glad for once I knew
> Not to look too much when
> *Really there*
>   Or try to write it down. (p. 51)

The premise of the earth as a mere construction yard of building resources is reiterated later in the sequence. The poet hears the log trucks in the early morning, reminding him 'of the world that is carried away' (p. 55). Snyder's poems and his essays bring to attention what he has called the 'art of the wild' – that is, to see art in the context of environment and nature. He urges us to see 'nature as process rather than as product or commodity . . . Seeing this also serves to acknowledge the autonomy and integrity of the nonhuman part of the world, an "Other" that we are barely beginning to be able to know'.[11]

A POETICS OF PLACE: GEOFFREY HILL, ROBERT HASS AND ANNE SZUMIGALSKI

According to Buell, place is 'a configuration of highly flexible subjective, social and material dimensions'.[12] He explains that for political geographer John Agnew, 'place' can be understood as 'a matter of (social) "locale", (geographical) "location" and a sense of place. It combines elements of nature (elemental forces), social relations (class gender and so on), and meaning (the mind, ideas, symbols)' (p. 60). While place can also evoke a physical relationship to the environment, or indeed 'a physical site', it also implies emotional and cognitive relationships – what Agnew refers to as 'a deeply personal phenomenon founded on one's life world and everyday practices' (p. 60). A configuration of place is also informed by 'the plural geographies associated with ethnic, political, economic, informational, cultural and religious forma-tions' (p. 60). As has been initially suggested in a cursory reading of Lefebvre, place also exerts effects on its inhabitants. Agnew concurs that 'those constructs are themselves, in turn, mediated ecologically by the physical environments that they also mediate' (p. 60).

Geoffrey Hill's *Mercian Hymns* (1971), takes as its geographical locus a specific area – the valley of the River Trent and its tributaries, once known as Mercia but now known as the English Midlands.[13] It has been suggested that the original old English 'Mierce' means border people. The book is written as a sequence of thirty discrete verses that Hill refers to as 'versets', which he describes as groupings of 'rhythmical prose':

The rhythm and cadence are far more of a pitched and tuned chant than I think one normally associates with the prose poem. I designed the appearance of the page in the form of versets. The reason they take the form they do is because at a very early stage the words and phrases begin to group themselves in this way. I did immediately see it as an extended sequence.[14]

The sonorous momentum of the sections is often incantatory, fusing private history with shards of broader historical narrative. A central figure in the sequence is the Anglo–Saxon King Offa who ruled Mercia during the eighth century. Geographical space and the historical figure cannot be disentangled from one another. Within *Mercian Hymns* there is also a strong autobiographical narrative. Hill admits a rather disturbing link between the king and childhood:

> The murderous brutality of Offa as a political animal seems again an objective correlative for the ambiguities of English history in general, as a means of trying to encompass and accommodate the early humiliations and fears of one's own childhood and also one's discovery of the tyrannical streak in oneself as a child.[15]

The opening of *Mercian Hymns* prepares the reader for an archaeological work, where buried in the text are strata of co-existent histories. Beginning the sequence with a panegyric, the speaker's praise of Offa includes titles such as King of 'holly groves', 'overlord of the M5' and 'architect of the historic rampart and ditch' (p. 105). Later, in section twelve, Hill presents a scene of excavation. Beginning with 'Their spades grafted through the variably-resistant soil', we are introduced to workers paid to 'caulk waterpipes' (p. 116). Confusion regarding time and period is deliberate, the most immediate anchor being the landscape and earth where 'Chestnut-boughs clash their inflamed leaves' (p. 116). The succeeding section presents the results of an archaeologist's dig which include Offa's hoard of coins: 'Trim the lamp; polish the lens; draw, one by one, rare coins to the light' (p. 117). The location of this find resonates as a space where history and ritual coalesce 'far from his underkingdom of crinoid and crayfish' (p. 117). This layering of the text enables Hill to introduce small narrative excerpts of his childhood. In the twenty-fifth section we are introduced to his grandmother's work in a nail shop. A visceral memory of the building is introduced: 'Sparks had furred its low roof. In dawn-light the troughed water floated a damson-bloom of dust' (p. 129). Hill's inclusion of compound colour-descriptors, musical resonances as well as Anglo-Saxon and Latinate phrases reinforces the density of the poem as strata of competing timeframes and languages.

Near the close, in hymnet twenty-eight, we are presented with a cartographer's view of the area depicting: 'The process of generations; deeds of settlement' (p. 132). Michel de Certeau's distinction between panoptic vision above a settlement, and the pedestrian experience of its inhabitants, offers a way of considering the different perspectives of place in *Mercian Hymns*. De Certeau's *The Practice of Everyday Life* (1984) suggests that the desire to view or map the city from such a height betrays a desire to theorise, with the panoptic spectator becoming a 'voyeur-god'.[16] By contrast, the practitioners of the settlement live 'down below' (p. 93). De Certeau's commentary draws an evocative description of the labyrinthine and the frequently illegible passage of people: 'The networks of these moving intersecting writings compose a manifold story that has neither author nor spectator, shaped out of fragments of trajectories and alterations of spaces' (p. 93). *Mercian Hymns* is intent on showing a landscape etched with 'tracks of ancient occupation' in 'Groves of legendary holly; silverdark the ridged gleam' (p. 132).

Robert Hass's work recreates with a keen botanist's eye the history and physical shaping of his environment. A native of Northern California, he inscribes the flora and fauna of the San Francisco Bay Area in his first volume, *Field Guide* (1973), as the titles of some of the poems indicate: 'On the Coast near Sausalito', 'Black Mountain, Los Altos', 'At Stinson Beach', 'Palo Alto: The Marshes'.[17] In this last long poem Hass delights in the naming of his environment:

> Walking, I recite the hard
> explosive names of birds:
> egret, kildeer, bittern, tern.
> Dull in the wind and early morning light,
> the striped shadows of cattails
> twitch like nerves. (p. 24)

The poem is dedicated to Mariana Richardson (1830–91), whose 'father owned the land / where I grew up' (p. 25). John Fremont and Kit Carson seized the land in Palo Alto during the US–Mexican War (1846–8). Given this historical context, Hass's resolute naming of what he sees can seem a sinister act of ownership. But when this adumbration of the landscape is performed near the close of the poem: 'sedge, flag, owl's clover, / rotting wharves' situated near a tank which 'lugs silver / bomb-shaped napalm tins' (p. 27), the impression and tone are distinctly different. Hass makes a link here with the untamed beauty of the marshes and the traffic of naplam to another, if remote, conflict in Vietnam. His sympathy with Richardson is emphasised at the poem's close:

> Again,
> my eye performs
> the lobotomy of description.
> Again, almost with yearning
> I see the malice of her ancient eyes (p. 27)

Here Hass criticises himself for what Ralph Waldo Emerson termed 'the tyranny of the eye' and what the poem refers to as 'the lobotomy of description'. The lure of taxonomy and the dissection of the landscape with a naturalist's eye find a shift in relations in Hass's second volume *Praise* (1979).[18]

Edward Casey stresses that 'Places are not so much the direct objects of sight or thought or recollection as what we feel *with* and *around*, *under* and *above*, *before* and *behind*'.[19] While Hass's 'Meditation at Lagunitas' is set in Marin County, the landscape of the poem forms the basis for an enquiry into the mechanics of language. Whereas *Field Guide* displays nostalgia for a naive relationship between language and the world (an Edenic state of taxonomy), 'Meditation at Lagunitas' intently assesses the role of language as a transparent vehicle of representation. Hass comments that his poem was read as a criticism of poststructuralism, in particular Derridean *différance*:

> There was a time when people took my work to be dumber than it was . . . Readings of *Praise*? A lot of people were ter-

rified about poststructuralism and seized on 'Meditation at
Lagunitas' as an antistructuralist Whitmanian affirmation.
They took me to be reopening the mindless door into the
American sublime.[20]

The poem begins with an evocation of absence, pointing us
towards the notion that 'All the new thinking is about loss' (p. 4).
The speaker takes elements from his environment as illustrations
of this idea. The woodpecker is 'by his presence, / some tragic
falling off from a first world of undivided light' (p. 4). Here references to an Edenic landscape where words are wedded to the
things they signify create an impression of a lost transcendent
language. However, Hass plays with these ideas by humorously
suggesting that since there is 'no one thing to which the bramble
of *blackberry* corresponds to / a word is elegy to what it signifies'
(p. 4). 'Meditation at Lagunitas' asks that if language is only a
system of pointing, gesturing to absence, then what becomes of
concepts such as justice, love and empathy? The speaker reflects
that 'After a while I understood that talking this way, everything
dissolves: justice, / *pine, hair, woman, You*, and *I*' (p. 4). Far from
inhibiting a narrative, these words create their own associations
and patterns of reminiscences. The poem not only inscribes a
series of losses, but transforms abstract thought into physicality and eroticism. Hass's speaker recalls a lover, which leads to a
recalling of desire, a 'thirst for salt, for my childhood river' (p. 4).
His use of personal narrative is juxtaposed with more theoretical pronouncements such as: 'Longing, we say, because desire is
full / of endless distances' (pp. 4–5). The meditation on language
theory, placed into the context of an absent lover, devolves into a
consideration of erotic love. These final lines reinforce a linkage
between the erotic and material world, pointing to moments when
'the body is as numinous / as words' (p. 5). The poem's close
attempts to fuse the natural world with language as the speaker
reflects upon: 'Such tenderness, those afternoons and evenings,
/ saying *blackberry, blackberry, blackberry*' (p. 5). The enforced
repetition of blackberry emphasises a delicious delight in the
physicality of the word. This appreciation for the physical world is
echoed in Hass's recent poetry where he claims 'It's not / Just the

violence, it's a taste for power / That amounts to contempt for the body'.[21]

Anne Szumigalski was known during her lifetime as a Canadian poet but was born in London before emigrating in 1951, and lived in Saskatoon, Saskatchewan, from 1956 until her death. For a few years before leaving for Canada she lived in North Wales. These are not incidental facts – since the terrain of her poetry is filled with what may be an unfamiliar landscape. A perception of strangeness or making the familiar and commonplace somewhat uncanny is not merely the experience of a different physical landscape, although Szumigalski has a keen botanist's eye. In an interview Szumigalski stated that the prairie landscape is key not only to the content of her poems, but more importantly as an enabling psychological space:

> I've lived in a lot of places and a lot of poems are about these places. But on the other hand the whole of my work is so much influenced by the prairie that even these would not exist . . . Somehow the prairies have given me a sort of licence its sort of . . . as though it were in fact a licence, a piece of paper on which is written 'Think as wide as you want to, infinite as the space up and down. Jump into it. Don't confine yourself.' And I know that's what I felt on the prairie, and I know that it's the foundation of all my poetry.[22]

In the narratives of Szumigalski's poetry there is sometimes a degree of slippage as the story suddenly moves to unexpected surrealism. Take for example the elegy 'A Celebration', where the focus on the grandmother's calcified knuckles becomes a fantastical site of regeneration:

> by September they poked out at the surface
> a wide circle of little chalky stubs
>
> *   *   *
>
> when All Souls' came we lighted
> eighty of them for holy candles.[23]

The poem ends with the hope that 'next year they may flower with rockroses / or stiff honeycomb corals'.[24] This attraction to meta-morphosis is what draws the poet to reconsider *The Mabinogion* in her erotic treatment of Pryderi in 'Hanner Hwch Hanner Hob – The Flitch'.[25] There is a comedy in the protagonist's wooing of the pig through Pryderi's tale, and also something disconcertingly atavistic at its close: 'he takes out his sharp pig little knife / and sticks her one / she's gone in a minute / with one happy sigh'.[26] Szumigalski judges this eroticism and suggestion of violation well, allowing us to reconsider the narrative of the trickster as a method of dangerous seduction.

Szumigalski's poems read as a desire to decipher marks in the world and translate them into significant meanings or linguistic signs. The most obvious clue to this impulse is given in the title of her third volume *The Doctrine of Signatures* (1983). Dating from the Renaissance, the concept of 'signature' proposes that a herbal-ist's use of various plants was dictated by their form. For example, lungwort, with its speckled leaves resembling the lungs, was used for bronchial illness. This impulse towards investing the world with decipherable meanings surfaces in 'The Musicologist'. In this poem a man, 'd', obsessively records and archives the sounds of daily life in an attempt to find some underlying structure or univer-sal code to be unscrambled:

> d shows
> her the place in the notebook where he's written down
> the melody all the sounds that ever were are stored in
> the void around us he claims the basis of some sort of
> symphony she asks he snorts with laughter at her simplistic
> approach.[27]

Szumigalski exhibits scepticism towards a doctrine of universality. It is not until 'I² = -1' from the volume, *Rapture of the Deep* (1991), that the poet addresses this ambition for a transcendent meaning directly. One cannot but read this poem as an investigation of *logos*, the divine order of language. Like Hass's 'Meditation at Lagunitas', the poem reveals a loss or mourning for the transcendent language where words are linked to the objects that they signified:

But it's true isn't it, that before something has become a
whole we may not refer to it as divided? The trick of the
word, the sag of the language, may mean it has always been
whole, even before the two halves were joined. Apartness.
Agglutination.[28]

What possible response can the poet grant in the face of such apparent 'apartness' between word and object? Szumigalski's answer is
simple: 'Invent me a set of pure symbols. Write me a letter in
unmistakable signs.'[29] Although this proposition is an untenable
one, the reader cannot help but be momentarily seduced by the
poem's demand to create a vocabulary of her own. '$I^2 = -I$' instructs
us in the creation of an imaginable compositional space: 'Now give
me an imaginary number; speak me an imagined word'.[30] In section
two of the long sequence poem 'Heroines', we are given a botanist's
description of an elderly Prairie woman's body. The descriptions
echo mythic transformations: her mouth becomes a repository for
herbal medicine 'planted with rue and artemesia', her shoulders
are 'shrubby branches' and her breasts 'hang like chokecherries'.[31]
The grandmother's body becomes an erotic and sexualised landscape of transformation since 'around your cunt grow stiff prairie
plants / whose withies are tough / whose leaves are aromatic'.[32]
Szumigalski adds to this sexualised landscape of the woman's
body a menstrual cycle in flowers: 'they flower orange red yellow
as locoweed / as buffalobean'.[33] The prairie plays an integral role
in establishing psychological space to enable the complex interplay
of ideas in Szumigalski's work. The prairie as a space of permis-
sion in Szumigalski's poetry enables a complex interplay of gnostic
meditations, family vignettes, gender relations, scientific theorems
and myths.

THE SPATIAL TURN

Lefebvre's *The Production of Space* furthers an understanding
of environment in spatial terms. Lefebvre is keen to bridge the
gap between theory and practice as well as creating connections
between mental and social space. Lefebvre states that: 'Not so

many years ago, the word space had a strictly geometrical meaning: the idea it evoked, was simply that of an empty area'.[34] Instead, he wishes to illustrate how '*(Social) space is a social product*' (p. 26):

> Social space will be revealed in its particularity to the extent that it ceases to be indistinguishable from mental space (as defined by the philosophers and the mathematicians) on the one hand, and physical space (as defined by practico-sensory activity and the perception of 'nature') on the other. What I shall be seeking to demonstrate is that such a social space is constituted neither by a collection of things or an aggregate of (sensory) data, nor by a void packed like a parcel with various contents, and that it is irreducible to a 'form' imposed upon phenomena, upon things, upon physical materiality. (p. 27)

Space, according to Lefebvre, is far from being a neutral container where events 'happen', but is always produced by social processes. His work claims a political practice for space, since it is always subject to battles for control. Moreover, he adds that one should not view space as a 'container of a virtually neutral kind, designed simply to receive whatever is poured into it' (p. 94). At its most elemental, space is created by humans, which are in turn affected by the spaces that they create.

The English translation of *The Production of Space* in 1991 disseminated Lefebvre's ideas to a broader audience. Critic Ian Davidson comments upon the 'spatial turn' around this time in the work of other writers on postmodernism – such as space–time compression in David Harvey's *The Postmodern Condition* and cognitive mapping in Frederic Jameson's *Postmodernism, The Cultural Logic of Late Capitalism*.[35] Davidson proposes that the fascination with spatial relationships, in both the arts and social sciences, includes the 'increased visibility of information and communication technologies that support processes of globalization, rapid movements of international capital, and an increasingly mobile global population' (pp. 94–5). As a consequence, Davidson adds that there has been 'an increased anxiety about ideas of identity in the wake of changes in relationships between place, language, and nationality, and an increased focus on the politics of gender and sexuality in relation to the "place" of the body' (p. 95). It is with these issues in mind that we turn to the representation of the city and its interaction with its inhabitants in poems by Edwin Morgan, Kathleen Jamie and Paula Meehan.

SPACE, THE CITY AND THE POEM: EDWIN MORGAN, KATHLEEN JAMIE AND PAULA MEEHAN

Edwin Morgan's sequence of ten Petrarchan sonnets, entitled *Glasgow Sonnets*, was published in 1972. As one of Morgan's most urban works, the sequence chronicles the consequences of modernisation in the city, the effects of planning upon social processes as well as the decimation of large-scale heavy industries. In an essay 'The Poet and the City' the poet traces writers' often ambivalent relationships to the cityscape:

> The city is just as capable of stirring a writer's creative imagination as the world of nature is, and this is true whether the relations are positive or negative. It may well be that the straightforward celebration of a city ... will not so easily achieve lift off in a doubtful and self critical age like ours, but the complexities of reactions to cities, especially in the last two centuries have initiated what is virtually a new kind of urban writing, in heightened prose as well as verse.[36]

Morgan draws attention to the work of nineteenth and early twentieth-century writers' responses to increased pressures of modernisation upon the city. He cites Charles Dickens's London, Charles Baudelaire and Victor Hugo's Paris, Fyodor Dostoevsky's St Petersburg, as well as the futurist cities in the poetry of Vladimir Mayakovsky, Tommasso Marinetti's prose poems and Thea von Harbou's *Metropolis* (1926).

Morgan's choice of the sonnet form creates a useful frisson with his subject matter – as tradition jostles with urban decay.

The sequence includes gobbets of vernacular and references to political unrest, and chronicles the impact of poor design on communities. The opening sonnet maps out the state of condemned tenement buildings: 'Four storeys have no windows left to smash' and an interior where 'Roses of mould grow from ceiling to wall'.[37] These, Morgan stresses, are inhabited buildings peopled by a mother and daughter and a man who lies late 'since he has lost his job' (p. 78). *Glasgow Sonnets* is a polyphonic text in that it is multi-voiced, sampling speech and dialect. In the third sonnet we encounter a landlord who is prepared to illegally rent 'a hoose' (p. 79) for £800. Morgan infuses the poem with Scots dialect, particularly in dialogue with the inhabitants whose spaces he depicts. Empathetically, the poet urges in the second sonnet: 'Don't shine a torch on the ragwoman's dram? / Coats keep the evil cold out less and less' as well as sadly acknowledging that 'The same weans never make the grade' (p. 78).

The urban spaces depicted in *Glasgow Sonnets* read as a complex interplay between history and the present. Morgan readily evokes literary history in his depiction of the streets, and makes comparisons between Hugh MacDiarmid's 'Glasgow 1960' written in 1935 and seventies Glasgow. This extends the implications of economic depression, and the poet in sonnet four questions the agency of his own work. Using mock political rhetoric and aphorisms, and paraphrasing *The Communist Manifesto*, Morgan's speaker taunts the city, its districts and himself:

> So you have nothing to lose but your chains,
> dear Seventies. Dalmarnock, Maryhill,
> Blackhill and Govan, better sticks and stanes
> should break your banes, for poets' words are ill
> to hurt ye. (p. 79)

The sequence questions the developers' attempts at regeneration and how a threatening exchange has occurred between labour and leisure. In the background to *Glasgow Sonnets* is the Clyde shipbuilders' strike of 1972, and the speaker poses that 'We have preferred / silent slipways to the riveters' wit' (p. 79). In shaping the city, Morgan has little time for the gentrification he associates with 'Environmentalists, ecologists / and conservationists', who are described as 'fine no doubt. / Pedestrianization will come out / fighting' (p. 80). He also laments the nondescript homogenisation of suburban areas which, treated by the 'sandblaster's grout', create 'pink piebald facades' that 'pout' at 'Mock-Venetianists' (p. 80). Space here becomes a simulation of building styles, design and textures that fabricate a past with no historical authenticity.

Midway in the sequence Morgan alerts us that the heavy industry has been supplanted by another, if remote, powerhouse. The amorphous but economically powerful space of the North Sea oil strike, while tilting 'east Scotland up', leaves the 'great sick Clyde' shivering in its bed (p. 80). In building roads around the city, the constructors give Glasgow's inhabitants a raw urban beauty: 'flyovers breed loops of light in curves' (p. 81). Yet, in the final sonnet this position of oversight upon the city space is associated with confinement, atrophy and immobility. In a block of flats built to replace the tenement building we witness a schoolboy reading from Shakespeare's *King Lear*: at the 'thirtieth floor windows at Red Road / he can see choughs and samphires, dreadful trade' (p. 82). Morgan evokes the samphire gatherers' dangerous work to evoke the modern constricted space, which becomes an incarceration of 'gentle load of souls in clouds' and the flats themselves are described as intimidating 'monoliths' (p. 82). For Morgan these vertical sites offer no immediate social space and only that of 'stalled lifts generating high-rise blues'; this perched immobility and restriction generates 'stalled lives' which 'never budge' (p.82). In this final image, Morgan's sequence reiterates Lefebvre's belief that space is a contested site of power relations. The philosopher proposes:

(Social) space is a (social) product . . . the space thus produced also serves as a tool of thought and of action . . . in addition to being a means of production it is also a means of control, and hence of domination, of power.[38]

As suggested by Davidson, the 'spatial turn' during the latter part of the twentieth century is often accompanied by an increased anxiety regarding identity, configurations of community and national affiliations. Scottish poet Kathleen Jamie and Irish poet Paula Meehan consider the relationship between civic and national pride and space. For Jamie the narrative is occasioned in 'Mr and Mrs Scotland are dead' by a visit to the detritus of the landfill site.[39] Meehan, by contrast, in 'Six Sycamores' considers the narrative space created within St Stephen's Green, Dublin.[40] Objects invariably litter the landscape of 'Mr and Mrs Scotland are dead'. Old-fashioned ladies' bags with 'open mouth spew postcards' (p. 9), and the voices from these missives inhabit the poem. Partly elegiac, and partly irreverent, Jamie embeds the words as litter in the environment of her poem. Death becomes a hand dealt 'fair but cool and showery' amid 'the lovely scenery' (p. 9). Slowly we piece together that these are the discarded items of the dead. Jamie asks that we re-assemble the stories of lives in the civic dump. The title suggests that we can take Mr and Mrs Scotland as an archetype of an era, and the poem displays nostalgia for a time when communal and local knowledge was commonplace. For example, Mr Scotland's *John Bull Puncture Repair Kit* becomes emblematic of better days when:

> he knew intimately
> the thin roads of his country, hedgerows
> hanged with small black brambles' hearts. (p. 9)

The deciphering of these objects and the lives linked to them results in an indignant questioning: 'Couldn't he have burned them?' Having found the stamping of 'SCOTLAND, SCOTLAND' on the husband's joiner's tools, the questioning becomes emphatic: 'Do we take them? Before the Bulldozer comes'. Jamie playfully asks, should we save 'these old-fashioned views addressed / after all to Mr and Mrs Scotland?' (p. 9). These lines can be read as gesturing to the postcard scenes of 'small Scots towns / in 1960: Peebles, Largs, the rock-gardens / of Carnoustie' (p. 9). But equally these 'views' can be interpreted as value systems that may now seem irrelevant to a conception of nationhood. In a final act of imagined appropriation the speaker incorporates these objects into her own domestic space, leaving us in a quandary about whether such an act betrays nostalgia. The closing brutal image is of the speaker's own effects being cleared by a person 'who enters / our silent house' performing 'this perfunctory rite' (p. 9). Jamie's poem pinpoints an anxiety of relationship: how objects frame our environment and remain as an elegy or fractured narrative on our death.

Meehan's poem sequence situates us in the park at the centre of Dublin: St Stephen's Green. 'Six Sycamores' was commissioned by the *Office of Public Works* in 2000 on the occasion of a new link between their offices at 51–2 St Stephen's Green, and was accompanied by a wall sculpture by Marie Foley. This immediate public occasion for Meehan's poetry places it in dialogue with civic space. A note at the opening of the poem informs us that: '*The original leaseholders around St Stephen's Green had to plant six sycamores and tend them for three years*' (p. 28). The six sycamores serve as a framing of the space of the Green and bear witness to major historical acts as well as acts of love, confession and dispute in the poem. Broken into six small subtitled lyrics, 'Six Sycamores' depicts different modes of relation within this space, and framing these individual narratives are six loosely constructed sonnets. Juxtaposed, these different formal strategies create different perspectives and voices. The opening sonnet, 'The Sycamore's Contract with the Citizens', is framed as a public document. The sycamore agrees to 'look up in autumn' and to release seeds 'helicoptering lazily down / to crashland on paths or on pads of weeds / when you were a child' (p. 28), The sonnet is immediately followed by a lyric with a time-monitored heading, '09.20 First Sycamore', which details a schoolgirl late for school, smoking a cigarette, listening to Bob Dylan on her Walkman. These shorter lyrics delineate the fleeting instances of encounter, mobility and exchange in the city park. '04.26 Second Sycamore' chronicles a drunken lovers' argument; '12.53 Third Sycamore' records a broken man asking for change; '14.48 Fourth Sycamore' grants us a perspective upon a woman's anxiety over the birth of her first child; '06.17 Fifth Sycamore' records a youth's ambition to win the Lotto and leave his 'McBoss with his McJob' (p. 32); and the final '19.38 Sixth Sycamore' recalls a man's admission that he hid behind the tree on his first date waiting for 'her' to arrive.

By contrast, the sonnets document the less ephemeral elements of city life and make an appeal to history, nature and time. The second sonnet, 'Number Fifty-One', envisages the 'dissolution' of 'the solid world' as building components return to nature, the red bricks to 'clay pit,' granite returns to the mountains 'above Ballyknockan', shutters 'ache' and the iron railings 'guard the memory of fire' (p. 29). This return of objects to their constituent elements is counterbalanced by the fourth sonnet's focus on the craftsmen and their work with 'chisel and clamp, diestock and drill / edgetools and files' (p. 31). Meehan reminds us that the Green's Georgian design is the result of intensive labour. The world of work creates a civic space procured by the 'makers and minders of our material world' (p. 31). In the fifth sonnet Meehan sketches for us how the park became a brief defence for the insurgents of the Easter Rising in 1916; and incidental details of the battle in the park are highlighted in a citation from the Park Superintendent's report on the damage: '*6 of our waterfowl were killed or shot, 7 of the garden seats broken and about 300 shrubs destroyed*' (p. 32). The view from a window overlooking the park prompts a scene from the past where buildings 'made mirror to smoke and fire / a Republic's destiny in a Countess' stride' (p. 32). The revolutionary nationalist Countess Constance Markievicz's bust is now displayed on the south side of the central garden. Importantly, Meehan suggests that the civic space's relationship with a national discourse is not a sacrosanct space. Indeed, the smaller lyrics of dailiness, desiring and loss which accompany the sonnets reinscribe the sense that living public spaces are constituted by ephemeral narratives and not only the dictates of civic pride.

PSYCHOGEOGRAPHY: THE POET IN THE CITY – IAIN SINCLAIR

Iain Sinclair's writing is often characterised as performing a form of literary psychogeography. Guy Debord in his 'Introduction to a Critique of Urban Geography' (1955) defined psychogeography as a practice that:

sets for itself the study of the precise laws and specific effects of the geographical environment, whether consciously organized or not, on the emotions and behaviour of individuals. The charmingly vague adjective *psychogeographical* can be applied to the findings arrived at by this type of investigation, to their influence on human feelings, and more generally to any situation or conduct that seems to reflect the same spirit of discovery.[41]

Psychogeography could be thought as an overlap where psychology and geography meet in assessing the behavioural impact of urban space. In Debord's original hypothesis, psychogeography proposes a new way of discovering the cityscape by relying upon tactics of errancy, as opposed to following conventional maps. In this way, the pedestrian travels outside of established and predictable paths to find a new understanding of the city that is not defined by the city's architectural forms. An important feature within Debord's discussion of psychogeography is the practice of dérive or drifting, which resembles a passage through varied ambiances. He proposes that dérives involve 'playful-constructive behaviour and awareness of psychogeographical effects, which are thus quite different from the classic notions of journey or stroll'.[42] It is a practice in which:

> One or more persons during a certain period drop their relations, their work and leisure activities, and all their other usual motives for movement and action, and let themselves be drawn by the attractions of the terrain and the encounters they find there.[43]

Sinclair's poetry *Lud Heat* (1975) and *Suicide Bridge* (1979), novels such as *Downriver* (1994) as well and the non-fiction *London Orbital* (2002) (which explores the M25 encircling London) engage with psychogeography's ways of discovering the cityscape. Moreover, his poetry is alert to the behavioural impression that the city makes upon its inhabitants.

The opening of Sinclair's poem 'hence like foxes' places its reader in unfamiliar terrain, and conventional methods of orientation vanish.[44] The title's citation from Lear's entreaty to Cordelia near the end of *King Lear*: 'He that parts us shall bring a brand from heaven / And fire us hence as foxes' (5.3), gives us an intense sense of affiliation as well as a threat of a brutal separation. Sinclair continues by highlighting the impression of imitation and role play. Drawing our attention to the word 'heat', he suggests that we link it with 'simple terms such as "Big" or "White"' to be impersonated by Lee Marvin. Both *White Heat* and *Big Heat* are films from the film noir era, the former starring James Cagney and the latter Marvin, whom the speaker considers to be the lesser actor, providing a mere simulation of Cagney's malevolent presence. These impressions prepare us for violent action and encounters with the law.

The poem negotiates the psychology of mass rioting in the city space and the spatial environment is perceived as a stream of associative impressions that intersect with one another. As Robert Hampson states, Sinclair's approach to the city interrogates 'its maps through purposeful drifting' in what he terms 'compulsive associationism'.[45] This impulse in Sinclair's poetry is described by Jenny Bavidge as encouraging 'a way of reading that is not concerned with excavating the city, with looking beyond surface detail to find a London sensibility . . . but which produces a constant stream of association on the horizontal plane of the text itself.'[46] 'hence like foxes' challenges any claim to authentic representation. The poem's law enforcers are reminiscent of 1980s television police dramas with Rover cars to 'haul 'em off' (p. 97). Linking the enforcers with fascism, they are described as fans of the 'simplest situation' (p. 97). Running with the rioting crowd, the speaker hallucinates a 'dazzling blonde' that then leads to an eroticisation of violence as men 'sublimate erections into truncheons' (p. 97). In 'scraps & green heaps' a walk past a scrapyard ends in the defamiliarising image of redevelopment in Canary Wharf as 'a whole tray of bright cutlery / exploiting opportunity' (p. 112). Sinclair sets up a formidable disjunction between locality and the architecture of economic power. Performing 'psychogeographically', Sinclair's writing displays a movement between localised sites and specific spaces as well as a constant revisiting and re-experiencing of spaces.

TRAVELOGUE FROM THE REGIONAL TO THE GLOBAL: ROBERT MINHINNICK AND LORNA GOODISON

Travel and mobility are important features in contemporary poets' negotiation of space as well as their representation of the global and the local. In 'Return of the Natives' from Robert Minhinnick's latest volume *King Driftwood* (2008), the speaker suggests wryly that 'could be I'm / back could be supplementary information / exists could be I never / left'.[47] Minhinnick's poetry is frequently cited as incorporating elements of travel writing as his poems often seek linkages between his native Wales and a global community. This claim is supplemented by his collections of prose essays that include meditations on travel, ecology, war and politics: *Watching the Fire Eater* (1992), *Badlands* (1996) and the more recent *To Babel and Back* (2005). Minhinnick states in an early essay that 'Living without nature is our last art, and we are bringing it to a state of perfection'.[48] Of his own seaside resort town, Porthcawl in South Wales, he remarks on the problems of consumption that tourism brings: 'Our town would die without tourists. And tourists are killing our town'.[49] Ian Gregson discerns not only the impact of the travelogue on the poet's work, but also how travel impacts upon the texture of Minhinnick's poetry. Gregson claims that the poet has invented 'a kind of travel poem which is distinctively his own' and even more importantly states 'his environmental anxieties have contributed to this because they lead to a sense of how local problems are also global problems – that, environmentally, there is one, shared planet which is being endangered everywhere'.[50] Minhinnick admits that 'North American landscapes made me want to write longer poems, but I also wished to write in a more variegated way'.[51]

In 'An Isotope, Dreaming' the poet combines the language of science with meditations on Porthcawl, as well as narratives highlighting the human impact of the war in Iraq. Minhinnick has already addressed some of his experiences of travelling to Baghdad following the first Iraq war, researching the use of depleted uranium in American weapons.[52] Nuclear waste and its radioactivity become both a benign and malign vehicle in the poem to illustrate the dissemination of ideas, birth of languages, acts of mobility and spirituality, as well as death and destruction. Beginning in South Wales, the speaker muses on redemption, which to him comes in the form of a reactor:

> Resurrection
> is in the reactor.
> It's the atom that's reborn
> The soul perishes
> but matter can never be destroyed. (p. 9)

The possible resurrection offered by a nuclear reactor is not only the provision of energy, but the deadly half-life of a decaying isotope. The speaker admits in a spiritual frenzy: 'we are all / fuel rods – spent, eternal' and 'the half-life of angels / that the world called waste' (p. 10). Writing in the early twentieth century Maria Rainer Rilke's poetry was accompanied by angels, whereas it is 'the isotope, dreaming' that inhabits Minhinnick's twenty-first century. The isotope moves beyond the 'iron womb of Sellafield', the 'cubist monument of Trawsfynydd' and the 'accelerator tunnel at Berkeley' (p. 9), making three journeys. The first is to an undisclosed 'nameless place' where the 'geiger talk / like a black habanero rattling with seeds' (p. 11). Yet even here the isotope is associated with birth and creation: 'I am the Isotope dreaming / Where they bury me an idea starts to grow' (p. 10). The second journey is to Iraq's Basra and the ancient city states of Nineveh and Babylon, while the third journey visits Belarus and the legacy of Chernobyl.

'An Isotope, Dreaming' enacts a present nightmare while providing a foretelling of the future. The recuperation of the isotope to indicate a spiritual awakening thwarts our expectations of radio-activity as the speaker pleads:

> Listen to this
> and imagine
> inside the reactor
> the soft mutation
> of a soul (p. 10)

Minhinnick's travelogue also looks for connections, for senses of connectivity and global links between communities. The form of the poem, with its drafted-in voices as well as stammers, visual performances on the page, repetitive clauses and pared-down lyrics, enacts an 'open field' poetics. First coined by the American poet Charles Olson in his manifesto 'Projective Verse', composition by field combines lyrics, speeches of different kinds, conversation, images and a collage of information.[53] This impression of a poetry written without predetermination enables the poet to enact multiple conversations throughout the journeys. In the second 'journey' we listen to a doctor in Iraq's damning indictment of the USA's involvement in the war: 'And no I don't feel sorry for your boys. / Let them anoint their blisters / with Exxon's frankincense.' He adds 'We all sign up for something' (p. 14). Minhinnick's vast poem returns us to the point of initial departure, but changed, with the imminent mutation threatened in 'the gamma / ghosting towards / the cell's gateway' (p. 17). This interrelationship between the local and the global is made evident in another poem from the volume, 'The Fairground Scholar', where one of the fair's main attractions is 'our Kingdom of Evil's Saddam Hussein' (p. 102). From the axis of evil to a small resort in South Wales, Minhinnick's work exhibits an awareness of global interconnections.

Jamaican poet Laura Goodison's 'Run Greyhound' from *Travelling Mercies* (2001) presents the more familiar expectations of a travelogue.[54] For Goodison the mythic status of the Greyhound bus enables a ludic narrative as well as vaudeville performances from her fellow travellers. Presented in unrhymed couplets, the movement of the poem enables the sense of an ongoing mobility. Goodison immediately interrogates elements of American cultural mythmaking. The legacy of the Beatniks becomes a humorous anecdote of an overheard conversation at the Ann Arbor station. A young woman admits that she set 'out after Jack Kerouac to write a road novel' but her car broke down (p. 20). Moreover, she panics once she learns that the man she is speaking to, who has travelled the 'vineyards of California and the peach groves of Georgia' (p. 20), has just been released from prison. Social anxiety ensues, as this most iconic of American institutions, representing mobility and freedom, becomes a 'convict bus' (p. 21) for men released from prison that morning. The characters include an impatient man in a bandana, a long-haired rocker, the twin of a country and western singer, two silent black men and a Native American man.

Humorously, through this anxious lens, the passengers begin to morph into threatening historical public figures and artists. A man with an eye patch looks like 'Henry Morgan, retired wicked buccaneer and born-again governor' (p. 21), whereas the driver becomes 'like J. Edgar Hoover' and the others 'like Tippu Tip / Augusto Pinochet, Margaret Thatcher, Émile Zola' (p. 22). Goodison juxtaposes internal clanging rhymes within the lines to create a sense of discord and heightened awareness. Travelling to Detroit becomes a nightmarish scenario, and Goodison dramatises wryly the fear of others joining the Greyhound bus: They have 'mad dogs and fouling pieces, sheep cloning pox blankets, / anthrax warfare, agent orange blunderbusses' (p. 22). From Vietnam warfare's 'agent orange' to the infection and dissemination of Native Americans through smallpox, each new passenger is a threat. But Goodison recognises that there is humour also in the situation as the speaker urges the Greyhound to 'Run, hound of the Pharaohs, run like the twinned Blue Nile' (p. 22). Goodison's poem creates a travelogue of significant cultural dislocation, but also generates self-deprecating comedy. Jahan Ramazani proposes that Goodison's lengthy periods away from Jamaica teaching at institutions around the world enables a form of 'poetic transnationalism' in her poetry.[55] Read in this light, we might concur with Ramazani that Goodison's depiction of that most American of cultural representations, the Greyhound bus, strives to counter the idea of a 'hermetically sealed national or civilizational bloc, but of intercultural worlds that ceaselessly overlap, intersect, and converge'.[56]

ECOPOETICS AND THE FUTURE

Considering poetry as a form of travelogue allows us to examine the relationship between the local and the global, as well as the poet's position as an observer of other cultures. Recent developments in ecocriticism further frame the relationship between environment and poetry. Ecocritic Buell suggests that the idea of a poet of 'nature' now has 'a suspiciously retro, neo-Victorian ring, even when the argument is recast to emphasize not just love of nature but proto-ecological knowledge and environmentalist commitment'.[57] Buell proposes that this is a problem which has troubled ecocriticism from its inception: 'the suspicion that it might not boil down to much more than old-fashioned enthusiasms dressed up in new clothes'.[58] Jonathan Skinner's magazine *ecopoetics* attempts to address these problems. Skinner asks: 'I wonder at the value of the term itself "nature writing", doesn't all writing have nature in it?'[59] He recognises that 'obviously there is a value and a need for writing focused specifically on the so-called natural world' (p. 127). Importantly, he notes the difference between nature writing and ecopoetry: the former for Skinner indicates empathy for the environment, while the latter suggests how economic forces create and impact on the environment. He admits that he is suspicious of the term 'ecopoetry' since it duplicates 'the "eco" already built into the ecology' especially if its premise is based on turning us 'away from the tasks of poetry, to more important or urgent concerns' (p. 127). Instead he proposes a conceptualisation of ecopoetics as a plurality of different artistic creations. Ecopoetics becomes in this way 'a site for poetic attention and exchange, where many different kinds of making (not just poetry or even just writing and certainly not just ecopoetry) can come to be informed' (p. 128).

Usefully, Skinner differentiates between four approaches to the umbrella term 'ecopoetics'. The first is *topological*, referring beyond the poem to a specific space or 'natural topos' (p. 128). Secondly, he identifies a *tropological* poetics, which indicates a hybrid fertilisation of the language of environmental sciences performing as 'exercises in analogy, casting poems as somehow functioning like ecosystems or complex systems' (p. 128). Next is an *entropological* poetics that is a practice 'engaged at the level of materials and process, where entropy, transformation and decay are part of the creative work' (p. 128). Finally, ecopoetics may also practise in an *ethnological* way. Ethnological poetics necessitates looking beyond Western languages and cultures to provide an understanding of environment. As Skinner states: 'whether nature contains the human or humanity contains nature is impossible to conclude. What we do know is that humans have been here a long time' (p. 129). Ethnological approaches look beyond a Western construction of landscape and involve 'an act of translation' (p. 129). Skinner's subheadings are not in themselves discrete categories. It is, for example, possible for a poet to perform both *topologically* and *tropologically* in the same poem. John Kinsella and Juliana Spahr's poetry offers illustrative approaches to an understanding of how ecopoetics may function in recent poetry.

APOCALYPTIC LANDSCAPES: JOHN KINSELLA

John Kinsella's poetry often depicts and examines the landscape in his native Western Australia. Spending time between Australia and Cambridge, he suggests that his writing encompasses both a regional and international perspective. Indeed, coining the term 'international regionalism', he believes is 'respecting the integrity of place, of a region, and at the same time opening avenues for communication and discourse'.[60] He proposes that 'regional identity is enhanced and best preserved by being part of the global community. Mutual understanding, mutual respect, and a willingness to tolerate difference best comes out of understanding what it is that makes and/or informs difference'.[61] His poetry is also associated with a form of ' "radical", or "neo", or "post", or (even) "poisoned" pastoral'.[62] Traditionally, pastoral poetry presents a romanticised, idealised or nostalgic impression of countryside spaces, often targeted at an urban audience. Kinsella suggests that his ' "radical" pastoral' arises from 'the bleak picture I paint of human destruction of landscapes and the external dismantling of indigenous cultures. Be they the Australian Aboriginal peoples or the early fenlanders colonised by drainage engineers and farmers'.[63] Kinsella's revisioning of the pastoral challenges established criteria of aesthetic beauty in poetry: his poems may contain 'The beauty horror of a polluted sky emanating a sickly red sunset, the exquisite crystalline formations resulting from clearing and degradation of land in the Western Australian wheatbelt'.[64] This radical pastoral embraces ideas of the mutated as a vehicle for change and activism:

I am trying to create a synthesis between the aesthetics
of creating the poem and its 'end' result, which I always
hope is deconstructive, and ultimately impermanent, and
certainly changeable . . . and using poetry to actively stop
land-damaging (and people and animal and plant-damaging)
practices.[65]

'The Ocean Forests: An Elegy and Lament' was written by
Kinsella during an ice storm in Ohio as a response to the 2004
tsunami in the Indian Ocean.[66] The poem considers submarine
ecology, the causes of a tsunami as well as human interaction with
the environment. Beginning with a TV live feed, the technological
process of newsgathering and dissemination is allied to the physical
sculptures of trees in the ice storm: 'trees tap inner heat / through
fibre-optics' (p. 104). 'Ocean Forests' performs tropologically,
since it borrows from the language of environmental science and
develops into an exploration of form as an organic system. The
speaker examines the causes of the tsunami scientifically as the
movement of convergent plates:

> an earthquake
> miles below the ocean's floor,
> plate slipping under plate,
> the massive release of energy
> and surge of water
> running the gradient
> of landfall: forcing entry. (p. 104)

The impact of this submarine world upon land is cataclysmic.
Kinsella later draws our attention to the morphing of map contours, which meld and curve, 'heaving re-alignment' to create 'the
seaweeds of new oceans / new shorelines' (p. 105). Juxtaposed to
scientific analysis is the perspective of ritual, myth and spiritual
belief. In these terms the tsunami is perceived as a vengeful god
seeking retribution: 'Calibrating prophesies / of the living, some
look for signs / of punishment' (p. 104).
    The poem reflects upon the ungovernable elements of envi-
ronmental processes in fire, air and water and their disruption

by climate change, and an associative patterning of reflections creates a poetic form that is fluid and organic. The appeal to 'we' in 'we search', 'we reflect', 'we are', 'we were' indicates the need for communal intervention in the human catastrophe of 'island wreckage' (p. 105). Kinsella asserts that human ownership of the sea's ecosystems cannot be claimed, since he evokes a pre-human history of 'hot coral forests, ice forests / and memories of mimosa / from the driest parts' (p. 105). 'Ocean Forests' presents a contracting of environmental space within a global economy and both locals and visitors are 'brought together' (p. 106). As the geographical size of the earth appears to contract, human societies have:

> grown fluid in the wobbling
> of the earth's rotation
> shortening all our days
> bringing palm trees and ice forests
> under the same cut-glass sky. (p. 106)

Kinsella's poem performs as both an elegy and lament, reminding us of our place in the earth's ecosystem, as well as a tribute to the lost and those vulnerable through economic disenfranchisement to climate change. One could claim that Kinsella's poem, in its discomfort with statically observing the human tragedies of the 'torn shores of an ocean / so close, so distant' (p. 107), echoes Lovelock's assertion that the earth is not owned by humanity. Lovelock puts us in our place: 'We are creatures of Darwinian evolution, a transient species with a limited lifespan, as were all our distant numerous ancestors'.[67]

CONCLUSION: JULIANA SPAHR'S ECOPOETICS AND IDEAS OF CONNECTION

Global information and newsgathering systems form a key component of Juliana Spahr's volume *this connection of everyone with lungs* (2005).[68] Spahr has insistently described poetry as medium of thought and enquiry:

Poetry moves words around. It rearranges them from their conventions. It re-sorts them. It uses more than one language. It repeats. It pursues aconventional language and divergent typography. It often experiments. It can be ephemeral and occasional. It often uses pleasing patterns as it does all this. And all that helps me think.[69]

this connection of everyone with lungs consists of two extended poems, one simply entitled 'Poem Written after September 11, 2001' and the second 'Poem Written from November 30, 2002 to March 27, 2003'. Set in long, prose-like lineation, the poems are intimate and epistolary, addressing two 'beloveds'. This hybrid form of poetic prosody intersperses factual information with lyric appeals and private meditation. Initially, one can frame Spahr's diaristic entries as responses to 9/11, but as Nicky Marsh suggests, the poems dramatise a desire 'to find the meaningful connections that allow Spahr to understand her own place in the machinations of international politics'.[70] Moreover, the poems are intent on examining the relationship between the local and global, or what the poet proposes as: 'I speak of boundaries and connections, locals and globals, butterfly wings and hurricanes' (p. 20). Increasingly, Spahr's desire to understand 'the interconnections between seemingly disparate world events, and her own role in them, is revealed as suspect in its hopelessness'.[71] This prospect is expressed in 'Poem Written from November 30, 2002 to March 27, 2003':

I speak of how the world suddenly seems as if it is a game of some sort, a game where troops are massed on a flat map of the world, and if one looks at the game board long enough one can see the patterns, even as one is powerless to prevent them. (pp. 20–1)

Taking Skinner's understanding of ecopoetics, one could add that *this connection of everyone with lungs* performs topologically, tropologically, entropologically and ethnologically. The first 'Poem Written after September 11, 2001' uses the analogy of lungs and air as a connective, uniting humanity across the globe. Moreover, the analogy with lungs and breath creates an ecosystem within the poem, not only in terms of the duration of the line, but also as a measure and unit of thought. The following section illustrates a pattern of breath between individuals, in domestic interiors, then countries and across continents:

There is space between the hands.

There is space between the hands and space around the
    hands.

There is space around the hands and space in the room.

There is space in the room that surrounds the shapes of
    everyone's hands and body and feet and cells and the
    beating contained within.

There is space, an uneven space, made by this pattern of
    bodies.

The space goes in and out of everyone's bodies.

Everyone with lungs breathes the space in and out as
    everyone with lungs breathes the space between the hands
    in and out

as everyone with lungs breathes the space between the hands
    and the space around the hands in and out. (pp. 4–5)

This accumulative patterning of phrases and clauses, as space around the hands becomes a space around a communal breathing, is evident in 'Poem Written from November 30, 2002 to March 27, 2003'. Written initially as response to the US government's intervention in Iraq, Spahr's poem delineates an overwhelming pressure to give form to information regarding the war. She was based in Hawaii at the time of writing, and the flora and fauna on the island are depicted in the midst of thinking about war. We are told that 'we reclined as we spoke' and 'we were surrounded by ditches, streams, and wetland areas, which serve as a habitat for endangered waterbird species' (p. 66). Spahr attempts to incorporate topical knowledge into a shape that forms connections with individuals. Working entropologically, transformation and decay become central to the poem's form as facts, once posed, unravel and are repelled by personal meditations. The movement of air in the first poem is replaced by fire in the second:

> When I wake up this morning the world is a series of isolated,
> burning fires as it is every morning.
>
> It burns in Israel where ten died from a bomb on a bus.
>
> Yesterday it also burned in the Philippines where twenty-one
> died from a bomb at the airport. And then it burned some
> more a few hours later outside a health clinic in a nearby
> city, killing one.
>
> It burns and the pope urges everyone to fast and pray for
> peace because it is Ash Wednesday. (p. 56)

This is a poet's desperate attempt to understand the interconnection between wars and her country's involvement in Iraq, as well as the religious rituals that are created to enable a decoding of the threat to individuals. Commenting on Spahr's more recent memoir examining climate change, *The Transformation* (2007), Eric Keenaghan proposes that her poetry:

> [e]xhibits a nostalgia for some acceptable way to talk about identity and community. Spahr reveals the problem of defining who 'they' are as ubiquitous in this age of Homeland Security. 'So it was a time of troubled and pressured pronouns'.[72]

In *this connection of everyone with lungs*, Spahr is not only looking for connections which bind communities together, but also to show how the machinery of war appropriates the environment. Her speaker demonstrates how Hawaii's status as a military base redefines the ecology of the island:

And because the planes flew overhead when we spoke of the cries of birds our every word was an awkward squawk that meant also AH-64 Apache attack helicopter, UH-60 Black Hawk troop helicopter. (p. 67)

Trevor Paglen suggests that experimental geographers aim to experiment with the production of space as: 'an integral part of one's practice. If human activities are inextricably spatial then new forms of freedom and democracy can only emerge in dialectical relation to the production of new spaces'.[73] Equally, Spahr's attempts to enable a poetry which performs an ecopoetics that is not only topological and tropological, but entropological and ethnological, creates new imaginative spaces for environmental enquiry.

SUMMARY OF KEY POINTS

- Ecological poetry can initially be understood as poetry that addresses the environment (often associated with nature poetry).
- An awareness of local spaces and cultures is often highlighted in the poetry of contemporary poets committed to region and locale.
- Contemporary poets examine the relationships of the individual to the cityscape through representations and psychological interpretations of urban space.
- Poetic travelogues offer a further perspective on identity, community and environment.
- Recent developments in ecocriticism consider the intersection of economic pressures and global concerns on the environment, a gesture which has been framed in poetry as 'ecopoetics'.
- Recent poetry engaged in exploring ecopoetics often presents future landscapes and spaces (frequently apocalyptic), and searches for ways of making global relations and connections.

NOTES

1. Lawrence Buell, *The Future of Environmental Criticism* (London: Blackwell, 2005), p. 2.
2. Jonathan Skinner, 'Statement for "New Nature Writing Panel" at 2005 AWP (Vancouver)' *Ecopoetics*, 4/5 (2004–5), 127–9 (p. 127).
3. Trevor Paglen, 'Experimental Geography: From Cultural Production to the Production of Space', in Nato Thompson (ed.), *Experimental Geography: Radical Approaches to Landscape, Cartography and Urbanism* (New York: Melville House, 2008), p. 29.
4. Cheryll Glotfelty, 'Introduction', in Cheryll Glotfelty and Harold Fromm (eds), *The Ecocriticism Reader: Landmarks in Literary Ecology* (Edinburgh: Edinburgh University Press, 1996), pp. xiii–xix.
5. Gary Snyder, *The Practice of the Wild* (Berkeley: Counterpoint, 1990); *A Place in Space* (Berkeley: Counterpoint, 1995).
6. Gary Snyder cited in Buell, *The Future of Environmental Criticism*, p. 13.
7. Gary Snyder, 'Riprap', in *Postmodern American Poetry* (New York NY: Norton & Norton, 1994), p. 215.
8. Gary Snyder, 'The Rediscovery of Turtle Island', in *A Place in Space: Ethics, Aesthetics, and Watersheds* (Berkeley: Counterpoint Press, 1995), p. 237.
9. Gary Snyder, *Axe Handles* (Washington, DC: Shoemaker and Hoard, 2005), pp. 49–58. All subsequent references to this edition are given in the text.
10. James Lovelock, *The Vanishing Face of Gaia: A Final Warning* (Penguin: London, 2009), p. 166.
11. Gary Snyder, 'Unnatural Writing', in *A Place in Space*, p. 168.
12. Lawrence Buell, 'The Place of Place', in *Writing for an Endangered World: Literature, Culture and Environment in the US and Beyond* (Cambridge, MA: Harvard University Press, 2001), p. 60.
13. Geoffrey Hill, *Collected Poems* (London: Penguin, 1985) pp. 105–34. All subsequent references to this edition are given in the text.

14. Geoffrey Hill, 'An Interview with Geoffrey Hill by John Haffenden', *Quarto*, 15 (1981), 19–22, p. 21.
15. Geoffrey Hill, 'An Interview with Geoffrey Hill by John Haffenden', in *Viewpoints* (London: Faber & Faber, 1981), p. 94.
16. Michel de Certeau, *The Practice of Everyday Life* (Berkeley: University of California Press, 1998), p. 93.
17. Robert Hass, *Field Guide* (New Haven, CT: Yale University, 1973). All subsequent references to this edition are given in the text.
18. Robert Hass, *Praise* (New York: Ecco, 1979). All subsequent references to this edition are given in the text.
19. Edward Casey, *Getting Back into Place: Toward a Renewed Understanding of the Place World* (Bloomington: Indiana University Press, 1993), p. 313.
20. Robert Hass, cited in Thomas Gardner, *Regions of Unlikeness: Explaining Contemporary Poetry* (Lincoln: University of Nebraska Press, 1999), p. 166.
21. Robert Hass, *Time and Materials: Poems 1997–2005* (New York: Ecco, 2007), p. 71.
22. John Livingstone Clark, 'Conversation with Anne Szumigalski', *Prairie Fire*, 18.1 (1997), 28–37 (pp. 33–4).
23. Anne Szumigalski, *Dogstones: Selected and New Poems* (Saskatoon: Fifth House, 1986), p. 8.
24. Ibid. p. 8.
25. Anne Szumigalski, *On Glassy Wings: Selected Poems* (Regina: Coteau, 1997), pp. 89–90.
26. Ibid. p. 90.
27. Szumigalski, *Dogstones*, p. 68.
28. Anne Szumigalski, 'I² = -1', in Susan McCaslin (ed.), *A Matter of Spirit: Recovery of the Sacred in Contemporary Canadian Poetry* (Victoria, BC: Ekstasis, 1998), p. 237.
29. Ibid. p. 237.
30. Ibid. p. 237.
31. Szumigalski, *On Glassy Wings*, p. 59.
32. Ibid. p. 59.
33. Ibid. p. 59.
34. Henri Lefebvre, *The Production of Space*, trans. Donald Nicholson-Smith (Oxford: Blackwell, 1991), p. 1.

35. Ian Davidson, 'Picture This: Space and Time in Lisa Robertson's Utopia', *Mosaic*, 40.4 (2007), 87–102.
36. Edwin Morgan, 'The Poet and the City', *Comparative Criticism*, 18 (1996), 91–105 (p. 92).
37. Edwin Morgan, *Glasgow Sonnets*, in *Selected Poems* (Manchester: Carcanet, 1985), pp. 78–82 (p. 78). All subsequent references to this edition are given in the text.
38. Lefebvre, *The Production of Space*, p. 26.
39. Kathleen Jamie, *The Queen of Sheba* (Newcastle: Bloodaxe, 1995) p. 9. All subsequent references to this edition are given in the text.
40. Paula Meehan, *Painting Rain* (Manchester: Carcanet, 2009), pp. 28–33. All subsequent references to this edition are given in the text.
41. Guy Debord, 'Introduction to a Critique of Urban Geography', in Harald Bauder and Salvatore Engel-Di Mauro (eds), *Critical Geographies: A Collection of Readings* (Kelowna, BC: Praxis e-Press, 2008), p. 23.
42. Guy Debord, 'Theory of the Dérive', in Joanne Morra and Marquard Smith (eds), *Visual Culture: Spaces of Visual Culture* (London: Routledge, 2006), p. 77.
43. Ibid. p. 77.
44. Iain Sinclair, *Penguin Modern Poets: Douglas Oliver, Denise Riley, Iain Sinclair* (London: Penguin, 1996), p. 97. All subsequent references to this edition are given in the text.
45. Robert Hampson, 'Spatial Stories: Conrad and Ian Sinclair', *The Conradian: The Journal of the Joseph Conrad Society*, 31.1 (2006), 52–71 (p. 69).
46. Jenny Bavidge, cited in Hampson 'Spatial Stories', p. 69.
47. Robert Minhinnick, *King Driftwood* (Manchester: Carcanet, 2008), p. 97. All subsequent references to this edition are given in the text.
48. Robert Minhinnick, *Watching the Fire Eater* (Bridgend: Seren, 1992), p. 21.
49. Ibid. p. 23.
50. Ian Gregson, 'The Baghdad Moon, the Pepsi Globe: Robert Minhinnick', *PN Review*, 31.6 (2005), 53.

51. Ian Gregson, 'Interview with Robert Minhinnick', *Planet* (2004), 49.
52. Robert Minhinnick, *To Babel and Back* (Bridgend: Seren, 2005).
53. See Chapter 3 for a discussion of performance and Charles Olson.
54. Lorna Goodison, *Travelling Mercies* (Toronto: McClelland & Stewart, 2001), pp. 20–3. All subsequent references to this edition are given in the text.
55. Jahan Ramazani, 'A Transnational Poetics', *American Literary History*, 18.2 (2006), 332–59.
56. Ibid. p. 355.
57. Buell, *The Future of Environmental Criticism*, p. 2.
58. Ibid. p. 3.
59. Skinner, 'Statement for "New Nature Writing Panel"', p. 127
60. John Kinsella, 'Interview John Kinsella', *The Poetry Kit*. Available online at www.poetrykit.org/iv98/kinsella.htm.
61. Ibid.
62. Ibid.
63. Ibid.
64. John Kinsella, 'Can there be a Radical "Western" Pastoral?', *Literary Review*, 48.2 (2005), 120–33 (p. 132).
65. John Kinsella, 'Geodysplasia: Geographical Abnormalities of an Activist Poetics', *Poetry Wales*, 44.4 (2009), 30.
66. John Kinsella, 'The Ocean Forests: An Elegy and a Lament', *Iowa Review*, 36.1 (2006), 104–7. All subsequent references to this edition are given in the text.
67. Lovelock, *The Vanishing Face of Gaia*, p. 6.
68. Juliana Spahr, *this connection of everyone with lungs* (Berkeley: University of California Press, 2005). All subsequent references to this edition are given in the text.
69. Juliana Spahr, in Claudia Rankine and Lisa Sewell (eds), *American Poets in the 21st Century* (Middletown, CT: Wesleyan University Press, 2007), p. 131.
70. Nicky Marsh, 'Going "Glocal": The Local and the Global in Recent Experimental Women's Poetry', *Contemporary Women's Writing*, 1.1/2 (2007), 192–202 (p. 199).
71. Ibid. p. 199.

72. Eric Keenaghan, 'Performance and Politics in Contemporary Poetics: Three Recent Titles from Atelos Press', *Post Modern Culture*, 17.3 (2007).
73. Paglen, 'Experimental Geography', p. 31.

CHAPTER 5

Dialects, Idiolects and Multilingual Poetries

GLOBAL POETRY OR, ENGLISH AS A GLOBAL LANGUAGE

Jonathan Arac voices concern for the situating of nation in a period of globalisation. In tandem with recent debates over ideas of 'post-nation' literatures, Arac identifies that the processes of globalisation are linked to the proliferation of English as a global language:

> Globalisation pluralizes: it opens up every local, national or regional culture to others and thereby produces 'many worlds'. Yet these many worlds can only be known through a single medium: just as the dollar is the medium of global commerce, so is English the medium of global culture, producing 'one world'.[1]

Almost 200 years after Goethe proposed the idea of *Weltliteratur* (1827), or a world literature, debates proliferate on how to respond to the impact of English upon the perception of national literatures. Romana Huk notes: 'There are very few conversations today that escape the g words global, globalization.'[2] Mostly associated with actions in 'market trading, corporate finance, mass media . . . political negotiations' (p. 758), Huk questions what such processes might mean for literary studies. Distinguishing between 'global' and 'globalisation', she suggests that the former indicates 'an already-existing state of things', whereas the latter suggests 'a process that's been inaugurated, a condition we're constructing' (p. 762). The utopian image inscribed at the heart of the proponents of a new global poetics raises key problems for Huk. For her, terms such as 'cross-cultural' and 'transnational' retain 'at least some traces of writing's sitedness and specific historied movements over borders' (p. 770). Huk is far more suspicious of terms such as 'Americas', 'world' and 'global' since these poetics correspondingly 'permit no intra-national, national or discreet group identifications or projects aside from the largest impossible ones' (p. 770). Central to Huk is what is lost in these larger totalities; she probes 'What gets elided in these constructions of negative totality . . . [i]n other words what have we got to lose (both in the possessive and imperative sense of that phrase)? Or perhaps what do we *want* to lose?' (p. 770).

While this chapter's focus is not upon the processes of globalisation per se, or the proposition of a world literature, it is important to discern how contemporary poetry addresses the development of English as a global language. Indeed, we may well ask how do contemporary poets respond to a plurality of Englishes? In the past it had become axiomatic to consider that processes of globalisation create a stylistic homogeneity. Jahan Ramazani, paraphrasing Kwame Anthony Appiah, suggests that as a response to globalisation people are 'constantly inventing new forms of difference, new hairstyles, new slang, even from time to time, new religion and we might add new forms of poetry'.[3] Ramazani's proposition of a transnational poetics explores how contemporary poets 'have also imaginatively transvalued and creolized these global forces to bring into expression their specific experiences of globalized locality and localized globality'.[4] Equally, Wai Chee Dimock reminds us that English-language poetries can no longer be seen as 'the product of one nation and one nation alone, analyzable within its confines'.[5]

In considering Anglophone poetries in tandem with the globalising tendencies of the post-war period, it is important to acknowledge Sujata Bhatt's ambivalence about how an 'oppressor's tongue' may eventually shift to grandchildren learning to 'love that strange language'.[6] Since English is a global language, we need to consider how one language can reflect plurality and diversity without reducing all identities to uniformity. Looking at specific examples of bilingualism and multiple language use, this chapter considers the differences between dialect, linked to a direct transcription of regional accent and idiom, and idiolects, often equated with the deformation of linguistic rules in an attempt to create an assertive identity. Frequently, contemporary poets evoke in their work an ongoing attempt at the translation between languages, which will be illustrated through processes of translation from Chinese to English, Welsh to English and Spanish to English. In addition, the chapter considers how contemporary poetry documents the experience and legacies of immigration.

DIALECT AND PHONETIC POETRY: TONY HARRISON, TOM LEONARD AND LIZ LOCHHEAD

In an early interview, Tony Harrison draws attention to his perception of hierarchical forms within English literature. He stresses that his evocation and negotiation of metrical verse were an attempt at ownership and occupation:

> Originally I was drawn to metrical verse because I wanted to 'occupy' literature as I said in 'Them and [uz]'. Now that I've occupied it in the sense that I can do it – I learned it as skilfully as I could in order that people would have to pay attention.[7]

The title of Harrison's second volume *From the School of Eloquence* (1978) was borrowed from E. P. Thompson's seminal book *The Making of the English Working Class* (1963). In the pivotal poem 'Them and [uz]', from this volume, Harrison shows how the instruction of so-called traditional English literature allowed no space for regional identifications. Neil Roberts suggests that the poem creates an initial focus upon 'the parallels between social and literary hierarchies in the Elizabethan period and later the imposition of RP and its stultifying association with the reading aloud of poetry'.[8] The teacher castigates Harrison's enunciation as a slur on 'our glorious heritage' (p. 122). The immediacy of the distinctions between classes, 'our' as opposed to 'your', mirrors the title 'Them and [uz]'. Roberts comments on how the title underlines phonically working-class speech patterns, since '[uz]' 'represents the word "us" as spoken with a working-class Leeds accent (long vowel, voiced consonant) as opposed to the short vowel, unvoiced consonant of Received Pronunciation' (p. 157). The speaker queries the proposition of uniformed pronunciation, allying his enunciation 'Littererchewer' to John Keats and Wordsworth's accented rhyming of 'matter / water' as 'full rhymes'.[9] The poet wages war on all those who seek to limit English literature to the confines of a perceived 'properly' enunciated speech, and promises to 'occupy / your lousy leasehold poetry'.[10]

Harrison's desire to inhabit the metrical structures of English verse evokes a desire to affirm regional identifications and negotiations against a monolothic positioning of English language. Terry Eagleton proposes that 'No modern English poet has shown more finely how the sign is a terrain of struggle where opposing accents intersect, how in a class divided society language is cultural warfare and every nuance a political validation.'[11] As a working-class 'scholar' trained as a classicist, Harrison's work creates a space for a variation of Englishes. This advancement of a poetic vernacular as a democratising art is evident in Harrison's attempt to promote poetry to a more general audience. The poem 'Book Ends' portrays an inchoate inability to express grief between son and father, since education separates the 'scholar me, you worn out on poor pay'.[12] His celebrated long poem v. (1985) caused controversy for a broader audience when it was broadcast as a poem-film in 1987 on Channel 4. Written by Harrison during the miners' strike (1984–5) – which arguably was one the most traumatic events visited upon post-war British working-class communities – v. documents the poet's visit to a Leeds graveyard to pay his respects to his parents. The graveyard is vandalised: graffiti on the gravestones proclaim tribal affinities to football through expletives. This long poem attempts to open a dialogue between the poet and the disenfranchised voices of the unemployed. Harrison's poem performs as a site of verbal interaction which theorist Mikhail Bakhtin associated categorically with the novel as heteroglossia, in comparison with the largely monologic or singular language of poetry.[13] The novel he suggests is a dialogic site with a diversity of social speech types, and allows for interaction between the multiple voices within the work. Bakhtin frequently describes the novel as 'saturated', 'impregnated' and 'contaminated'.

Bakhtin's implication of a 'contaminated' language is evident in the use of expletives which litter the text. The poem's construction in iambic pentameter creates a space for the voice of a young skinhead. As the epithet at the beginning of *v.* by Arthur Scargill emphasises, an ideal of mastery of language dominates the opening section: 'My father still reads the dictionary every day. He says your life depends on your power to master words'.[14] Harrison admits that his linguistic knowledge has made him more aware of his working-class background: 'I thought that somehow language would take me away, but – on the contrary – the more I became articulate, the more I was conscious of what I owed to the goad of the inarticulate'.[15] The footballing failures of Leeds United make the vandals 'lose their sense of self-esteem' (p. 236):

> and taking a short cut home through these graves here
> they reassert the glory of their team
> by spraying words on tombstones, pissed on beer (p. 236)

Importantly, the remnant of heavy industry casts a shadow over the burial ground since the graveyard 'stands above a worked-out pit / Subsidence makes the obelisks all list'. The rhymes that are now found are 'CUNT, PISS, SHIT and (mostly) FUCK!' (p. 236). The versus or *v.* of the poem's title informs the divisions orchestrated in the poem, the conflicts between football clubs, educated and uneducated, workers and jobless, racist and ethnic groups, British working-class ambition and post-industrial unemployment, poet and graffitist. As Harrison puts it: 'These Vs are all the versus of life' which also include 'man and wife', 'US and THEM / personified in 1984 by Coal Board MacGregor and the *NUM*' (p. 238).

When the poet questions whether the graffiti is 'just a *cri-de-coeur* because man dies', another voice intrudes in the poem with a vehement riposte:

> *So what's a cri-de-coeur, cunt? Can't you speak*
> *the language that yer mam spoke. Think of 'er!*
> *Can yer only get yer tongue round fucking Greek?*
> *Go and fuck yourself with cri-de-coeur!* (p. 241)

This division between voices imprints a further element of conflict in the work. In an attempt to enable conversation, the poet assumes the vernacular:

> 'Listen, cunt!' I said, 'before you start your jeering
> the reason why I want this in a book
> 's to give ungrateful cunts like you a hearing!
> A book, yer stupid cunt 's not worth a fuck! (p. 242)

As Roberts notes there is a measured degree of discomfort once the poet enters into the vernacular of the vandal. He contrasts the poet 'who grew up poor but in a full employment economy' trying to access 'the world of the unemployed and alienated youth of the early 1980s' (p. 165). In his articulation of the skinhead's voice, Harrison questions the efficacy of poetry as a political weapon: '*Don't talk to me of fucking representing / the class yer were born into any more*', ending with the assertion '*it's not poetry we need in this class war*' (p. 244).

Tom Leonard, well known for his poetic compositions in Glaswegian dialect, declares in 'The 6 O'Clock News' that the newscaster has a BBC or RP accent: 'coz yi / widny wahnt / mi ti talk / aboot thi / trooth wia / voice lik / wanna yoo / scruff'.[16] Leonard's mordant and sardonic work transcribes speech patterns and dialect into staccatoed lines. The implication of this poem is that other accents do not have the authority of 'trooth'. Leonard is, however, emphatic that his poetry does not aim to inscribe nationalistic sentiment at the heart of poetry. On his website he has posted a note for all GCSE students countering the BBC Education website's pedagogical reading of his poem:

> The poem's take on accents has nothing to do with the writer 'being Scottish' as a BBC 'GCSE bitesize' model answer on the poem suggests, it is instead about social *class*.

The six o'clock news is as unlikely to be read by a working-class Liverpudlian, London, Birmingham, Swansea, Belfast, Portsmouth, Aberdeen etc etc voice as by a Glaswegian. This has nothing to do with any difficulty in understanding, as audiences have no difficulty understanding lower class accents in phone-ins, gameshows, 'Eastenders' etc.

Why can't someone with for example a strong East London accent read the six o'clock news? The speaker of the poem suggests the answer lies in an attitude about who and what is considered to be 'authoritative', and this attitude is the hidden 'news' inside the six o'clock news itself. 'Scruff' means 'scum' or the muck gathered at the top of dirty water, and is used as a term of social disdain. 'belt up' means 'shut up!'[17]

Usefully, Leonard points out in an interview that he does not see himself as a nationalist, but instead 'I suppose I have to use "-isms" – as a localist and an internationalist'.[18] Leonard's movement away from standardised dictionary spelling marks an attempt to politicise his poetry. He requires a different form of literacy from his reader, which is far more dependent on the simultaneous translations and modification of sound. As he writes in *Six Glasgow Poems*, 'Good Style': 'helluva hard tay read theez init' while declaring humorously a poetic power: 'ahmaz goodiz thi lota yiz so ah um'.[19] Within these six poems we read a plurality of voices, from the grumpy poet to the voice counselling his son in 'The Miracle of the Burd and the Fishes': 'thirz a loat merr fish in thi sea', to the raucous voices of women in 'A Scream': 'o yi shooda seeniz face / hi didny no wherrty look'.[20] Leonard's poems take play with audience challenging our expectations by stressing the phonetic valences of linguistic use. Take for example 'the burd', which in colloquial use points to female or lover, and 'the scream', not as angst or fear, but as having a laugh. Leonard in a review declares that it is important to acknowledge:

how a language is seen to have status according to whether it is used by the governing or the governed; whether professional linguists have published academic works on it; whether it can be shown to have a grammar, a distinctive sound-pattern, a 'full' range of reference; whether agreed value has been, or can be, placed on works of literary art that use it as a medium; above all, whether ways have yet been found of agreeing a form of the language in serious dictionary, thus – more even than fixing meanings to words – fixing pronunciations to fixed spellings.[21]

Both Harrison and Leonard recognise that class is displayed in linguistic hierarchies.

Helen Kidd reflects upon the relationship of dialect to the works of women poets. Responding specifically to the work of Scottish women poets, Kidd suggests that 'Scots dialect is recognisable by certain tropes whereas women do not have a language that is specifically female, nor a specific set of dialects which are identifiable to women from other cultural contexts'.[22] In place of such an emphatic dialect, she suggests that the subversive linguistic experimentation is offered in the work of female poets: 'ironies, digressions, musicalities as well as a sense of the dangers of certain male discourses which lace the female subject in a subordinate position'.[23] In Liz Lochhead's poem 'Lady Writer Talkin' Blues', the figure of the female poet asserts her voice through an intonation of blues rhythm, but this appropriation of the blues is rendered more complex by the intrusion of syntax and grammar which inscribe a Scots inflection.[24] Lochhead plays with the melodies of both clashing intonations and the phonetic texture of colloquial speech. The speaker is told by her partner that 'Mah Work was a load a' drivel / I called it detail, he called it trivial' (p. 38). Substitution, or the rewriting of the speaker's voice, enacts hierarchies of power and an enforced editing. The male voice intrudes upon the blues rhythm to damn the speaker: 'I was woolly in my politics / And personal poetry gave him the icks' (p. 39). Finally, we are told that 'He couldn't do His brainwork in the same house as me / Because I screwed up his objectivity' (p. 39). Lochhead's redeployment of the blues enables her work not only to present the intonation of a Scots idiom, but to place the woman poet's voice on a vast stage of call and response, as well as humorously jostling with the ego of the male artist.

THE 'BIG ONE, BETTER TONGUE': JACKIE KAY

The intervention of Scots dialect in Jackie Kay's poetry emphasises the relationship of language to a sense of place, tribalism and identity. Kay is the child of a Nigerian father and white Scottish mother (later adopted by a white Scottish couple). Her poetry documents the difficulty of her positioning in a Scottish landscape, and how language use asserts affiliations while also presenting diversities. Nancy Gish suggests that 'Kay's self-conscious play on voices, dialects and discourses destabilizes any notion of a consistent unified self.'[25] Kay states that 'people can't contain being both things, being Black and being Scottish without thinking there is an inherent contradiction there'.[26] These tensions come to the fore in 'In My Country', in which the poet is asked by a woman, 'Where do you come from?' and Kay's response is, 'Here. These parts'.[27] Finding a space of identification is key to many of Kay's poems and this sense of in-betweenness or liminality, Scottish-Nigerian, gay vs straight, Scots dialect vs English, permeates her work:

> If you are brought up in a place, you get that identity very, very fixedly. And you don't necessarily get a sense of your being Black, because there's nothing around you affirming that you are. So although I was steeped in Scottish culture, of which I'm very appreciative, I never had any sense of Black culture at all, until I went about finding that and creating that for myself.[28]

In 'Old Tongue' from *Life Mask* (2005), Kay negotiates her relationship with received pronunciation and Scots dialect. Describing a child's journey 'south', the poem portrays the colour and vibrancy of dialect language against the staid confines of so-called 'correct' enunciation. This movement from place is coupled with an abstracted sense of loss. Words are mourned since the poem chronicles not only the loss of accented speech, but of an alternative language use. Attempting to fit into a new environment, the child suffers the loss of an alternative language which gives expression to emotion and even insult: 'eedyit' for idiot, 'heidbanger' for someone out of control.[29] Other words describe the timbre of an emotional state such as *crabbit*, ill tempered, or *dreich* as drab or dreary. Emphatically, Kay illustrates how this loss is a visceral sensation, with the defecting words described as having their own anarchic personalities. Hence, the speaker admits that if she had found the words 'wandering' she would have 'swallowed them whole, knocked them back' (p. 50). The imposition of a new accent is also seen in physical terms, since her 'vowels start to stretch like my bones' (p. 50). Kay's description of a linguistic metamorphosis indicates how identity can be inhabited in a language. This dual inhabiting becomes towards the end of the poem a struggle for the restitution of identity, dramatised as 'My dour soor Scottish tongue' (p. 50). The closing vigorous statement 'I wanted to *gie it laldie*' (p. 50), with its emphasis on giving it all, affirms not only a Scottish identity but the role of a minor language as a powerful vehicle of self-expression.

Kay's sensitivity to minority languages and dialects takes centre stage in 'Sign', from *Other Lovers* (1993). 'Sign' dramatises the failure to recognise alternate languages as having any agency or role. This failure to acknowledge is perceived as a brutalising statement of '*no language at all*' (p. 20). The poem focuses upon the role of sign language as a space of immediacy where body and abstract thought conjoin in the presence of 'Everything grows / in the right place', where things are seen in 'the present tense: a flashback is something held between her thumb and her index finger' (p. 20). Kay places the focus on the spatial relationships created in signing between 'mouth, eyes and hands', which become a cosmic map of 'space between' planets (p. 21). The intricacy of the patterning of space through body language, gesture and eyes creates an important inter-subjective space. Yet, through the perspective of those who cannot read these actions they become mere '*miming*' or '*pantomime*' (p. 21). A dominant drive towards vocal expression is portrayed in distressing terms where the subject of the poem has her hands tied behind her back and is forced to repeat words without signing 'until / she has no language at all' (p. 21). Provocatively, Kay uses the startling perceptions of signing as a language of space and body where abstracted thought becomes tangible to chart the threat posed to minority languages: 'The *little languages* / squashed, stamped upon, cleared out / to make way / for the big one, better tongue' (p. 21). This attention to multiple language use and challenge to a dominant English tongue is articulated in Kay's work through its multiple references to inclusion and multiplicity. As Gish states in her assessment of contemporary Scottish poets: 'these poets who are complicating these linguistic borders are creating not something in between "mainstream" and "experimental" but culturally specific experimentation demanding of those who have internalized the dominant dialect the effort required to read genuinely different cultural work'.[30]

FROM ORALITY TO TEXT: ETHNOPOETICS IN SIMON ORTIZ AND JOY HARJO'S POETRY

In a recent interview, Native American poet Simon Ortiz, a member of the Acoma Pueblo tribal community in New Mexico, discusses the fate of indigenous languages of the Americas and the subsequent domination of English and Spanish:

> After 1492, European languages became the prominent and dominant colonial languages that helped to achieve settlement, invasion, occupation, also known as conquest of the Americas. English was introduced to North America in the 1600s along the eastern or Atlantic seaboard, although by then Spanish was already the strongest European colonial instrument of social, economic, political control and dominance in the Caribbean and North American continental lands known now as Mexico and Guatemala.[31]

Responding specifically to the situation of Native Americans, Ortiz states that English in the USA has invariably become 'the language-cultural choice that has determined the lives of Indigenous peoples. Go to reservations anywhere in the US, and you'll hear English as the common language' (p. 7). While he stresses that there are exceptions and that indigenous languages are spoken in both South and North America, he emphasises that English has become the first language for most indigenous poets and writers: 'Why not? It is the language that has to be dealt with face to face personally, socially, and politically' (p. 6). For him 'Indigenous language can be a strong part of this consciousness, but it doesn't have to be the only or main ingredient' since 'language is only one part of cultural consciousness, while physical engagement and involvement in spirited activities is a bigger part of consciousness' (p. 8). Central to Ortiz is the sense of being communal beings within a holistic universe and the 'principle of continuance' (p. 8).

Ortiz and Harjo's poetry enables a sense of continuance through their transfer of oral histories, ritual and mythology into text. This approach to poetry has been read under the moniker 'ethnopoetics', meaning writing that offers a questioning of the traditional Western literary canon. Often combining an interest in anthropology and linguistics, ethnopoetics considers a history of non-Western and indigenous literatures while questioning the division between so-called primitive and civilised cultural production. As a general analytic approach, a form of ethnopoetics existed before the twentieth century, but the term was first introduced to public attention by Jerome Rothenberg in 1968 as part of a momentum guided towards issues formed by race and ethnicity:

> Closely related to the primitive is the approach that focuses on the idea of oral poetry – though the dominance of the oral clearly continues in cultures that could by no stretch of the imagination be thought of as technologically 'primitive'. The approach through 'performance' over a wide range of cultures might almost be synonymous with that through the oral while spilling over as well into cultures with a fixed system of writing.[32]

Rothenberg in this more recent revisiting of the term is keen to emphasise that ethnopoetics must not be seen as a dichotomy between so-called primitive and advanced societies and cultures.

Ortiz's poem 'Telling about Coyote' uses ideas from the trickster tradition to present his narrative.[33] In folklore and myth the trickster is a figure or spirit (often represented anthropomorphically) who breaks rules and challenges hierarchies. Drawing from the Coyote as a trickster figure in Native American folklore, Ortiz presents a character who defies multiple deaths. Gary Snyder suggests that the Coyote in Native American folklore is: 'a trickster . . .

he is always traveling, he's really stupid, he's kind of bad . . . most of the time he's just into mischief'.[34] Jarold Ramsey adds that the basic narrative is that coyotes are 'unkillable' and although 'they may suffer bad luck or just retribution in the form of starvation, poisoning, dismemberment, ingestion by monsters, incineration, drowning, fatal falls . . . it is a universal convention that they survive'.[35] Ortiz's Coyote, travelling to his own wedding, gets sidetracked into a gambling party. The inflection of the poem is a casual orality which communicates a guarded affection for the Coyote: '. . . you know, Coyote / is in the origin and all the way / through' (p. 434). Placed in a literary framework, the Coyote is described humorously as 'an existential man / a Dostoevsky Coyote' (p. 434). We are told that, losing dramatically at cards, he had quite literally lost everything including his skin and fur. Some mice, finding Coyote in the cold, take pity on him and reclaim pieces of fur, pasting them onto his body, the result being an 'old raggy blanket' which looks like 'scraps of an old coat' (p. 434). Ortiz frames Coyote as dependent upon those who are around him. Wai Chee Dimock comments upon this interdependency: 'Coyote is literally what others make of him. His stories have to be about other animals, for they need to be there if these stories are to have their customary semi-happy ending'.[36] In effect, Ortiz uses the Coyote story as a way of indicating strong bonds of community and inter-subjectivity. The conversational and discursive framework he establishes enables the poetic text to perform the retelling of an oral narrative with immediacy.

Joy Harjo is of Cherokee descent and a member of the Muscogee Nation of Oklahoma. Her prose poem 'Deer Dancer' is a lament for the disconnection of contemporary native experience with ancestry and an affirmation of reconnecting with ancient rituals and beliefs.[37] Set in a run-down bar, the tale is narrated by a community 'we', who identify themselves as 'Indian ruins' or 'broken survivors, the club of the shotgun, knife wound, of poison by culture' (p. 5). A stranger enters to dance for and amongst them: 'No one knew her, the stranger whose tribe we recognized, her family related to deer' (p. 5). Harjo evokes as a basis to her poem the Native American mythology of a deer woman. Interpreted as a siren, the deer woman is associated with dancing, seduction, danger and even personal transformation. As with the trickster mythology, the deer woman is aligned with shape-shifting, and her figuration as a woman is betrayed by having deers' hooves instead of feet. The speaker's dual vision portrays the conflict between contemporary and Native cultures. As the woman finishes the dance, we are told she is dressed in 'a stained red dress with tape on her heels' (p. 6). Yet during the dance she is portrayed as a myth-maker 'slipped down through dreamtime', becoming eventually a collective ideal: 'The promise of feast we all knew was coming. The deer who crossed through knots of a curse to find us' (p. 6). Key to the poem is the difficulty of finding the words to describe the experience of the dance that the community witnesses:

> In this language there are no words for how the real world collapses. I could say it in my own and the sacred mounds would come into focus, but I couldn't take it in this dingy envelope. (p. 5)

Harjo skilfully presents the tensions between the spiritual and material; the poem searches for reparation with the world as a holistic presence. At the close, a promise of reaffiliation exists in 'her fawn a blessing of meat, the ancestors who never left' (p. 6). We can extend Stuart Cochran's analysis of Simon Ortiz's poetry to Joy Harjo's poem. Cochran proposes that Ortiz's ethnopoetics 'speak of identities inseparable from particular landscapes and of the spiritually and culturally disintegrative impact of the loss of that connection'.[38] Through this perspective, we can concur that Harjo and Ortiz also affirm 'the primacy of storytelling and the significance that stories give to the land and its people'.[39]

BILINGUALISM AND TRANSLATION IN POETRY

For some poets, the relationship with an Anglophone culture necessitates elements of translation, a process which is made evident through the act of writing. Lawrence Venuti considers that literary translation is often reliant upon the translator's invisibility.

He argues for translations to be read as 'texts in their own right permitting transparency to be demystified, seen as one discursive effect among others'.[40] Venuti emphasises the destabilising element in the translation practice – the contingency of signification: 'the chain of signifiers that constitutes the foreign text is replaced by a chain of signifiers in the translating language' (p. 13). He alerts us to multiple valences of interpretation:

> Because meaning is an effect of relations and differences among signifiers along a potentially endless chain (polysemous, intertextual, subject to infinite linkages), it is always differential and deferred, never presents as an original unity. Both foreign text and translation are derivative; both consist of diverse linguistic and cultural materials that neither the foreign writer nor the translator originates, and that destabilize the work of signification, inevitably exceeding and possibly conflicting with their intentions . . . Meaning is a plural and contingent relation, not an unchanging unified essence. (p. 13)

Three poets – Gwyneth Lewis, Li-Young Lee and Lorna Dee Cervantes – perform different acts of translation in their poetry. Their work dramatises a keen awareness of the erotic, authoritarian and often homogenising characteristics of English. An exploration of how bilingualism is performed in their work provides insights into the cultural conflicts which arise in multiple language use – an experience which Li-Young Lee describes as 'You live / a while in two worlds / at once'.[41]

'MY GLOSSOLALIA SHALL BE MY PASSPORT': GWYNETH LEWIS

As a poet writing both in Welsh and English, often translating her own poetry, Lewis emphasises that her translations must be read as departures from the original, if not new explorations. In considering the inter-relationship between both languages, Lewis reflects in one of her essays that:

The smuggling of familiar material from one language to another seemed to me on reflection, too easy a way of exploiting a Welsh subject matter in English. I wanted to be a full English language poet when I wrote in English and not just a translator of material which might not work in Welsh.[42]

Provocatively, Lewis adds that 'translation doesn't just happen between languages – it's sometimes needed within one', which suggests that it is not only bilingualism which establishes a fertile textuality in the poetry.[43] 'Pentecost', the opening poem of *Parables & Faxes* (1995), alerts us immediately to the gift of languages or 'glossolalia', which enables the speaker's safe passage through the checkpoints of Europe to Florida. Lewis suggests that linguistic multiplicity is a passport, a point of entry into a 'perpetual Pentecost'.[44] As is often the case in Lewis's work, language is linked to the erotic and the tactile: 'I shall taste the tang / of travel on the atlas of my tongue / salt Poland, sour Denmark and sweet Vienna' (p. 9). This entry into language (or languages in this case) is presented as a quest for symbolic significance, resonant of Jacques Lacan's interpretation of the child's initiation into language as a manifestation of a lack. According to Lacan, language offers a symbolic order in which the subject can represent desire and so compensate, albeit inadequately, for the experience of lack.[45] This is a process that Lewis correlates to an understanding of her bilingualism:

They say that language develops in infants as the baby finds itself alone and calls out for its absent mother. At its very root then, language is about needing your mother and about responding to your desolation without her . . . A truly bilingual person has not one mother tongue, but two. Welsh was my blood mother, English my stepmother.[46]

Lewis's poem celebrates linguistic multiplicity, its speaking in tongues while also seeking correspondence with the immediate world of things. Drawing from a cabalistic notion of language as a supreme order ordained from God, the poem suggests that there is continuity between how things are represented through language and an innate symbolism:

> Then the S in the tail of the crocodile
> will make perfect sense to the bibliophile
>
> who will study this land, his second Torah.
> All this was revealed. Now I wait for the Lord
> to move heaven and earth to send me abroad
> and fulfil His bold promise to Florida. (p. 9)

This desire for a unity between word and object becomes a pilgrim's quest. Lewis is alert to the humorous ambitions of such a journey. Indeed, even God intervenes at the end, closing the Atlantic, bridging the gap between the continents of Europe and the Americas, allowing the speaker's immediate passage. The poem points towards a landscape where there was once not only geographical unity but a divine linguistic order.

Lewis's sequence 'Welsh Espionage' navigates with clarity the immediate cultural clash between English and Welsh. A father teaches his daughter English through gesturing to parts of the body. As a consequence Lewis embeds Welsh names with English, such as 'penelin' for elbow, 'gwallt' for hair, 'dwrn' for fist, 'gwefusau' for lips and 'llygaid' for eyes' as part of the 'fetishist quiz' (p. 42). We are told that 'Each part he touched in their secret game / thrilled as she whispered its English name' (p. 42). Critics have commented upon the suggestion of sexual abuse in this poem, and it is clear that the site where the two languages intersect is the body. On first glance the translations seem straightforward, but on closer consideration both languages are jostling for ascendancy and power. Italics switch their roles; pedagogy is represented through the English and a certain active agency in Welsh. The duality of what the poet refers to as having two mother tongues is underwritten with unease and guilt. Lewis's commentary is insightful:

> I suspect that this sinister suggestion was a way for me to explore the discomfort I felt at being born between two cultures. Early on I had an acute sense of the cultural clash

between the social values tied up in both languages. I suppose, that in some way, I still feel guilty about being Daddy's girl and writing in English at all.[47]

To harness the poem solely to a reading of sexual abuse would be to narrow its focus. Lewis examines the complex process of establishing and transgressing boundaries be they sexual, cultural or linguistic. The poem's resistance to a singular reading (malign or benign) indicates that it is precisely this ambiguous relationship between the two languages which the poem depends upon.

Deryn Rees-Jones points to a consideration of the dualities of 'Welshness' and 'Englishness', suggesting that the future for such writing may be found in establishing correspondences between binary oppositions. This would be a poetics which 'while celebrating differences, works towards the exploration and interrogation of connections'.[48] Yet, there are occasional resistances in the text by a bilingual poet that cannot be solely resolved by mobility between cultural identities. Lewis proposes that 'If you're truly bilingual it's not that there are two languages in your world, but that not everybody understands the whole of your personal speech'.[49] One way of considering her words is to think about bilingualism as a sort of simultaneity in the writing, not just as the inclusion of Welsh words in an English-language text. Tzvetan Todorov urges us not to think of bilingualism as two distinctive languages operating independently. Instead, he suggests that we must approach bilingualism as the simultaneous existence of more than one cultural model, or what he refers to as a form of 'dialogism'. This in turn becomes a sort of excess or intractable multiplicity:

> Placing bilingualism within the framework of dialogism also allows us, rather than turning it into a purely linguistic question, to consider it in direct relation with two phenomena: the problem of the co-existence of cultural models within the same society, and the internal multiplicity of personality.[50]

Todorov's essay gives a troubling prognosis for any bilingual poet.

In 'Oxford Bootlicker', from the extended sequence *Parables & Faxes*, the speaker starts off eating a religious scroll, moves to Tolstoy and 'nourishing' Kafka, then proceeds to 'lick the fat' (p. 56) from all the other books in the vicinity. Religious symbolism, knowledge and fantasy intertwine as the speaker states:

> I am voracious
> for the Word – a lexicon is wine
> to me and wafer, so that home, at night,
> I ruminate on all that's mine
>
> inside these messages. I am the fruit
> of God's expressiveness to man. (p. 56)

The speaker imagines that once she is 'ripe', multiple languages, texts and even a metropolis of inhabitants will be evacuated from her body: 'I spew up cities, colonies of words / and flocks of sentences with full-stop birds' (p. 56). This is taking Todorov's internal multiplicity to an extreme, but satisfyingly humorous, conclusion. Syntactical disruption and the radical dislocation of language on the page are perhaps not viable options for a bilingual poet, especially one sharply attuned to the literal silencing of a language. Lewis chooses discursiveness over estrangement. As the epilogue to *Parables & Faxes* reminds us, such a position would restrict Lewis's poetry to '*a partial vision*' and halt a productive conversation '*scarcely begun*' (p. 77).

IMMIGRATION AND LINGUISTIC DIFFERENCE: LI-YOUNG LEE

Following the establishment of the People's Republic of China, Li-Young Lee's parents fled to Indonesia, where he was born. Lee eventually settled in the USA, and his experience as a child immigrant with no English is dramatised in his early poetry. In a memoir, *The Winged Seed* (1995), Lee remarks on his awareness of linguistic and cultural difference:

> I noticed early on that accents were not heard alike by the dominant population of American English speakers. Instead each

foreigner's spoken English, determined by a mother tongue, each person's noise fell on a colouring ear, which bent the listener's eye and consequently the speaker's countenance . . . While some sounds were tolerated, even granting the speaker a certain status in the instances of say French or British, other inflections condemned one to immediate alien.[51]

Lee's 'Persimmons' presents this sense of linguistic exclusion or difference as well as interrogating a cultural legacy.[52] The poem examines ideas of integration, the mourning of a mother language and the importance of memorialising what survives the process of immigration. Zhou Xiaojing comments that 'Persimmons' conceives of the past as consisting of 'memories, experiences, received knowledge, established notions, and culturally and historically constructed ethnic identity', all of which are 'reconstructed, questioned, challenged, and re-created'.[53] Initially, the poem recalls the violence of the sixth-grade teacher Mrs Walker, who hits the child for mispronunciation, for not knowing the difference between '*persimmon* and *precision*' (p. 17). Lee shows how processes of cultural translation and equally importantly *mis*translation operate. The teacher, rather than naming the fruit persimmon, refers to it as a '*Chinese Apple*' (p. 18) and failing to identify it as unripe, is exposed herself as failing in 'precision'. Within the poem, persimmons are associated with the child's need to integrate, a physical sexuality and the attempt to retain a cultural legacy through processes of memory. These linkages in the text are asserted as exploratory performances within the poem. A key section recreates a scene of erotic translation as the speaker attempts to teach a lover Chinese. Onomatopoeia guides the speaker initially, but amnesia also intervenes as he tries to translate the setting: 'Crickets: *chiu chiu*. Dew: I've forgotten / Naked: I've forgotten. / *Ni, wo*: you and me' (p. 17).

Lee presents a relationship to an unfamiliar language in experiential terms. The differences between words such as 'fight and fright' and 'wren and yarn' (p. 17) are described in terms of agency, action and family activity. 'Fight' is what the child does 'when he was frightened', and 'fright' (p. 17) is what the child feels while fighting. Equally, wrens are presented as indistinguishable from domesticity. While the child recognises that wrens are birds, and yarn is knitting material, the translation becomes magically alive when the speaker comments that 'wrens are soft as yarn / my mother made birds out of yarn' (p. 18). It is in these small micro-narratives that family histories become tangible. Moreover, the persimmon is identified by his mother in spiritual and nurturing terms since 'every persimmon has a sun / inside, something golden, glowing, / warm as my face' (p. 18). Lee proposes that the initial 'strangeness' of English language helped his writing: 'I can't tell if my being Chinese is an advantage or not, but I can't imagine anything else except writing as an outsider.' He adds that: 'It's bracing to be reminded [that] we're all guests in the language, any language'.[54] Usefully in this context, poet Lyn Hejinian's reflection on the Greek word *xenos* – suggestive of foreigner or stranger – creates a meditation upon the figure of the border as a point of both reciprocity and differentiation. Hejinian suggests that encounters with difference create a site of 'contradiction and confluence' since 'the stranger it names is both guest and host . . . The guest / host relationship is one of identity as much as it is of reciprocity'.[55] For Mikhail Bakhtin, the meeting of the outsider with the dominant culture necessitates dialogue and in many ways a sense of cultural translation and examination:

> In the realm of culture, outsidedness is a most powerful factor in understanding. It is only in the eyes of another culture that foreign culture reveals itself fully and profoundly . . . A meaning only reveals its depths once it has encountered and come into contact with another, foreign meaning: they engage in a kind of dialogue, which surmounts the closedness and one-sidedness of these particular meanings, these cultures. We raise new questions for a foreign culture, ones that it did not raise itself; we seek answers to our own questions in it; and the foreign culture responds to us by revealing to us its new aspects and new semantic depths.[56]

At the close of the poem Lee presents us with the immigrant's perspective of cultural memory. The poem is infused with indications of amnesia and its close affiliation to acts of memorialisation.

Returning home as an adult, the son finds three scrolls, one which details two persimmons 'so full they want to drop from the cloth' (p. 19). He presents this picture to his blind father who reasserts through touch, memories of the past as well as a sensual patterning of evocation. These are persimmons he has painted 'blind' with his eyes closed 'hundreds of times' (p. 19). Evoking both familiarity and cultural identification, the persimmons are finally translated into a pattern of mourning and remembrance; the memory of their shape and texture are equated with the immediacy of recollecting 'the scent of the hair of one you love' (p. 19).

INTERLINGUAL POETICS: LORNA DEE CERVANTES

Lorna Dee Cervantes's first volume of poetry *Emplumada* (1981) was credited with showing the barrio life from a Mexican-American woman, or Chicana's perspective. The emergent wave of first-generation Chicana poets writing in English was responding to a degree to the emergent politics of Chicano writers beginning in the 1960s. Appeals for the reclamation of a spiritual homeland lineated in the Amerindian myth of Aztlán were key to the early Chicano manifesto by Alberto Baltazar Urista, 'El Plan Espiritual de Aztlán' (1969):

> We the Chicano inhabitants and civilizers of the northern land of Aztlán from whence came our forefathers reclaiming the land of their birth and consecrating the determination of our people of the sun, declare the call for our blood is our power, our responsibility, and our inevitable destiny.[57]

The rewriting of these rhetorical positions from a female perspective was central to the development of Chicana writing. The pivotal writer and critic Cherrie Moraga describes that, as women: 'we sought and believe we found non-rhetorical, highly personal chronicles that present a political analysis in everyday terms'.[58] Cervantes suggests that Chicana poetry is a poetry of 'the observer class' and points towards gendered differences:

Whereas the men's poetry was more linguistically free, when Chicanas started publishing it was all about perceptions, what was observed. To me, it's not history, oral history, written. It's a matter of the relationship between power and language. But again, that kind of participation through the language was for us one of our strengths. It's the keen power of observation.[59]

This drive towards personal female experience is validated by critic theorist Gloria Anzaldúa, who echoes the perspectives of Moraga and Cervantes by emphasising that 'The danger in writing is not fusing our personal experience and world view with the social reality we live in, with our inner life, our history, our economics and our vision'.[60] She adds that '*No topic is too trivial*', since the danger for the Chicana writer is 'in being too universal and humanitarian and invoking the eternal to the sacrifice of the particular and the feminine and the specific historical moment'.[61]

An immediate feature of Cervantes's early poems is the intersection of Spanish and English language. Born in the Mission District of San Francisco and raised in San Jose, Cervantes was deprived of speaking Spanish – or, as she puts it: 'Mama raised me without language / I'm orphaned from my Spanish tongue'.[62] As a consequence, her poetry is splintered with phrases from the Spanish that often assert a disjunctive and warring texture in the poem. 'Poema para los Californios Muertos' is inscribed with the epithet: 'Once a refuge for Mexican Californios, plaque outside a restaurant in Los Altos California, 1974.' Cervantes meditates on the battles of the Californian–Mexican Wars of the 1840s. The Amerindian narrative of Aztlán is read here in a feminised description of the original Mexican California (inhabited by native Californios), with its present-day landscape of the freeway exerting 'a clean cesarean / across belly valleys and fertile dust' (p. 42). This rewriting of the Aztlán myth is accompanied by reflections in Spanish on revenge for the loss of life and native inhabitants: '*Yo recuerdo los antepasados muertos*' (p. 42) [I remember the dead ancestors]; '*Soy la hija pobrecita pero puedo maldecir estas fantasmas blancas*' (p. 42) [I am only your poor daughter, but I can curse these white ghosts]. The intersection of both languages excavates a violent history of conquest and subordination. Commenting on the development of Chicana writing, Norma Alarcón poses that her aim was to encourage those who challenged linguistic hierarchies: 'the silence and silencing of people begins with the dominating enforcement of linguistic conventions, the resistance to relational dialogues, as well as the disablement of people by outlawing their forms of speech'.[63] Moreover, Louis Reyes Rivera proposes that: 'When you speak the language of your oppressor you either absorb all of his values or your recreate your tongue to change each image and syllable into weapons for the people's awakening'.[64] Read within these critical contexts, Cervantes mounts an attack, using Spanish as an agency for recovery and reaffirming cultural complexity. The actions of revenge and memory are also viewed in gendered terms: '*tierra la madre*' (p. 42) [mother earth], as well as '*Los recuerdo en la sangre, / la sangre fértil*' (p. 42) [I remember them in my blood, my fertile blood]. It seems particularly apt that the poem closes with a reflection upon the Californian indigenous tree, the eucalyptus, as 'the pure scent of rage' (p. 43).

Cervantes comments on her use of Spanish that 'I don't want to pretend I know more / and can speak all the names. I can't' (p. 45). The amalgam of English and Spanish in 'Freeway 280' grants an intimate perspective on the speaker's relationship to the land, culture and past wishes of escape. Opening with the Spanish description of 'Las casitas' (p. 39) [small houses] next to an industrial site, a sense of intimacy is continued by the description of the 'abrazos' [embraces] of wild roses around the houses (p. 39). Chicano critic Juan Bruce-Novoa proposes that this form of combined language use differs from the experience of bilingualism:

The two languages inform one another at every level. There are certain grammatical usages, words, connotations, spellings which to a native speaker of Spanish or English, or to the true bilingual appear to be mistakes, cases of code switching or interference in linguistic terms, but which to the Chicano native speaker are common usages, the living reality of an interlingual space.[65]

In addition, for Bruce-Novoa 'Bilingualism implies moving from one language code to another', whereas 'interlingualism implies the constant tension of the two at once'.[66] This tension is illustrated in the images of the reclamation of land near the freeway by indigenous plants. The apricot, cherry and walnut trees are named as '*Albaricoqueros, cerezos, nogales*', and we are told that old women come to collect the spinach, purslane and mint: '*Espinaca, verdolagas, yerbabuena*' (p. 39). One effect of the interlingual processes of the poem is to present the neglected physical spaces as defamiliarised, yet also emotionally proximate. Cervantes seeks a placing of these conflicts within what she names 'los campos extraños de esta ciudad' [the strange fields of this city] (p. 39). The transcription of these tensions between warring languages creates a form of poetic realism that challenges assumptions and preconceptions.

IDIOLECTS OR IDEOLECTICAL POETRIES

The inclusion of dialect in poetry is often a way of affirming identities – often regional, national, economic and racial – that may be seen in a dialectical relationship with standard English use. Derek Walcott's book-length *Omeros* (1990) is often cited as a poetics of creolisation, with its complex inflection of epic, Caribbean speech acts and local history. We may also consider the advent of a distinct topography of Caribbean speech of the late sixties which Brathwaite has taken to be the affirmation of 'nation language'.[67] A further understanding might also include idiomatic linguistic use, often referred to as idiolectical language use. The *OED* suggests that an idiolect refers to 'the linguistic system of one person, differing in some details from that of all other speakers of the same dialect or language'.[68]

The word 'idiolect' surfaces in Charles Bernstein's provocative essay of 1996 'Poetics of the Americas', where it is transmuted to 'ideolect'. In this essay Bernstein argues for an 'ideolectical' approach to an American poetry, reliant less on a multiplicity of identities, than a plurality of different languages. Taken at its broadest sense, Bernstein's 'ideolects' draw a vast perimeter around an experimental poetics and the conceptualisation of a shared language. As opposed to dialect in poetry, Bernstein argues that an 'ideolectical' approach creates a 'virtual' poetics of the Americas, allowing in effect for a range of different idioms. Above all, Bernstein stresses that an 'ideolectical' poetics is provisional, unlike dialect in poetry which is still 'informed', if not regulated, by its difference to 'standard' language practices:

> By linking dialect and ideolect I wish to emphasize the common ground of linguistic exploration, the invention of new syntaxes as akin to the invention of new Americas, or of new possibilities for America . . . nonstandard writing practices share a technical commonality that overrides the necessary differences of interpretation and motivation, and this commonality may be the vortical prosodic force that gives us footing with one another . . . dialect understood as nation language, has a centripetal force, regrouping often denigrated and dispirited language practices around a common center; ideolect in contrast, suggests a centrifugal force moving away from normative practices without necessarily replacing them with a new center of gravity, at least defined by self or group.[69]

Bernstein is proposing languages of differentiation, not merely the placing of words in unusual grammatical orders. Initially, this development in the poet's conceptualisation of poetic language appears to promote a solipsistic enquiry advocating multiple forms of 'private' language. Yet, Bernstein in an early essay categorically states that 'the idea of a private language is illusory because language itself is a communality, a public domain. Its forms and contents are in no sense private – they are the very essence of the social'.[70] On reflection, what is shared in this enterprise of an 'ideolectical' approach to poetry is the creation of a common social space for these linguistic endeavours, and an attempt to decentralise the informing role of rule-governed practices in poetic language:

> The use of dialectical or ideolectical language in a poem marks a refusal of standard English as the common ground of

communication. For poets wishing to obliterate or overcome such marks of difference, the choice of the conventional literary language whether understood as mask or not, reflects a willingness to abide by the linguistic norms of a culture and to negotiate within these norms. Nonstandard language practice suggests an element of cultural resistance that has as its lower limit dialogic self-questioning and as its upper limit secession and autonomy.[71]

It could be argued that Bernstein's reliance upon multiplicity may only promote an increasingly atomised resistance to the conventions he wants to challenge. Paradoxically, Bernstein also argues that the problematising of identity that an 'ideolectical' approach provides may, in effect, 'forge new collective identities'.[72] Already we can see how a poet such as Tom Leonard challenges the centralising role of standard English in his language. Bernstein's harnessing of an 'ideolectical' approach to an experimental poetics can be seen as overtly idealistic. It perhaps acknowledges the development of multiple Englishes, a process of devolution which the performance poet cris cheek acknowledges as a dispersal of 'the sounds of Englishes' and the loss of a centralising authority: 'I celebrate that loss, as a positive sign that is a language in a turmoil of great promise, opening rather than resistant to, that vibrant plethora of influences and change which has enabled it to become so translocal'.[73] Bernstein's appeal to an 'ideolectical' poetics can also be read in recent criticism's fascination with establishing an aesthetic for a post-national literature, or what Ramazani terms a transnational literature: 'a nation-crossing force that exceeds the limits of the territorial and judicial norm'.[74] Key to Ramazani's identifications are the practices of creolisation and hybridisation which he reads not only as essential to the 'formal advancement or the growth of discrete national poetries', but as 'cross-cultural dynamics . . . among the engines of modern and contemporary poetic development and innovation'.[75] However, Ramazani's transnational poetics does not advocate a vapid idea of a global aesthetic, as we are reminded that given the complex nature of current poetic practice 'the homogenizing model of globalization is inadequate for the analysis of specifically poetic transnationalism'.[76]

LINGUISTIC CROSS-FERTILISATION: TUSIATA AVIA

Tusiata Avia's poetry shows how the poetic text can become a space for linguistic cross-fertilisation and the exploration of idiomatic, or idiolectical, texture. Of Samoan decent, Avia was raised in Christchurch, New Zealand. As a performance poet, her poetry engages with oral storytelling, often focusing on the intervention of folklore from her Samoan heritage and modern New Zealand. The opening poem of her volume *Wild Dogs Under My Skirt* (2004) offers a rendition of the Samoan alphabet – 'O le pi tautau' – through a series of poetic narratives, as well as a glossary of words at the back of the volume.[77] The stories in this work seek to translate between two idioms and two cultures. We are told that 'A is for Afakasi' [half-caste], and represented as a 'child / left at the crossroads' about whom the poem asks: 'Who will save her from the snakes? / Who will save her from the darkness?' (p. 9). This position of being in-between two cultures, identities or at a 'crossroads' is enforced by the doubling positions enacted in 'O le pi tautau'. 'T' for example stands for 'teine lelei / good girl' and also 'T is for teine leaga / bad girl' (p. 12). Through this alphabetised poem Avia also enforces a sense of pedagogy and the imposition of what might be considered 'correct' pedagogy. It comes as no surprise that 'V' stands for virgin, and the speaker communicates confusion regarding religious doctrinal thought:

> Mary was a virgin
> and God was her husband
> but Joseph was her husband
> and Jesus was her baby. (p. 12)

The positioning of women is crucial in Avia's volume, as are the narratives inherited by the young female child that dominates the volume. In 'O le pi tautau', 'S' we are told is for 'Slut' which is then translated into Samoan: 'I know what it means / it means pa'umuku / like my mother' (p. 12). Avia uses Samoan as a method for framing the contesting representations of both women and female sexuality. Her prose poem 'Alofa', translated as 'love', uses the Samoan firstly as a name for young woman, then for framing gestures that are misinterpreted. The idiomatic stress on a Samoan background suggests sexual naiveté and innocence. A simple equation is created between love and pleasure. Alofa goes for a walk and finds 'alofa everywhere in da bush in da tree under da tree in da dark alofa . . . plenty alofa in da dark' (p. 62). In the poem 'alofa' also becomes a currency to be traded, since Alofa sings and prays to Jesus: 'Jesus bring me plenty alofa plenty money too Jesus make me win da bingo den I make da big donation show my alofa to all da peoples in da church' (p. 62). When she does win she goes to the town and a nightclub to perform with 'fa'afafine' [drag queens or transsexuals], as well as 'Palagi mans' (p. 62) or white men. The poem eventually chronicles Alofa's exchange of her body for alofa – 'Alofa making alofa in da Seaside Inn with da Palagi man name Bruce' (p. 63). On return to her community Alofa becomes the 'pa'umuka kirl' pregnant with an illegitimate child – 'an when it's finish – Alofa call it Alofa too' (p. 63). Avia's ideolectical tenor to the poem adds to a sense of cyclicality; it also frames a brutal encounter with racial prejudice and the tensions between community and urbanity.

CONCLUSION: DALJIT NAGRA

The publication of British Asian poet Daljit Nagra's *Look We Have Coming to Dover* (2002), was heralded as a new male perspective and voicing of minority poetry in the UK. As Dave Gunning notes, Nagra's poetry 'leads to important questions about what is being promoted as an authentic British Asian poetic voice, and to what extent he is being authorized to speak as a representative for the plurality of cultures that make up British Asian communities'.[78] Gunning argues that Nagra's texts are open to a plurality of different voices from the experiences of immigration, as well as those of first- or second-generation Indian immigrants. More than even Avia's poems, Nagra's work performs 'ideolectically' in Bernstein's configuration by creating a text which acts not only against the established hierarchies of English grammar, but which is sonically adventurous, pushing boundaries through challenging expectations. Gunning offers an insightful reading of the texture and porosity of Nagra's poetry:

> Nagra's portrayal of working class Punjabis is always less about verisimilitude to a reified culture, or an authentic capture of an idiom, as it is concerned with the possibilities of refracting this speech into his poems and of dislocating the expectations of an audience who receive a racialized performance as indicative of a particular way of being in the world. The voices that speak in Nagra's verse are alienated; they reveal less of the worlds that their named speakers inhabit than of the poet's concerns that his enunciation will always be over-determined by the pre-text of racist or patronizing liberal-multicultural expectations of the British Asian poet.[79]

This textual density and transcription of radical speech patterns is evident in 'The Man Who Would Be English'. Seeking assimilation into a community through football, the speaker becomes part of a group: 'we plundered up gulps of golden rounds for the great game.'[80] Within this poem there lies a carefully orchestrated tension between vernacular such as 'just for kicks', and the more archaic language of 'lark-about days of school' (p. 15). These phrases add an intertextual intrusion into the layering of the text – performing a ventriloquising of familiar phrases. This need to assimilate phonetically is a survival strategy, which requires that the speaker's voice is 'passed' 'into theirs' (p. 15). A desire to be unobtrusive is asserted by the negatives: 'I wasn't Black or Latin or / managed by a turbaned ghost' (p. 15). But the assertion is challenged by the intrusion of a wife's voice, clearly marked in staccatoed syntax, taking her husband to task for his affiliation. The wife brutally emphasises the degrees of difference: 'Lookk lookk ju nott British ju rrr blackkk . . .!!!' (p. 15). Another poem, 'The Speaking of Bagwinder Singh Sagoo', renders a voice which criticises the sexualisation of the 'western' woman selected for him in the UK. Malapropisms add to the texture of his berating. His beau's actions towards the praying father threaten to 'give him cardigan arrest' and cosmetics are described as 'odour toilet' (p. 27). The language of television advertising and consumption intrudes upon the descriptions of the relationship. His friends work at the 'Sugar Puff factory' and his partner is described as dressed in 'film-star red' as well as 'Dulux of British poodle pink' and is accompanied by her doctor, 'the Avon Lady' (p. 26). Nagra presents cultural complexities which require assiduous deciphering.

This process of interpretation is made complex by Nagra's positioning of the speech patterns in his poetry. Gunning proposes that Nagra's poems are 'Trapped between racist expectations that delimit the meanings open to the racialized or ethnicized subject, and the burden of representation that would deny the particularity of his enunciation in order to impose a derogatory function upon it'.[81] Nagra's poetry illustrates that for many twenty-first century poets writing in English, the complexities of cultural expression necessitate not only an intricate linguistic texture, but a poetics that can enact ventriloquism *and* critique.

SUMMARY OF KEY POINTS

- While English is recognised as a global language, poets across the world writing in English embrace variations in language use, emphasising a plurality of Englishes as opposed to a monolithic or totalising language.
- The way that poets insist upon the particularity of language use in their poetry is through the inclusion of dialects and idiolects in their poetry.
- The poetry of native cultures is often marked by the transformation of orality into text.
- For poets such as Li-Young Lee, Gwyneth Lewis and Lorna Dee Cervantes, bilingualism is key to their poetic practice, and the texture of their poetry is informed by translation and interlingual practices.
- The deformation of established rules and grammatical practices may also be thought of as an ideolectical poetics.
- In the poetry of Tusiata Avia and Daljit Nagra the cross-fertilization of different language use results in the exploration of not only idiom, but also cultural expression.

NOTES

1. Jonathan Arac, 'Anglo-Globalism?', *New Left Review*, 16 (2002), 35–45 (p. 35).
2. Romana Huk, 'A New Global Poetics?', *Literature Compass*, 6.3 (2009), 758–84 (p. 758).
3. Jahan Ramazani, *A Transnational Poetics* (Chicago: University of Chicago Press, 2009), p. 10.
4. Ibid. p. 10.
5. Wai Chee Dimock, *Through Other Continents: American Literature Across Deep Time* (Princeton, NJ: Princeton University Press, 2006), p. 3.
6. Sujata Bhatt, *Point No Point: Selected Poems* (Manchester: Carcanet Press, 1997), pp. 24–5.
7. John Haffenden, 'Interview with Tony Harrison', in Neil Astley (ed.), *Tony Harrison: Bloodaxe Critical Anthologies 1* (Newcastle: Bloodaxe, 1991), p. 236.
8. Neil Roberts, *Narrative and Voice in Postwar Poetry* (Basingstoke: Palgrave, 1999), p. 157.
9. Tony Harrison, *Selected Poems* (London: Penguin, 1987), p. 123.
10. Ibid. p. 123.
11. Terry Eagleton, 'Antagonisms Tony Harrison's *v.*' in Astley, *Tony Harrison*, p. 349.
12. Harrison, *Selected Poems*, p. 126.
13. For a full reading of Bakhtin, see Chapter 2.
14. Harrison, '*v.*', in *Selected Poems*, pp. 235–49 (p. 235). All subsequent references to this edition are given in the text. Arthur Scargill is a former president of the NUM, National Union of Mineworkers.
15. Tony Harrison, 'Interview', *Poetry Review*, 73.4 (1984), reprinted in Astley, *Tony Harrison*, pp. 227–46, (p. 234).
16. Tom Leonard, personal webpage. Available online at www.tomleonard.co.uk/main-publications/intimate-voices/the-six-oclock-news.html.
17. Ibid.
18. Tom Leonard, 'Interview with Tom Leonard by Attila Dosa 2003'. Available online at www.tomleonard.co.uk/

online-poetry-a-prose/interview-with-tom-leonard-by-attila-dosa-for-hungarian-literary-magazine-2003.html.

19. Tom Leonard, 'Glasgow Poems'. Available online at www. tomleonard.co.uk/main-publications/intimate-voices/six-glasgow-poems.html.

20. Ibid.

21. Tom Leonard, 'Review of *Language and Power*'. Available online at www.tomleonard.co.uk/online-poetry-a-prose/review-roxy-harris-language-a-power.html.

22. Helen Kidd, 'Writing Near the Fault Line: Scottish Women Poets and the Topography of Tongues', in Vicki Bertram (ed.), *Kicking Daffodils: Twentieth Century Women Poets* (Edinburgh: Edinburgh University Press, 1997), p. 100.

23. Kidd, 'Writing Near the Fault Line', p. 100.

24. Liz Lochhead, *True Confessions & New Clichés* (Edinburgh: Polygon Books, 1985), pp. 37–9. All subsequent references to this edition are given in the text.

25. Nancy Gish, 'Complexities of Subjectivity', in Romana Huk (ed.), *Assembling Alternatives: Reading Postmodern Poetries Transnationally* (Middletown, CT: Wesleyan University Press, 2003), p. 268.

26. Jackie Kay, *Sleeping with Monsters*, ed. Rebecca Wilson and Gillean Somerville-Arjat (Edinburgh: Polygon, 1990), pp. 121–2.

27. Jackie Kay, *Other Lovers* (Newcastle: Bloodaxe, 1993), p. 24.

28. Kay, 'Interview', in *Sleeping with Monsters*, p. 122.

29. Jackie Kay, *Life Mask* (Newcastle: Bloodaxe, 2005), p. 50. All subsequent references to this edition are given in the text.

30. Gish, 'Complexities of Subjectivity', p. 273.

31. Janet McAdams, 'A Conversation with Simon Ortiz', *Kenyon Review*, 32.1 (2010), 1–8 (p. 6).

32. Jerome Rothenberg, *Poetics and Polemics 1980–2005* (Tuscaloosa, AL: University of Alabama Press, 2008), p. 132.

33. Jerome Rothenberg and Diane Rothenberg (eds), *Symposium of the Whole: A Range of Discourse Toward an Ethnopoetics* (Berkeley: University of California Press, 1983), pp. 433–6.

34. Gary Snyder, 'The Incredible Survival of the Coyote', in Rothenberg and Rothenberg, *Symposium of the Whole*, p. 426.

35. Jarold Ramsey, *Reading the Fire* (Lincoln: University of Nebraska Press, 1983), p. 42.
36. Dimock, *Through Other Continents*, p. 180.
37. Joy Harjo, *In Mad Love and War* (Middletown, CT: Wesleyan University Press, 1990). All subsequent references to this edition are given in the text.
38. Stuart Cochran, 'The Ethnic Implications of Stories, Spirits, and the Land in Native American Pueblo and Aztlán Writing', *MELUS*, 20.2 (1995), 69–91 (p. 70).
39. Ibid. p. 70.
40. Lawrence Venuti, *The Translator's Invisibility* (London: Routledge, 2008), p. 13.
41. Li-Young Lee, 'Indigo', in *Rose* (Rochester, NY: BOA Editions, 1986), p. 31.
42. Gwyneth Lewis, 'Whose Coat is That Jacket? Whose Hat is That Cap?' *Columbia: A Journal of Literature and Art*, 27 (1996–7), 58–68 (p. 63).
43. Ibid. p. 67.
44. Gwyneth Lewis, *Parables & Faxes* (Newcastle: Bloodaxe, 1995), p. 9. All subsequent references to this edition are given in the text.
45. Jacques Lacan, *The Four Fundamental Concepts of Psychoanalysis*, ed. Jacques-Alain Miller, trans. Alan Sheridan (Harmondsworth: Penguin, 1979).
46. Gwyneth Lewis, *Sunbathing in the Rain* (London: Flamingo, 2002), pp. 40–2.
47. Lewis, 'Whose Coat is That Jacket?', p. 59.
48. Deryn Rees-Jones, 'Editorial', *Poetry Wales* 32.2 (1996), 2–3 (p. 3).
49. Lewis, 'Whose Coat is That Jacket?', p. 58.
50. Tzvetan Todorov, 'Bilingualism, Dialogism and Schizophrenia', *New Formations*, 17 (1992), 16–25 (p. 16).
51. Li-Young Lee, *The Winged Seed: A Remembrance* (New York: Simon & Schuster, 1995), p. 76.
52. Li-Young Lee, 'Persimmons', in *Rose*, pp. 17–19. All subsequent references to this edition are given in the text.
53. Zhou Xiaojing, 'Inheritance and Invention in Li-Young Lee's Poetry', *MELUS*, 21:1 (1996), 113–32, p. 123.

54. Li-Young Lee, in Earl G. Ingersoll (ed.), *Breaking the Alabaster Jar: Conversations with Li-Young Lee* (New York: BOA Editions, 2006), p. 94.
55. Lyn Hejinian, 'Barbarism', *The Language of Inquiry* (Berkeley: University of California Press, 2000), p. 326.
56. Mikhail Bakhtin, *Speech Genres and Other Late Essays*, ed. Caryl Emerson and Michael Holquist, trans. Vern W. McGee (Austin, TX: University of Texas Press, 1990), p. 7.
57. Alberto Baltazar Urista, *Aztlán: Chicano Journal of Social Sciences and the Arts*, 1.1 (1970), iv–v.
58. Cherríe Moraga and Gloria Anzaldúa (eds), *This Bridge Called My Back: Writing by Radical Women of Color* (Berkeley: Third Women Press, 2002), p. liv.
59. Lorna Dee Cervantes, 'Poetry Saved My Life: Interview with Lorna Dee Cervantes', *MELUS*, 32.1 (2007), 163–80 (p. 178).
60. Gloria Anzaldúa, 'Speaking in Tongues: A Letter to Third World Women Writers', in Jennifer Browdy de Hernández (ed.), *Women Writing Resistance: Essays on Latin America and the Caribbean* (Cambridge, MA: South-End Press, 2005), pp. 79–90 (p. 85).
61. Anzaldúa, 'Speaking in Tongues', p. 85.
62. Lorna Dee Cervantes, 'Refugee Ship', in *Emplumada* (Pittsburgh, PA: University of Pittsburgh Press, 1981), p. 41. All subsequent references to this edition are given in the text.
63. Norma Alarcón, 'The Theoretical Subject(s) of *This Bridge Called My Back* and Anglo American Feminism', in Héctor Calderón and José David Saldívar (eds), *Criticism in the Borderlands Studies in Chicano Literature, Culture and Ideology* (Durham, NC: Duke University Press, 1991), pp. 28–39 (p. 36).
64. Louis Reyes Rivera, 'Introduction', in Sandra María Esteves *Yerba Buena: Dibujos y Poemas* (New York: Greenfield Review, 1980), p. xvii.
65. Juan Bruce-Novoa, cited in Nina M. Scott, 'The Politics of Language: Latina Writers in Unites States Literature and Curricula', *MELUS*, 19.1 (1994), 57–71 (p. 61).
66. Ibid. pp. 63–4.
67. See Chapter 3.

68. *Oxford English Dictionary* (Oxford: Oxford University Press, 1989).
69. Charles Bernstein, 'Poetics of the Americas', *Modernism/Modernity*, 3.3 (1996), 1–23 (p. 7).
70. Charles Bernstein, 'Thought's Measure', in *Content's Dream* (Los Angeles: Sun & Moon Press, 1986), p. 81.
71. Bernstein, 'Poetics of the Americas', p. 11.
72. Ibid. p. 19.
73. cris cheek, cited in *Assembling Alternatives*, p. 248.
74. Ramazani, *A Transnational Poetics*, p. 2.
75. Ibid. p. 3.
76. Ibid. p. 8.
77. Tusiata Avia, *Wild Dogs Under My Skirt* (Wellington: Victoria University Press, 2004). All subsequent references to this edition are given in the text.
78. Dave Gunning, 'Daljit Nagra, Faber Poet: Burdens of Representation and Anxieties of Influence', *Journal of Commonwealth Literature*, 43.3 (2008), 95–109 (p. 96).
79. Gunning, 'Daljit Nagra, Faber Poet', p. 98.
80. Daljit Nagra, *Look We Have Coming to Dover* (London: Faber & Faber, 2002), p. 15. All subsequent references to this edition are given in the text.
81. Gunning, 'Daljit Nagra, Faber Poet', p. 107.

Conclusion

In his poem 'Killing Time', Simon Armitage describes a human-oid built out of technological bric-a-brac. Far from the utopian-ism of early twentieth-century conceptions of the robotic human, Armitage's creature is a 'monkey gone wrong' with 'loud speakers for earlugs' and 'a microphone tongue'.[1] This creature, with body parts made from communication and information hardware, sub-sists on news and information networks, even having a 'mouse for a hand'. We are told that observers sit at the monkey's feet 'switched on and tuned in' (p. 4), while the creature is sated by its consump-tion of electronic information: 'After booting up with a virtual fart / it flickered and started to sing' (p. 4). Armitage's humorous if dystopic poem exhibits an anxiety about our relationship with technology; any technological advance is portrayed with a corre-sponding brutish behaviour.

Do all poets share Armitage's concerns? If not, how does tech-nology impact upon our reading of the present and future scene of contemporary poetry? It has become somewhat axiomatic, in con-sidering poetry of the early twentieth century, to equate the advent of new technologies with a corresponding impact upon literary form. The genuine impact of the Internet upon contemporary poetry is less immediately quantifiable. However, one element is evident in considering twenty-first-century poetry: the exchange of instantly accessible information has an impact upon the content and texture of writing. Certainly, not all poets share Armitage's alliance of networked information with brutishness. American poet Juliana Spahr, for example, admits in an interview from 2003: 'Now I can't imagine how one wrote poetry before the Internet. When I write poetry I spend a lot of time with search engines like *Google* and *Nexis*'.[2]

My conclusion offers a reading of the impact of multimedia and web technologies upon poetic language and form. The inflection of web technologies – as we will see in the case of Claudia Rankine – can result in creating mock-epic poems that juxtapose a litany of facts with personal meditation. For some poets the overwhelming perception of a vast information resource is perceived as a threat. To others, such as John Cayley, the possibilities of technology are celebrated as a site for visual and textual experimentation, otherwise known as 'electronic writing'. These sites do not share the identity of magazines, presses or poetry organisations, but are conceived primarily as websites. Other poets consider the Internet as a tool of poetic composition, and chance operations such as 'Flarf' poetry. Most obviously, the Internet enables a mass audience and speedy dissemination. On one level this dissemination can be of poetic material itself to a broader audience – such as in the response to *100 Poets Against the War*.[3] From a further perspective, new technologies enable the awareness of breaking news material instantly, which proves vital to the work of Labour activist and poet Mark Nowak. It will become evident that poetry is always grappling and responding to the 'new'– be it new artistic, scientific or technological developments. But we might also need to consider whether new technologies can overall be viewed as a panacea to political activism, or as supplement to more traditional forms of response and protest.

WHAT IS ELECTRONIC WRITING?

The proliferation of media technologies over the past decades and the possibilities that they offer in the construction of literary texts have invariably impacted on the composition of poetry in a digital age. The critic of contemporary poetry is well accustomed to accessing materials through digital archives, or entering into conversations and debates through litservs as well as through individual blogs. Poets such as John Cayley, Peter Finch, Ingrid Ankerson, Megan Sapnar and Jenny Weight have all used web technologies, computer programming and multimedia presentations in different ways with varying intentions. One of the key commentators on the impact of technology and literature, N. Katherine Hayles, argues that the umbrella term 'electronic literature' or 'electronic writing' (which might characterise some of the work by the poets mentioned above), can be thought of as excluding 'print literature that has been digitized' since it is 'by contrast "digital born", a first generation digital object created on a computer and (usually) meant to be read on a computer'.[4] Within the categorisation of 'digital object', one might include the familiar term 'hypertext' which could be understood, according to Ted Nelson, as 'series of text chunks connected by links which offer the reader different pathways'.[5] Or, as Jakob Nielsen proposes: 'Hypertext is non-sequential writing, a directed graph where each node contains some amount of text or other information . . . Hypertext should also make users feel that they can move freely through the information according to their own needs'.[6] Other categories we might associate with digital forms could be interactive fiction, generative texts, installation video and sound poetry. Poet-critics, such as Loss Pequeño Glazier, consider that there is an ongoing conversation between electronic writing and a tradition of experimental verse, that the digital field in effect extends a published tradition. For poet Brian Stefans, electronic writing encapsulates a compendium of identifications. His online entry 'What is Electronic Writing?' offers a most useful overview.[7]

Stefans argues that electronic writing could be thought of as a genre in its own right, but at its most general it 'takes advantage of the possibilities afforded by digital technology – such as the Internet, or graphics programs such as Illustrator or Photoshop, or animation / audio / interactive programs such as Flash in their creation and presentation'. Most importantly, he suggests that the forms that the writing may take are 'informed by new ways of thinking brought on by the way digital technology has impacted our world'. Specific to poetry, he identifies the following: the hypertextual work, a poetic narrative which enables interaction, the 'animated poem' where the viewer or reader 'is not asked to do anything but watch and listen while the text performs', 'conceptual blogs or websites', 'word toys' where the user is 'invited to play with an experimental interface' in effect creating her own text, poetic works which are generated by computer programme, and documentary websites such as *UBU.com* which Stefans credits as offering 'a collection of concrete, audio and avant-garde video files'. In addition he adds collaborative poetic practices which 'take advantage of the forms of communication peculiar to electronic media' such as email. It should be noted that the recent CD-ROM anthology *Electronic Literature Collection* (also available online at http://collection.eliterature.org), advances the following explanation of poetic electronic writing. Poetry in this context can be understood as:

> Writing native to the electronic environment is under continual construction (poiesis) by its creators and receivers. Works of electronic literature are 'poietic,' in this sense, and are often constructed by strategies analogous to those found in experimental print poetry, or cinema, as well as by strategies native to the digital environment.[8]

In this definition electronic poetry straddles two objectives: it establishes an ongoing conversation with an established trajectory of experimental writing while also highlighting an electronic process of revision and remaking.

CONTENT-SPECIFIC *ELECTRONIC WRITING*: JOHN CAYLEY, JENNY WEIGHT, INGRID ANKERSON AND MEGAN SAPNAR, REINER STRASSER AND M.D. COVERLEY

Anglo-Canadian poet John Cayley is one of the most established of electronic poets. He began experimenting with compositional techniques on personal computers during the late seventies. Speaking retrospectively, Cayley notes:

There were a small number of practitioners, a small number of systems for composing text in digital media and a growing realization that at some indeterminate point in the future . . . text and textual practice would migrate to the new "writing space" of networked programmatons.[9]

Cayley's work *windsound*, winner of the 2001 *Electronic Literature Award for Poetry*, can be labelled under the following categories: 'ambient', 'appropriated texts', 'audio', 'multilingual' and 'text movie'.[10] It is not an interactive work, but demands that the reader watch carefully the morphing letters on the screen. Initially, a paragraph forms that eventually is set and spoken in English. Sound recordings of wind and ambient noise are also ever-present. Immediately lyrical, the opening includes lines such as 'taut winds listen as the inn-keeper's footsteps fade deep across the court-yard'. Cayley's text is algorithmically generated, that is words and letters are gradually replaced onscreen, chronicling a move-ment from illegibility to legibility that is constantly reviewed on a twenty-three-minute program. The work includes intertexts from Cayley's own translation of a song lyric 'Cadence: Like a Dream' by Qin Guan (1049–1100), which also is subject to textual mor-phing based on letter replacement. Stefans suggests that Cayley has exploited the 'programmaton' – 'the poetic object that is both literary language and the language of code'.[11] Hints of a psycho-logical landscape emerge and retreat in lines such as 'long sunk long drowned in the far waters of the night' and 'I cannot sleep'. In her adjudication of *windsound*, Heather McHugh proposes that the work challenges established reading practices by revealing 'the power of letters, even as it plays with the limits of literal intelligi-bility' and 'explores the power of sequences, even as it plays with non-sequitur'.[12] Central to Cayley's poetics is that electronic media enable the creation of provisional yet dynamic communities, since he argues that: 'On the net and in new media this – potentially and in a number of demonstrable instances – translates to the spawning of radical, marginal, evanescent, provisional text art communities and collaborations that come together in software virtuality'.[13]

Jenny Weight's *Rice* (1998) by contrast, depends on hypertex-tual links.[14] Enacting a travelogue, this interactive travel poem requires that the reader select her way through sixteen items of tourist memorabilia from Vietnam, including a hotel information card, a tin of lip balm and a fragment of manuscript. Each object reveals a narrative, giving sixteen aspectual readings of Vietnam. One direction, clicking on a small red cardboard box with a crocodile branded upon it, reveals that: 'The previous things never / happened to me in Vietnam. I / acquired the Vietnam experience / on the internet before I left / Australia. It was vastly more / efficient. Then, to get them out of / the way, I wrote these poems. / Whew.' Radically transforming our expectations of the travel narrative, Weight playfully indicates how we create the conditions of our experience through a pre-established narrative. Moments of lyrical intensity emerge from the setting of Vietnam such as: 'At dawn a sampan splits / the silence on the / Mekong River'. These are placed in conjunction with ironic commentary on advertising images: when one clicks on an icon for *Wrigley's* chewing gum, three words are thrown up on the screen: 'TRUTH FREEDOM HAPPINESS'. Weight explains that *Rice* examines 'my experience as a Western tourist in Vietnam. Issues of colonialism, war, poverty, and cultural difference arise. Technically and aesthetically, *Rice* belongs to an early period of web-based poetry. It uses Shockwave, popup windows, and frames'.[15]

Most alluring and self-referential is the search elicited in the poem for the 'poem factory' since 'The cyclo drivers say they know where it is, / but we never actually get there.' As we continue through the hypertext we are told 'On the third-last day / we found the poetry factory' which turns out to be a 'Temple of Literature' where / they made 'laws, / letters and literature for over 900 years.' Against the accolades made to scholars '500 years dead. They are / engraved into the backs / of stone tortoises' and we are faced with the 'Army Museum / (where touching / photos of War Mothers / serve like slaves / for poetry).' On clicking a red script with ideograms, Weight gives us a history lesson of the '12-point plan' which includes the 'stimulating poem', 'Long live the victorious Resistance!' and citations from Ho Chi Min extolling 'victory is built with the people as / foundations'. Through the hypertext Weight presents an aspectual impression of Vietnam, rendering in effect multiple Vietnams which succeed in fracturing the authoritative and often appropriative narrative of the travel guide.

As a flash poem, *Cruising* (2001) uses oral recitation written from the perspective of a young teenage girl driving in her friend's car up and down Main Street in small-town Wisconsin.[16] Ingrid Ankerson and Megan Sapnar's collaboration presents filmic black-and-white images played at varying speeds and sizes, showing neon signs, billboards and shop hoardings. In addition a ribbon of script is also performed throughout, and can be rewound or fast-forwarded in varying sizes. The recitation describes a coming-of-age ritual in the form of cruising: 'we wanted love maybe in a pick up truck'. The poem mirrors the cinematic visual world which is created, since the speaker associates night rolling through Mary Jo's father's station wagon with movie credits. As an example of visual poetry, Ankerson and Sapnar enter into the adrenalin-fuelled world of the young women. The speaker declares that, 'I was the skinny girl in the bag sniffing the street like a dog' and that they all were 'eyeing life in a car we couldn't yet take to the world'. Above all the interaction required by *Cruising* creates an experiential poem, as the authors' notes indicate:

> *Cruising* reinforces the spatial and temporal themes of the poem by requiring the user to learn how to 'drive' the text. A new user must first struggle with gaining control of the speed, the direction, and the scale in order to follow the textual path of the narrative . . . The viewer moves between reading text and experiencing a filmic flow of images – but cannot exactly have both at the same time. In this way, the work seeks to highlight the materiality of text, film, and interface.[17]

Finally, Reiner Strasser's poetic collaboration with M. D. Coverley, *ii – in the white darkness* (2004), explores the experience of Alzheimer's and Parkinson's patients.[18] Building from the experiential element that an electronic poem can offer, the text explores dimensions of memory. Coverley states that: 'It was not the erasure that mattered so much as the act of trying to recover what we no longer can identify'.[19] The interface consists of pulsing dots, which once activated by a pointer, trigger different images and sounds in varying combinations. As the poets explain:

> In this process the experience of remembering and loss of memory can be re-created in the appearance and disappearance of words, pictures, animations and sounds. Memories (readable with a general metaphorical meaning) are unveiled and veiled in transition at the same time, arranged by or using your own memory.[20]

The network of materials created by the random patterning of dots in this electronic text is not dissimilar to the pulsating of synaptic ends. An initial quotation 'guides' the exploratory text: 'Just a whisper at least of the persistence of this memory, this forgetfulness.' This linking of reminiscence with forgetfulness is an overarching momentum of the work. We are shown images of interiors to houses we cannot quite navigate, seascapes which fade and words which appear, shift and refuse to be captured. An image of sunrise has a loop of recurring text upon it: 'a sunrise is a sunrise is sunrise'. Another click on a dot leads to a blurred image of a passing train with a successive display of words: 'pass by / passed by / past'. The possibility of simultaneously accessing and viewing these images and words makes for a densely textured interactive poem. These processes of encountering memories reinforce the complexities of mnemonic patterns which guide life histories. As the text itself asks, 'we build our history thru the experience of our life / do we lose our history when we lose our memory?'

ELECTRONIC EXPERIMENTATION AND LANGUAGE: PETER FINCH AND TREVOR JOYCE

Poets whose work is read in conventional print format often engage with electronic media as a way of enquiry, experimentation with form, and collaboration. Peter Finch's poetry is engaged with an inventive rewriting of the Welsh cultural landscape. There is often something distinctly uncanny about the spaces that his poetry creates. Psychoanalytically, this sense of cultural defamiliarisation could be read in Freudian terms as *unheimlich*, when a quotidian over-familiarity is dispersed in a synchronous haunting. Finch has systematically experimented with methods of rewriting original documents, poems, essays and manifestos. These techniques include filleting a government text such as the poem 'Words beginning with "A" from the Government's Welsh Assembly White Paper', which introduces key phrases from cultural policy making. Finch in the 1980s went as far as to create a computer program that aimed to create the archetypal Anglo-Welsh poem:

> Back in the early 80s when the best home computer in the world was the BBC B with 32k memory, no printer and a cassette-tape A-drive I wrote a program in Basic which would compose Anglo-Welsh poems for me. I set up a number of word pools containing the sort of vocabulary the Anglo-Welsh were famous for – sheep, stipple, cariad, hillside, hiraeth, chapel, pit – and then a couple of rules for how these words could be combined. Up it all came on screen.

> > slate fences on farmer's hillsides,
> > shrouded cockles and grass-polished deacons,
> > the nation majestically watered.[21]

Drawing from techniques of *ostranenie* or defamiliarisation, Finch enacts a dialogue with earlier modernist techniques and experimentation, which enables him, however randomly, to interrogate a legacy of Anglo-Welsh poetry. It is this sense of a recuperated and adaptive modernism which energises a reading of Welsh cultural history and its evolution without retreating to struggles with poetic precedents, and even in this early example of experimentation, by using technology as an impertinent wordsmith. His ongoing cybertextual 'R. S. Thomas Information Project' relies for its formation on the hypertext.[22] The work presents information on the Anglo-Welsh poet R. S. Thomas, instructed by biography, bibliography and Thomas's own texts. Finch declares that Thomas's vocabulary is 'broken down and re-ordered and filled with fixed and random links. There are side leaps into descriptions of some of his recent mind-states and into critical coverage of his work (appropriately redrawn and reworked)'.[23] But most central to the work is that it comes into being digitally and has not existed in any prior form:

> The information (the essence of the web) becomes a new piece of creative work in itself and is then, in turn, remade to become further information as an end in itself . . . 'The poem is never finished only abandoned' – certainly this one. And it simply cannot exist in any other medium.[24]

For Irish poet Trevor Joyce, electronic information technologies offer possibilities as well as problems of surveillance. Joyce has approached electronic resources as a field for exploration in a collaborative project entitled 'Offsets'. Including poets cris cheek, Alison Croggon, Billy Mills and Mairéad Byrne, the project was dependent on submissions to create a collaborative poem, using a structure not dissimilar to a listserv and asking poets to compose by free association. Marthine Satris comments that, as the electronic submissions increased, the identification of individual authorship became more difficult:

> One loses the flow that gives each series of poems its cohesion, and so essentially what results is that in this mode of publication, the author's individuality is subsumed to the group poetics, as they are required to be influenced by someone unknown, and that first person's words are then added to, sometimes in very similar form to what they wrote. There is no ownership of the poem, no copyright, and it would be challenging to say the least to pick out the Irish vs. the British vs. the Icelandic vs. the born in Ireland but now lives in the USA, as each addition to the poem incorporates the idiom of at least one other.[25]

Joyce's poetic sequence *Syzygy* (1997), was dependent for its composition upon the transformation of twelve lyric poems by a computer spreadsheet. The sequence also evokes medieval poet's Guillaume de Machaut's cancrizans, which, as Joyce explains, is a musical form where 'one or more parts proceed normally while the imitating voice or voices give out the melody backwards'.[26] Yet, his work also shows an acute awareness of how electronic data do not work in our interest. Joyce comments about the sinisterly entitled 'Data Shadows':

> The 'data shadow' cast by an individual in a series of electronic transactions (via ATM, credit card or Internet usage for example) can be assembled into a pattern which will allow a profile of that person to be developed, including personal habits and buying power and preferences. Information collected on one context is routinely re-used in entirely unanticipated and even hostile ways without the knowledge or consent of the individual involved. (p. 239)

This poem combines data, technological and ecological language with the presentation of an unnamed landscape of no definite historical time. 'Data Shadows' makes us aware of 'systems hunger', 'dear instruments', 'the clock', 'databases' (p. 167), as well as 'systematic breakdowns' (p. 167) and 'behaviour banks.' The sequential repetition of key clauses in the poem affirms a systematic industry at work, a world of data retrieval 'without managed rivers or cultivated fields / only human bodies massed in their billions / will flash before you here' (p. 168). The unsettling decompositional process outlined in the opening, with its 'swarming vermin that / disarticulate the fast frame' (p. 163), is allied to a landscape of data – 'a vastness stretching towards all horizons' (p. 168). Joyce's ironic use of the childish phrase 'losers keepers finders weepers' (p. 165) alerts us to the dystopic scene of managing information.

POET'S PLAYGROUND: 'FLARF' POETRY

The Internet has spawned a loosely defined movement of poets (particularly in the USA) who use Internet search engines as a tool for composition of what is sometimes known as 'spam' poetry, 'Google sculpted' poetry, but more often than not as 'Flarf' poetry. Michael Gottlieb proposed that Flarf is a 'self dubbed group' of young poets mainly associated with both east and west coasts.[27] He adds that: 'A defining characteristic of their work can be said to be the embrace of the dizzying opportunities proffered to those who are inclined to engage in chance-generated poetry, or artistic composition, by the stunningly voracious, simply overwhelming power of the Internet's search engines'.[28] The texts can veer from whimsy, with a focus on bizarre and humorous facts, to collaborative enterprises. 'Flarf' was coined as a descriptive term by Gary Sullivan, and has been described as 'the first recognizable movement of the 21st century, as an in-joke among an elite clique, as a marketing strategy, and as offering a new way of reading creative writing'.[29] A loose grouping emerged in 2001 under an email list entitled 'The Flarflist'. As Sullivan adds, 'The Flarflist Collective is hardly the first e-mail based collaborative enterprise, but it has been, despite the relatively occult nature of the project, one of the most visible'.

A special edition of the online journal *Jacket* (2006) was dedicated to Flarf poetry and focused upon the work of early key names associated with the collective impetus. These included Benjamin Friedlander, Anne Boyer, Drew Gardner, K. Silem Mohammad, Rod Smith and Christina Strong. Turning to an example of collaborative web-based work gives a sense of how Internet information and poetry collide with one another. In 'Infinity Revisited', the poets have collaged elements of information from animal experimentation reports as a basis to their collaboration: 'As I said to my Spontaneously Obese Rat Friend, I said'.[30] We are told that the aim of the poem is 'to assess weather produced from rat feed, grain, / and four doses.' Using the language of scientific report, the poem asserts:

> The study used 480 male and female rats
> and their little rat cell phones (under Simulated Microgravity)
> which did not have cancer. One will study acupuncture.
> The other will look at the old rats.

Dan Hoy notes that using the Internet as a collage machine presents ethical dilemmas to the poet. He asks: 'The flarfists may be aware of the webpage from which they borrow material, but the only reason they're aware of that webpage is because Google (or AskJeeves, or Yahoo!, or . . .) showed it to them – so the question is, are they aware of why they're aware of that webpage?'[31] Hoy contends that Flarfists need to recognise that business and market interests often dictate the results that search engines feature as their most immediately popular. He adds: 'Do they wonder how it is that their poem is determined as it is – that is, of the process at work on their work by an outside force, one not divine or natural but corporate? This is a fundamental aesthetic concern as well as a socioeconomic one.' It should be recognised that for most Flarfists the Internet is a perfect playground for creating biting playful social critique and satire, but an awareness of the data offered must also be regarded with a sceptical eye.

DOCUMENTATION AND POETRY: MARK NOWAK'S *COAL MOUNTAIN ELEMENTARY*

The possibility of making a politically responsible poetry from Internet source materials is evident in the work of labour activist and poet Mark Nowak. His recent book of poems *Coal Mountain Elementary* (2009) combines photo-document, reportage, government reports, workers' testimony and academic primers.[32] One could even add that Nowak's role is as an arranger or compositor of source material. Nowak in his 'Notes Toward an Anti-Capitalist Poetics II' makes it clear that poetry must be linked with political activism. He asks: 'As the US economy transitions from a modernist manufacturing economy to late capitalism's service economy, what would a service economy poetry and poetics look like and who among us is prepared to step forward and imagine it?'[33] The questions that Nowak seeks to address are enacted through 'poetry and through on-the-ground organizing work in corporate bookstores and throughout working-class communities and anti-capitalist social movements'.[34] He adds that his own poetics are a form of *writing* 'that is to me, dialogue and dialectical materialism, and documentary and drama all rolled into one, *writing* as a vehicle through which I form and inform'.[35]

Coal Mountain Elementary juxtaposes three categories of source material, which are interspersed throughout the volume and combined with photographs taken by Nowak and Ian Teh. Nowak places in bold, verbatim extracts from the transcripts of testimony of mineworkers who survived a methane gas blast in Sago, West Virginia, on 2 January 2006, when twelve miners lost their lives and fourteen were rescued. The testimonies were recorded between 17 January 2006 and 19 June 2006 and the 6,300 pages uploaded to the West Virginia mine safety website.[36] Secondly, Nowak uses three lessons excerpted from the American Coal Foundation's 'Lesson Plans'.[37] Finally, sources placed in italics throughout focus on Chinese mining disaster news reports and bulletins accessed from the web. Nowak's relentless use of news material informs the sickening regularity of mineworkers' deaths – to this end he has also established an ongoing web page which records recent disasters and reports.[38] The dispersal of these different documents enables the distinct textures of pedagogical instruction, intimate account and reportage to reflect upon one another. Frequently, Nowak uses these materials against one another as ironic commentary, or counterpoint. A deliberate contrast is created by his juxtaposition of an extract from a lesson plan and a report of a mine blast in the Sihe Coal Mine in North China's Shanxi province:

> Procedure (cont):
>
> 5. Have each student
>   purchase 'mining equipment'
>   (flat and round toothpicks
>   and paper clips).
>   More than one piece of equipment
>   may be purchased,
>   but no tools may be shared among students
>   Sell a flat toothpick for $2,
>   A round toothpick for $4
>   And a paper clip for $6.
>   Sell replacement tools when necessary. (p. 110)

A colliery gas blast on Wednesday killed at least 23 miners and sickened 53 others in North China's Shanxi Province, local mine safety authorities said yesterday. Altogether 697 miners were working in the pit when the blast went off around 7:00 p.m. at the Sihe Coal Mine under the State-owned Jincheng Mining Group, said an official with the provincial coalmine safety supervision bureau who declined to be named. 'No more deaths will occur in the mine as the rest of the miners are all safe,' Tai Jie, an employer of the general office of the mining group, told China Daily in a telephone interview yesterday. She was the only person on the managerial staff who could be reached to comment on the fates of the more than 600 miners. The tragedy happened on the fourth day of the Year of the Dog, according to the lunar calendar. Local sources told China daily that most of the miners were from villages nearby who had hoped to earn some extra money by working during the Spring Festival holiday. (p. 111)

The first extract is an attempt by the American Coal Foundation to integrate the processes of mining as a pedagogical classroom game, illustrated by 'cookie mining' (or removing the chocolate chips from cookies). The overall aim of the exercises is to find ways of maximising profit. Nowak's scathing juxtaposition of these materials foregrounds the disparity between toothpicks, paperclips, human bodies and machinery. *Coal Mountain Elementary* – through its arrangement and filleting of this primer – communicates contempt for the intrusion of corporate interests into the teaching of elementary school mathematics. This is highlighted with a later extract which encourages: 'Working in tandem to complete the profit/loss worksheet might be helpful for those with math-related learning disabilities' (p. 130). On the facing page the citation from *China Daily* reports in bald facts the Sihe Coal Mine disaster and the subsequent inability of authorities to immediately comment or accept any responsibility. The bare reportage does, however, present a humanising of the disaster with the general comments on nearby villagers aiming to earn extra income by working through the holiday. Compare these rather clinical statements with an extract from one of the Sago testimonies:

When we got back to the fresh air base, the backup team had performed a task that we were initially sent in to recover the first miner that they located. And he was on a stretcher that was loaded in another scoop in

the intake, but he wasn't in a body bag. So our team took the bag over and prepared him to be brought out. Otherwise he was just covered up in a blanket. And it wasn't very – I don't want to paint a disparaging comment. It wasn't really a professional, I guess, way of bringing the gentleman out. He was strapped on this backboard with a blanket covering him up. So we took him off the backboard and put him in a body bag, put him back on the stretcher. And I said backboard, but I think it was a stretcher. Put him back on the scoop. And then we waited for further instructions from command. (p. 98)

The graphic human cost of mining is made evident as well as the co-worker's desire to enact the retrieval of bodies with respect and dignity, hence the reference to 'the gentleman' and ideas of professionalism. Apparent also is the worker's grief and shock, which are indicated in the conflicting reporting of 'backboard' and 'stretcher'. The extract conveys the traumatic scenes awaiting accident response teams, and how the tally of numbers reported by newsgathering agencies translates into immediate experience.

It is important to note that Nowak's work builds upon a tradition of poetry as documentary in American poetry. Earlier poets writing in the 1930s and 1940s, such as Muriel Rukeyser and Charles Reznikoff, used poetic forms as a way of examining social inequity through their own investigations. Examples are Rukeyser's serial poem *The Book of the Dead* (1938) and Reznikoff's account of the fate of Jewish families in *Holocaust* (1975), which was composed solely of Holocaust survivor testimony taken from twenty-six volumes of documentation of the Eichmann and Nuremberg trials. There are parallels that can be drawn between Rukeyser's investigation of one of the worst industrial accidents at Gauley Bridge, West Virginia, and Nowak's work. In examining Union Carbide's tunnelling of the Gauley tunnel, and the subsequent cases of recurring silicosis amidst miners (due to mismanagement of health and safety issues), Rukeyser's documentary sources included local geography, medical reports, design plans, congressional reports, personal testimonies and accounts of legal action. The arrangement of these materials, combined with lyric interludes, creates in Rukeyser's work a poetry that can 'extend the document'.[39] In a similar way, Nowak's organisation of web-based materials into a poetic form creates a composition that highlights the cruelty of social inequities in a way that a governmental report cannot. Tim Dayton comments that Rukeyser 'challenges any poetics that removes poetry from the ugliness and conflict of the real world of labor and politics'.[40] Dayton's comment is clearly applicable to the contemporary industrial landscape explored by *Coal Mountain Elementary*.

TEXTURED INFORMATION: JOSHUA CLOVER AND CLAUDIA RANKINE

Hazel Smith's 'Visibility and the Generation of the Text' asks us to consider how we quantify ideas of poetic form at a time when twenty-first-century formats challenge our vocabulary for ideas of time, space and reception. Smith suggests that 'reader interactivity, real-time imaging, morphing and text generation can all produce textual variability . . . new media has the capacity to change how we think about textual variability in general both on and off the page'.[41] Already we have seen how new media and information technology offer ways for sourcing material, performing poetry, organising material as well as enabling political poetry. Finally, we can offer a reflection on how interaction with global information networks may impact on poetic form and poetic language, as well as the representation of subjectivity in the contemporary poetry volume. Joshua Clover and Claudia Rankine's poetry offers insights into how poetic language responds to the pressures of a perceived giddying arena of information. In a poetic manifesto Clover draws attention to the premise of 'superinformation':

Data is a phenomenon of life organized by survival; superinformation hangs out near where the waves of data crash against the seawall of the sublime, mixing metaphors in the infinite. Superinformation is a manifesto; the manifesto is the most passionate hoax. Categories are preparation for thinking, but the mighty superinformationists are no Boy Scouts.[42]

This combination of different textures of writing and the pressures exerted by rapid movements between different forms of language are evident in Clover's volume *The Totality for Kids* (2006).[43] In 'Early Style' language is presented 'promenading' around 'the failures of the codex' (p. 8). 'Whiteread Walk' takes on the role of nineteenth-century Charles Baudelaire's Parisian *flâneur*, or walker of the cityscape. Strange and unexpected formulations of language appear as the speaker is identified with the 'illbiquitous promenaders' near the square, which becomes part of what Clover refers to as 'social forms of grieving' (p. 56). Far from being offered a direct spatial commentary upon Georges Haussmann's Parisian boulevards, we are thrown into sonic overload in 'hardcore Autumnophage echolocation' (p. 56). This phrase draws reference to the sensory overload of extreme music in a neologism which conveys seasonal shifts and repeated sound. The poem then closes with a visual implant of 'Brooklyn Bombs over Baghdad' (p. 56). 'Whiteread Walk' is a poem which multitasks: it simultaneously explores city space in tandem with a focus on American foreign policy.

Finally, Claudia Rankine's *Please Don't Let Me Be Lonely* (2004) examines the possibilities for autobiography by combining the format of her work with media imagery and commentary.[44] Diverse texts ranging from photographs, TV news, labels on pharmacy bottles, Google and medical textbooks prompt the telling of a personal meditation which splays in different directions. The narrative of Mr Tools, 'the only person in the world' (p. 71) with an artificial heart, prompts one such meditation:

Mr Tools had the ultimate tool in his body. He felt its heaviness. The weight on his heart was his heart. All his apparatus – artificial heart, energy coil, battery and controller – weighed more than four pounds. The whirr, if you are not Mr Tools, is detectable only with a stethoscope. For Mr Tools that whirr was his sign that he was alive. (p. 71)

Rankine moves the personalised lyric into a realm of bizarre and micro-narratives that fill newsprint and media networks. The impact of solitude is made evident in the book, but co-exists with a disturbing need to verify the sentiment through data and information. Walking alone to her apartment one night, the speaker meditates:

> After we part and I am climbing the stairs to my apartment, I think surely some percentage of women hasn't been raped. I don't know though really. Perhaps this is the kind of thing I could find out on *Google*. Then I think, maybe, that 'what woman hasn't been raped' could be another way of saying 'this is the most miserable day of my life'. (p. 72)

Moreover, the book dramatises how religion and science fiction merge into a futuristic field of data and information. Responding to the evangelist with her pamphlet 'BE LIKE JESUS', she is drawn to reflect upon the character of Neo from *The Matrix Reloaded*: 'I say aloud to Neo, be like Jesus' (p. 121). Rankine adds:

> Neo can't save anyone; Morpheus will have to have another dream: the one in which salvation narratives are passé; the one in which people live no matter what you dream; the one in which people die no matter what you dream; or no matter what, you dream. (p. 121)

Performing 'in between' different texts in this way enables Rankine to probe how autobiography and subjectivity are formed and created. These tissues of intersecting and often-found narratives recuperate a life story from an overwhelming volume of competing data.

DISSEMINATING POETRY

My conclusion has attempted to show how poetry is responsive to technological advancement, as well as the pressures that may be placed upon poetic language in some future poetries. It remains to be stated that technology has offered important avenues for the dissemination of poetry on a global scale. In entering the twenty-first century, the possibilities inherent in a web-based dissemination of poetry were realised with the creation of the e-book, *100 Poets Against the War*. The trilogy of chapbooks were first published online on 27 January 2003 as a response to the threat of entry into a war against Iraq by both the UK and USA. The editor, Todd Swift, explains that the anthology was timed to correspond with the appearance of Hans Blix's weapons inspections report to the United Nations. As Swift adds, *100 Poets Against the War*

> may hold the record for being the fastest assembled global anthology . . . Only the speed of the Internet, and the overwhelmingly positive support of so many poets, who shared the project with their colleagues and personal networks, could have made it happen. These poets are from Ireland, Scotland, Wales, England, Canada, Australia, India, France, America and elsewhere; many are cultural and/or peace activists; some are emerging poets, others very well-known.[45]

The anthology has been followed by French, German and Brazilian versions, which denotes quite literally a global poetic dissemination. The introduction to the electronic version made it clear that poetry could have agency and a power for change through its circulation of protest. The readers of the original version were encouraged 'to spread the word about the *100 Poets Against the War* project – in your community, and beyond'. Technology and poetry can thus make significant interventions in the public sphere. The *Retort* group from the San Francisco Bay Area, reflecting upon the subsequent global demonstrations against the Iraq war in February 2003, concedes that:

> One ingredient of the February dynamic was the appearance on the world stage of something like a digital 'multitude', a worldwide virtual community, assembled . . . in the interstices of the net and that some of the intensity of the moment derived from the actual experience of seeing – or hearing, feeling, facing up to – an *image* of refusal become a reality.[46]

One fragile possibility is that poetry's conversation with information technology imagines a possible reconvening of community and political engagement. Such reconvening and creation of communities, however virtual they may be, can still respond with agency in the face of adversity.

NOTES

1. Simon Armitage, 'Killing Time', in *Killing Time* (London: Faber & Faber, 1999), pp. 3–4. All subsequent references to this edition are given in the text.
2. Joel Bettridge, 'A Conversation with Juliana Spahr', *How 2*. Available online at www.asu.edu/pipercwcenter/how2journal/archive/online_archive/v2_3_2005/current/workbook/spa/media/spa.pdf.
3. Todd Swift (ed.), *100 Poets Against the War* (Cambridge: Salt, 2003). Available online as e-book at www.nthposition.com/100poetso.pdf.
4. N. Katherine Hayles, *Electronic Literature: New Horizons for the Literary* (Notre Dame, IN: University of Notre Dame Press, 2008), p. 3. All the electronic writing discussed is available online at http://collection.eliterature.org/1/index.html.
5. Ted Nelson, cited in Loss Pequeño Glazier, *Digital Poetics: The Making of E Poetries* (Tuscaloosa: University of Alabama Press, 2002), p. 87.
6. Jakob Nielsen, cited in Glazier, *Digital Poetics*, p. 87.
7. Brian Kim Stefans, 'What is Electronic Writing?' 21 February 2006. Available online at www.arras.net/brown_ewriting/?page_id=54. All immediate citations from Stefans, unless noted, refer to this online source.
8. 'Contents by Keyword', in N. Katherine Hayles, Nick Montfort, Scott Rettberg and Stephanie Strickland (eds), *Electronic Literature Collection Volume One*. Available online at http://collection.eliterature.org/1/aux/keywords.html.
9. Brian Kim Stefans, ' "From Byte to Inscription": An Interview with John Cayley', *The Iowa Review Web* (February 2003).

Available online at http://iowareview.uiowa.edu/TIRW/
TIRW_Archive/tirweb/feature/cayley/index.html.

10. John Cayley, *windsound*. Available online at http://collec-
tion.eliterature.org/1/works/cayley__windsound.html. All
further citations from *windsound* refer to this online source.

11. Stefans, 'From Byte to Inscription'.

12. Heather McHugh, cited in description of *windsound*. Available
online at http://collection.eliterature.org/1/works/cayley__
windsound.html.

13. Stefans, 'From Byte to Inscription'.

14. Jenny Weight, *Rice*. Available online at http://collection.elit-
erature.org/1/works/geniwate__rice.html. All further citations from *Rice* refer to this online source.

15. Ibid.

16. Ingrid Ankerson and Megan Sapnar, *Cruising*. Available
online at http://collection.eliterature.org/1/works/anker-
son_sapnar__cruising.html. All further citations from *Cruising*
refer to this online source.

17. Ibid.

18. Reiner Strasser and M. D. Coverley, *ii — in the white darkness*.
Available online at http://nonfinito.de/ii. All further citations
from *ii — in the white darkness* refer to this online source.

19. Ibid.

20. Ibid.

21. Peter Finch, 'Real Cardiff'. Available online at www.peter-
finch.co.uk/btidc.htm.

22. Peter Finch, *R. S. Thomas Information Project* web page, www.
peterfinch.co.uk/depot.htm.

23. Peter Finch, 'Binary Myths: Andy Brown Interviews Peter
Finch'. Available online at www.peterfinch.co.uk/binary.htm.

24. Ibid.

25. Marthine Satris, 'Paper Spaces and Spatial Places'. Available
online at www.cltc.ucsb.edu/roundtables/papers/satris.doc.

26. Trevor Joyce, *With the First Dream of Fire They Hunt the Cold:
A Body of Work 1966–2000* (Dublin: New Writer's Press,
2003), p. 237. All subsequent references to this edition are
given in the text.

27. Michael Gottlieb, 'Googling Flarf', in Craig Dworkin (ed.),

The Consequence of Innovation: 21st Century Poetics (New York: Roof Books, 2008), pp. 199–203 (p. 199).

28. Ibid. p. 199.

29. Gary Sullivan, 'Introduction', *Jacket*, 30 (2006). Available online at http://jacketmagazine.com/30/fl-intro.html.

30. Flarf Collective, 'Infinity Revisited'. Available online at http://mainstreampoetry.blogspot.com.

31. Dan Hoy, 'The Virtual Dependency of the Post-Avant and the Problematics of Flarf: What Happens when Poets Spend Too Much Time Fucking Around on the Internet', *Jacket*, 29 (2006). Available online at http://jacketmagazine.com/29/hoy-flarf.html.

32. Mark Nowak, *Coal Mountain Elementary* (Minneapolis, MN: Minneapolis Coffee House Press, 2009). All subsequent references to this edition are given in the text.

33. Mark Nowak, 'Notes Toward an Anti-Capitalist Poetics II', in Claudia Rankine and Lisa Sewell (eds), *American Poets in the 21st Century: The New Poetics* (Middletown, CT: Wesleyan University Press, 2007), pp. 333–4.

34. Ibid. p. 334.

35. Ibid. p. 334.

36. See www.wvminesafety.org/sagointerviews.htm.

37. See www.teachcoal.org/lessonplans/index.html.

38. Dedicated site for *Coal Mountain Elementary*, http://coal-mountain.wordpress.com.

39. Muriel Rukeyser, 'Note', in *US 1* (New York: Covici and Friede, 1938).

40. Tim Dayton, 'Lyric and Document in Muriel Rukeyser's *The Book of the Dead*', *Journal of Modern Literature*, 21:2 (1997–8), 223–40 (p. 225).

41. Hazel Smith, 'Textual Variability in New Media Poetry', in Annie Finch and Susan M. Schultz (eds), *Multiformalisms: Postmodern Poetics of Form* (Cincinnati: WordTech Communications, 2008), pp. 485–516 (p. 512).

42. Joshua Clover, 'Once Against (Into the Poetics of Superinformation)', in *American Poets in the 21st Century: The New Poetics*, p. 163.

43. Joshua Clover, *The Totality for Kids* (Berkeley: University

of California Press, 2006). All subsequent references to this edition are given in the text.

44. Claudia Rankine, *Please Don't Let Me Be Lonely* (Saint Paul, MN: Graywolf Press, 2004). All subsequent references to this edition are given in the text.

45. Todd Swift, *100 Poets Against the War*.

46. Iain Boal, T. J. Clark, Joseph Matthews and Michael Watts, *Afflicted Powers: Capital and Spectacle in a New Age of War* (London: Verso, 2005), p. 4.

Student Resources

ELECTRONIC RESOURCES

There is an extensive range of materials available for students of contemporary poetry on the Internet. Here is a cross-section of sites representing a diverse range of work from essay and text-based poems to performances, recordings and visual poetries.

General

Academi

www.academi.org
A Welsh National Literature Promotion Agency and Society for Authors, Academi runs events, competitions (including the Cardiff International Poetry Competition), conferences, international exchanges, events for schools, lectures and festivals. It offers resources for writers and information for readers and is responsible for the National Poet of Wales project.

The Academy of American Poets

www.poets.org
Has a wide range of material on modern and contemporary poets. A good site for background information, manifestos, bibliographies and critical responses.

The Archive of the Now

www.archiveofthenow.com
An online and print collection of recordings, printed texts and manuscripts, focused on innovative contemporary poetry written or performed in Britain. The site is hosted by Queen Mary College, London.

The Argotist

www.argotistonline.co.uk
Publishes non-mainstream contemporary poetry. Also offers interviews, reviews and critical works.

Australian Poetry Centre

www.australianpoetrycentre.org.au
A promotional site that offers archive material and information regarding performances and events.

BEPC: British Electronic Poetry Centre static site

www.soton.ac.uk/~bepc
Launched in May 2002, a joint venture of the Contemporary Poetics Research Centre in the School of English and Humanities at Birkbeck College, the Poetic Practice Group at Royal Holloway College, and the Department of English at University of Southampton. The site offers a guide to the work of contemporary British poets from an experimental tradition.

Contemporary Poetics Research Centre

www.bbk.ac.uk/cprc
This centre hosted by Birkbeck College London 'is a forum for the study and performance of contemporary poetries, and research into their historical, political and theoretical contexts'. It holds readings, performances, workshops, exchanges, seminars, lectures and conferences. The site offers two web journals.

Electronic Literature Collection

http://collection.eliterature.org
Offers access to a range of contemporary electronic writing via the site.

Electronic Poetry Center

http://epc.buffalo.edu
One of the earliest websites specialising in avant-garde and experimental American poetry. Offers a vast amount of single poet pages, criticism and discussions as well as oral poetries, bibliographies and extracts from essays.

Electronic Poetry Review

www.epoetry.org
A US-based ezine spanning a range of contemporary poetry from North America and beyond.

How2

www.asu.edu/pipercwcenter/how2journal
This site specifies that it explores 'non-traditional directions in poetry and scholarship by women.' Provides critical material on performance, ecology, poetry and poetics. Offers an extensive archive of material.

Jacket

http://jacketmagazine.com
A vast online magazine from Australia which offers a variety of English-language poetries. The archived issues in particular are impressive. Issues can be thematised and *Jacket* covers a range of issues from ecocriticism to feminism.

Meshworks: The Miami University Archive of Writing in Performance

www.orgs.muohio.edu/meshworks
A site dedicated to documenting and preserving video and sound recordings of writing in performance.

Modern Australian Poetry

www.cultureandrecreation.gov.au/articles/poetry
A showcase site for Australian poetry. Offers some useful links and website resources.

National Poetry Foundation

www.poetryfoundation.org
Hosts a range of poetries and offers some practical guides to poetry as well as information about reading, publications and profiles of poets. A very comprehensive site.

New Zealand Electronic Poetry Centre

www.nzepc.auckland.ac.nz
Offers online material and digital poetics, as well as more traditional text-based material. Includes native poetries as well as archive material relevant to New Zealand.

Nthposition

www.nthposition.com
An online political magazine, offering poetry. Site which initially circulated *100 Poets Against the War*.

PennSound

http://writing.upenn.edu/pennsound
One of the most impressive and cavernous websites for contemporary poetry and poetics. Offers up-to-date information, podcasts,

archived readings and discussions, all run through the University of Pennsylvania Poetics programme.

Poemtalk

http://poemtalkatkwh.blogspot.com
Downloadable as a podcast, this is a poetry show hosted by PennSound and fronted by Al Filreis. A group of poet-theorists discuss at length a single poem, often featuring archive poetry readings. Versatile and often very enlightening.

The Poetry Archive

www.poetryarchive.org/poetryarchive/home.do
Includes a wealth of contemporary and historic recordings, as well as information for students and teachers.

Poetry Daily

http://poems.com
Showcases new work daily with featured poets. Also collates essays from around the world to showcase the website for a week. Essays are then archived for a year.

Poetry International Web

www.poetryinternationalweb.org
A site which covers a range of worldwide poetries ranging from Australia to Zimbabwe, and in between. Offers introductions, bibliographies, biographies and further links to poetry-related websites.

The Poetry Library

www.poetrylibrary.org.uk
On the South Bank, the Poetry Library is the national public library devoted to poetry. Contains a wealth of information and many links to other websites.

poetrymagazines.org.uk

Gives access, with search facility, to some back issues from a range of UK magazines from the Poetry Library's archives, including: *Angel Exhaust*; *10th Muse*; *Ambit*; *Fire*; *Oasis*; *Painted, spoken*; *Poetry Nation*; *Shearsman*; *The Interpreter's House*; *The London Magazine*.

Poetry Society

www.poetry.society.org.uk
Hosts National Poetry Day in the UK. Also has information regarding the society's magazine *Poetry Review*. Information regarding poets as well as poetry events in the UK.

Salt Poetry Directory

www.saltpublishing.com/links Folder/index.php
On the poetry publisher's website, this dedicated resource lists: agents, archives, authors, blogs, bookstores, centres, competitions, conferences, courses, directories, festivals, funding, libraries, magazines, organisations, prizes, publishers, radio shows, television programmes, venues and workshops, worldwide.

The Scottish Poetry Library

www.spl.org.uk
Offers annual lists of the best Scottish poems and a range of Scottish poetry.

Silliman's Blog

http://ronsilliman.blogspot.com
American poet Ron Silliman's blog, which offers responses to recent work as well as pithy essays on all kinds of poetic histories and materials. Allied to the experimental vein in American poetry.

UBU

www.ubu.com
A site dedicated to non-writing-based texts: visual, concrete and sound language spanning twentieth- and twenty-first-century experimentation.

Publishers' Websites

Arc: www.arcpublications.co.uk
Barque: www.barquepress.com
Bloodaxe: www.bloodaxebooks.com
Carcanet: www.carcanet.co.uk
Equipage: www.cambridgepoetry.org
Etruscan: http://llpp.ms11.net/etruscan/index.html
New Directions: www.ndpublishing.com
Salt: www.saltpublishing.com
Seren: www.serenbooks.com
Shearsman: www.shearsman.com

QUESTIONS FOR DISCUSSION

Chapter 1: Lyric Subjects

How do contemporary poets present subjective states in their work?

What are the characteristics of a 'discursive lyric'?

Examine how a contemporary poet uses elegy to convey intense emotion.

Consider the different ways that autobiography can be represented in contemporary poetry.

Explore how autobiography offers a way into exploring race and ethnicity in the work of contemporary poets.

How do contemporary poets represent more than one perspective in their work?

Consider how two poets use the practice of self-portraiture as a way of investigating the processes of writing and composition.

Is indeterminacy a compelling factor in writing the self in contemporary poetry?

Explore how contemporary poets play with constructions of subjectivity in their work.

How do poetic forms aid or hinder the representation of subjectivity in recent poetry?

Chapter 2: Politics and Poetics

What do you consider Adorno meant by his statement 'to write poetry after Auschwitz is barbaric'? And how have contemporary poets responded to his statement?

W. H. Auden famously stated that 'poetry makes nothing happen'. Do you agree?

How political is the poetry from 1980s Northern Ireland?

It has been suggested that language for the poet is always political. Do you agree?

What do you understand by poetry acting as 'witness'?

Examine the use of reportage in recent poetry.

Consider the role served by allegory in representing the political in contemporary poetry.

How does poetry represent the perspective of the exile?

Compare two contemporary poets' different approaches to composing anti-war poems.

Why do contemporary poets often use challenging forms to make a political statement?

Chapter 3: Performance and the Poem

Consider the importance of Charles Olson's 'Projective Verse' to ideas of performance in the work of recent poets.

Compare the way two poets present a poetic 'voice'.

How does poetry perform a countercultural critique?

Examine how contemporary poetry uses jazz compositional techniques as a method for poetic writing.

What do you understand by the term 'dub poetry'?

Consider the relationship between Olson's ideas of 'open form' and an oral poetry.

What techniques do contemporary poets use to present humour in their work?

Is there a relationship between the body and poetic performance?

Examine whether ideas of the 'performative' aid a reading of contemporary poetry.

How does poetry perform an understanding of gender in language?

How spontaneous is performance poetry?

Chapter 4: Environment and Space

Consider the impact of ecocriticism on the work of contemporary poets.

To what extent are contemporary poets suspicious of language as a vehicle of representation?

Examine how two contemporary poets represent the impact of environment on human communities.

Consider the relationship between civic spaces and the everyday in the work of one poet.

Illustrate how contemporary poets reimagine spaces in their work.

Examine how two poets map the cityscape in their work.

What do you understand by the term 'psychogeography'?

Consider the relationship between the global and the local in the work of a poet.

How do contemporary poets respond to the challenge of writing an ecopoetics?

Chapter 5: Dialects, Idiolects and Multilingual Poetries

As a global language, how is English 'made different' by poets from different countries?

Examine how the use of dialect creates a sense of affiliation to a region.

Consider how class may be represented through poetry.

How do native cultures deal with the transformation of oral story into poetic text?

What techniques do poets use to dramatise the intersection of competing languages in their work?

How do two poets represent minority languages and identities in English?

Is the relationship between minority languages and English in the work of contemporary poets always a problematic one?

Is Charles Bernstein's configuration of an 'ideolectical' poetics particularly useful to an understanding of recent poetic practice?

Examine how poetic experimentation furthers the reinvention of English use in poetry.

GLOSSARY

avant-garde

The term has a military origin ('advance guard') and in the context of the literary arts denotes work which is pathfinding, experimental, ahead of its time and exploratory. Often associated with a revolutionary ambition; always associated with innovation.

cancrizans *or* cancrine

In Latin, meaning 'crab-wise'. Poetry which reads both ways, as a palindrome.

confessional poetry

The term is often confined to the work of poets in the 1950s and 1960s associated with what was termed a 'movement inward'. The poetry associated with confessionalism often examines and reveals extreme states of being as well as states of violence. Yet it is worth being reminded that there is also a strong element of performance implicit in this revelatory impulse.

dialect

Often referred to as 'idiom', a language or manner of speaking indicative of a particular class or regional identity. In poetry, the term frequently denotes a deviation from so-called standard English.

dub poetry

Allied to the Caribbean practice of speaking while 'DJing', often called toasting. Dub poetry is often performed with music dependent on a strong reggae beat, and is also associated with ideas of spontaneity and political responsibility. Dub poets in the past have used their poetry to comment on social inequities, racism and violence.

ecocriticism

The study of literature and the environment with the aim of providing solutions for endangered environments. The work often stresses its interdisciplinary nature. In the past ecoliterature would often focus on idealised depictions of landscape and wilderness. Increasingly ecocriticism and literature take into account the economic and political forces which harm the earth's sustainability.

electronic writing

Writing which is digitally 'born' and not literature which has been digitised. Often the practitioners embrace new media in innovative ways, combing text with audio and visual imageries. Practices we might associate with electronic writing forms could be interactive fiction, generative texts, installation video and sound poetry.

elegy

Poetry of a commemorative nature, often to mark a death or express an experience of mourning and loss.

epic poetry

A long narrative poem vast in scale and ambition, often addressing the deeds of warriors and heroes. Frequently epics are attached to ideals of nationhood embodying a country's aspirations. The form often contains references to myths, history, folklore and legends.

epistle

An intimate poem addressed to a close companion or friend, often reading like a conversational letter in verse.

ethnopoetics

Often combining an interest in anthropology and linguistics, ethnopoetics considers non-Western and indigenous literatures while questioning the division between so-called primitive and civilised cultural production.

Flarf poetry

A poetry which is occasioned by text from the Internet. The title covers an array of approaches, with some poets using the Internet for chance operations, and others seeking humorous narratives to arrange into poetic forms. For yet others it takes the form of a range of different material sutured together with disconcerting shifts in subject matter and texture.

found poetry

A form of poetic composition which takes texts from other sources to create new work. Often the original texts are placed into an entirely new context.

free verse

Poetry which has no regular meter or line length, often dependent upon natural speech rhythms and musical counterpoint.

globalisation

Often associated with actions in mass media, corporate finance, market trading, and the political negotiations where interests are interlinked or interdependent across nations. What such processes might mean for literary studies is complex, but for some critics it can be seen as a celebration of multilingual practices and formal approaches which are transnational. For others there is a fear that globalisation will ultimately lead to a corporate similarity, in effect challenging and eroding difference. Frequently these fears are couched in relation to the fate of minority languages, in the face of English as a global language.

hybridity

Literally means a mixture or mixing together, often contextualised in terms of race and ethnicity. In literary production the term is often associated with the creation of new transcultural forms.

identity poetics

The literary exploration of what is referred to as identity politics. Identity politics, premised upon distinctions between groups according to race, ethnicity, gender and sexual orientation, finds a fertile and often recuperative role in contemporary poetry. Essentially identity politics focuses upon the experience of often marginalised identities as an enabling possibility for political discussion and action.

idiolect

A form of language unique to an individual or individual use. In linguistics, however, the term is often used to refer to the speech acts of a particular community.

intertextuality

An expansive term which is used to refer to the inclusion of many texts or references within a work. For the literary arts, intertextuality may also denote a history of earlier writing, as well as the inclusion of contemporary cultural references.

lyric

A broad umbrella term to encompass a range of different poetries often associated with the expression of the subject's wishes, desires and recollections. Traditionally associated with music and song: many contemporary poets insist on the musicality of their work. In contemporary practice, the lyric has mutated into different forms. An 'analytic lyric' or 'self-reflexive' lyric will often draw attention to the linguistic textual making of its own utterance. A 'discursive' or 'expressive' lyric offers the poet's voice in a conversational mode, often meditating on the world around her.

malapropism

The misuse of a word, or its use in a wrong context. For some contemporary poets the error may be deliberate in a spirit of play, humour or performance.

narrative poetry

Essentially a poem which tells a story, often traditionally divided into three categories: epic, romance and ballad.

nation language

A term first coined by poet-theorist Edward Kamau Brathwaite. It offers a challenge to the imperial 'correctness' of English, and acknowledges the infusion of different languages, idioms and dialects spoken in Caribbean English.

panegyric

A praise poem, often celebrating an individual, institution or group, and frequently associated with rhetorical prowess.

performance writing

A form of writing which stresses its interdisciplinarity and links with performance. The field of performance writing can be defined in its widest sense as the investigation of the performative nature of language.

periphrasis

In Greek *peri* as a preposition means 'around', 'about' or 'beyond'. Another equivalent term would be 'circumlocution', generally a roundabout description of something. In poetry it can show itself as a tendency to journey around an object or situation, often generated by the movement and patterning of words themselves, as opposed to a direct recalling of events or action.

petrarchan sonnet

Named after the fourteenth-century Italian poet, Francesco Petrarch, the petrarchan sonnet is a fourteen-line poem of iambic verse usually divided into two parts. The first eight lines are known as an octave or octet, with a typical rhyming scheme of abbaabba. The last six lines are known as the sestet. Petrarchan love poems often feature a distant and unobtainable object of devotion.

phenomenology

A philosophical movement whose origins can be traced back to the philosopher Edmund Husserl. Broadly speaking the aim of phenomemology is to provide an 'objective' account of the nature of subjectivity, consciousness and how things are perceived. Key practitioners associated with phenomenology are Maurice Merleau-Ponty and Martin Heidegger.

poetics

For our context it is useful to think of 'poetics' as a philosophy of poetry, the 'thinking' of the art of poetic composition. Key early philosophers and thinkers whose work is associated with the creation and discussion of a poetics are Aristotle, Horace and Dante. *The New Princeton Dictionary of Poetry and Poetics* states that poetics is at its most specific 'a systematic theory of poetry'.

polyphony

At its most literal, the term refers to a work which has more than one voice and is therefore multi-voiced. Users of the term often pay homage to Mikhail Bakhtin's theory of the novel as a democratic form of writing 'saturated' or 'impregnated' with different types and levels of language, which undermine the univocal nature of authoritative/authoritarian discourse.

psychogeography

Associated with the French theorist Guy Debord, the term refers to inventive and experimental ways of representing the landscapes and cityscapes around us, which extend beyond the way they are represented in cartography (or mapping). As Debord stated in 1955, psychogeography can be thought of as the study 'of the precise laws and specific effects of the geographical environment, consciously organized or not, on the emotions and behaviour of individuals'.

terza rima

Associated with Dante's epic poems, terza rima consists of three interlocking three-lined stanzas, in which the second line of each one rhymes with the third line of the successive tercet.

villanelle

Originally used for pastoral poetry sometimes called chain poetry. It is a strict traditional form which is fixed into five three-lined stanzas or tercets with a final quatrain. The first and third lines of the first tercet recur in alternation as a refrain in the following stanzas, forming a final couplet.

POETRY ANTHOLOGIES

Abbs, Peter, *Earth Songs: A Resurgence Anthology of Contemporary Eco-Poetry* (Totnes: Green Books, 2002).

Allen, Donald (ed.), *New American Poetry, 1945–1960* (Berkeley: University of California Press, 1999).

Alvarez, Al (ed.), *The New Poetry: An Anthology* (London: Faber & Faber, 1962).

Astley, Neil (ed.), *New Blood* (Newcastle: Bloodaxe, 1999).

Bertram, Vicki (ed.), *Kicking Daffodils: Twentieth-Century Women Poets* (Edinburgh: Edinburgh University Press, 1997).

Bornholdt, Jenny, Gregory O'Brien and Mark Williams (eds), *An Anthology of New Zealand Poetry in English* (Melbourne: Oxford University Press, 1997).

Burnett, Paula (ed.), *The Penguin Book of Caribbean Verse in English* (London: Penguin, 2005).

Caddel, Richard and Peter Quartermain (eds), *Other: British and Irish Poetry since 1970* (Middletown, CT: Wesleyan University Press, 1999).

Conquest, Robert (ed.), *New Lines* (London: Macmillan, 1956).

Couzyn, Jeni (ed.), *The Bloodaxe Book of Contemporary Women Poets: Eleven British Writers* (Newcastle: Bloodaxe, 2000).

France, Linda (ed.), *Sixty Women Poets* (Newcastle: Bloodaxe, 1993).

Gioia, Dana, David Mason and Meg Schoerke (eds), *Twentieth-Century American Poetry* (Maidenhead: McGraw-Hill, 2003).

Heiss, Anita and Peter Minder (eds), *Anthology of Australian Aboriginal Literature* (Montreal and Kingston: McGill-Queen's University Press, 2008).

Herbert, W. N. and Matthew Hollis (eds), *Strong Words: Modern Poets on Modern Poetry* (Newcastle: Bloodaxe, 2000).

Hilson, Jeff (ed.), *The Reality Book of Sonnets* (Hastings: Reality Street, 2008).

Hoover, Paul (ed.), *Postmodern American Poetry: A Norton Anthology* (New York: Norton, 1994).

Hulse Michael, David Kennedy and David Morley (eds), *The New Poetry* (Newcastle: Bloodaxe, 1993).

Kinsella, John (ed.), *Landbridge: Contemporary Australian Poetry* (Todmorden: Arc, 1999).

—— (ed.), *The Penguin Anthology of Australian Poetry* (Camberwell: Penguin, 2008).

—— and Paul Henry (eds), *The Salt Anthology of Contemporary American Poetry* (Cambridge: Salt, 2008).

Lasell, Michael and Elena Georgiou (eds), *The World in Us: Lesbian and Gay Poetry of the Next Wave* (New York: Saint Martin's Press, 2001).

Leonard, John (ed.), *Contemporary Australian Poetry: An Anthology* (London: Gollancz, 1991).

McClatchy, J. D. (ed.), *The Vintage Book of Contemporary American Poetry* (New York: Vintage, 1990).

Markham, E. A., (ed.), *Hinterland: Caribbean Poetry from the West Indies and Britain* (Newcastle: Bloodaxe, 1989).

Marsack, Robyn and Andrew Johnstone (eds), *New Zealand Poetry* (Manchester: Carcanet, 2009).

Mengham, Rod and John Kinsella (eds), *Vanishing Points* (Cambridge: Salt, 2004).

Messerli, Douglas (ed.), *From the Other Side of the Century: A New American Poetry 1960–90* (Los Angeles: Sun & Moon Classics, 1994).

Miller, Kei (ed.), *New Caribbean Poetry: An Anthology* (Manchester: Carcanet, 2007).

Muldoon, Paul (ed.), *The Faber Book of Contemporary Irish Poetry* (London: Faber, 1986).

Ormsby, Frank (ed.), *A Rage for Order: Poetry of the Northern Ireland Troubles* (Belfast: Blackstaff, 1992).

Paterson, Don and Charles Simic (eds), *New British Poetry* (Minneapolis, MN: Graywolf Press, 2004).

Ramazani, Jahan, Richard Ellman and Robert O'Clair (eds), *The Norton Anthology of Modern and Contemporary Poetry* (New York: Norton, 2004).

Rankine, Claudia and Juliana Spahr (eds), *American Poetics in the 21st Century: The New Poetics* (Middletown, CT: Wesleyan University Press, 2007).

Rees-Jones, Deryn (ed.), *Modern Women Poets* (Newcastle: Bloodaxe, 2005).

Roberts, Andrew and Jonathan Allison (eds), *Poetry and Contemporary Culture* (Edinburgh: Edinburgh University Press, 2002).

Ross, Jack and Jan Kemp (eds), *New New Zealand Poets in Performance* (Auckland: Auckland University Press, 2008).

Rothenberg, Jerome (ed.), *Shaking the Pumpkin: Traditional poetry of the Indian North Americas* (Berkeley: University of California Press, 1983).

—— and Pierre Joris (eds), *Poems for the Millennium* (Berkeley: University of California Press, 1995).

Rumens, Carol (ed.), *New Women Poets* (Newcastle: Bloodaxe, 1990).

Shepherd, Reginald (ed.), *Lyric Postmodernisms: An Anthology of Contemporary Innovative Poetries* (Denver, CO: Counterpath Press, 2008).

Sinclair, Iain (ed.), *Conductors of Chaos* (London: Picador, 1996).

Swensen, Cole (ed.), *American Hybrid: A Norton Anthology of New Poetry* (New York: Norton, 2009).

Thayil, Jeet (ed.), *The Bloodaxe Book of Contemporary Indian Poets* (Newcastle: Bloodaxe, 2008).

Tuma, Keith (ed.), *Anthology of Twentieth-Century British and Irish Poetry* (New York: Oxford University Press, 2001).

GUIDE TO FURTHER READING

General Resources

Buell, Lawrence, *Writing for an Endangered World: Literature, Culture and Environment in the U.S. and Beyond* (Cambridge, MA: Harvard University Press, 2003).

Donnell, Alison and Sarah Lawson Welsh (eds), *The Routledge Reader in Caribbean Literature* (London: Routledge, 1999).

Garrard, Greg, *Ecocriticism* (London: Routledge, 2004).

Matterson, Stephen and Darryl Jones, *Studying Poetry* (London: Bloomsbury Academic, 2000).

Padley, Steve, *Key Concepts in Contemporary Literature* (Basingstoke: Palgrave, 2006).

Waugh, Patricia and Philip Rice (eds), *Modern Literary Theory: A Reader* (London: Bloomsbury Academic, 2001).

Wisker, Gina, *Key Concepts in Postcolonial Literature* (Basingstoke: Palgrave, 2006).

Wolfreys, Julian, *Introducing Criticism at the 21st Century* (Edinburgh: Edinburgh University Press, 2002).

Contemporary Poetry Resources

Acheson, James and Romana Huk (eds), *Contemporary British Poetry: Essays in Theory and Criticism* (Albany: State University of New York Press, 1996).

Alderman, Nigel and C. D. Blanton (eds), *A Concise Companion to Postwar British and Irish Poetry* (Oxford: Blackwell, 2009).

Altieri, Charles, *Self and Sensibility in American Poetry* (Cambridge: Cambridge University Press, 1984).

——, *The Art of Twentieth-Century American Poetry: Modernism and After* (London: Blackwell, 2006).

Armand, Louis, *Contemporary Poetics* (Evanston, IL: Northwestern University Press, 2006).

Baker, Peter, *Obdurate Brilliance: Exteriority and the Modern Long Poem* (Gainesville: University of Florida Press, 1991).

—— (ed.), *Onward Contemporary Poetry and Poetics* (New York, NY: Peter Lang, 1996).

Barry, Peter, *Contemporary British Poetry and the City* (Manchester: Manchester University Press, 2000).

——, *Poetry Wars: British Poetry of the 1970s and the Battle of Earls Court* (Cambridge: Salt, 2006).

Beach, Christopher, *Poetic Culture: Contemporary Poetry Between Community and Institution* (Evanston, IL: Northwestern University Press, 1999).

——, *The Cambridge Introduction to Twentieth-Century American Poetry* (Cambridge: Cambridge University Press, 2003).

—— (ed.), *Artifice and Indeterminacy: An Anthology of New Poetics* (Tuscaloosa: University of Alabama Press, 1998).

Bernstein, Charles (ed.), *The Politics of Poetic Form: Poetry and Public Policy* (New York: Roof Books, 1990).

—— (ed.), *Close Listening: Poetry and the Performed Word* (Oxford: Oxford University Press, 1998).

Bertram, Vicki, *Gendering Poetry: Contemporary Poetry and Sexual Politics* (London: Rivers Oram Press, 2005).

Boykoff, Jules and Kaia Sand, *Landscapes of Dissent: Guerrilla Poetry & Public Space* (Long Beach: Palm Press, 2008).

Brinton, Ian, *Contemporary Poetry: Poets and Poetry since 1990* (Cambridge: Cambridge University Press, 2009).

Broom, Sarah, *Contemporary British and Irish Poetry: An Introduction* (Basingstoke: Palgrave, 2005).

Buell, Lawrence, *The Future of Environmental Criticism* (Oxford: Blackwell, 2005).

Butling, Pauline and Susan Rudy, *Writing in Our Time: Canada's Radical Poetries in English (1957–2003)* (Waterloo: Wilfrid Laurier University Press, 2004).

Campbell, Matthew, *The Cambridge Companion to Contemporary Irish Poetry* (Cambridge: Cambridge University Press, 2003).

Caplan, David, *Questions of Possibility: Contemporary Poetry and Poetic Form* (Oxford: Oxford University Press, 2006).

Clark, Heather, *The Ulster Renaissance: Poetry in Belfast 1962–1972* (Oxford: Oxford University Press, 2006).

Corcoran, Neil, *English Poetry Since 1940* (London: Longman, 1993).

—— (ed.), *The Cambridge Companion to Twentieth-Century English Poetry* (Cambridge: University of Cambridge Press, 2007).

Damon, Maria and Ira Livingstone (eds), *Poetry and Cultural Studies: A Reader* (Chicago: University of Illinois Press, 2009).

Davidson, Michael, *The San Francisco Renaissance* (Cambridge: Cambridge University Press, 1989).

——, *Ghostlier Demarcations: Modern Poetry and the Material Word* (Berkeley: University of California Press, 1997).

Dawes, Kwame and Kadija Sesay (eds), *Red: Contemporary Black British Poetry* (Leeds: Tree Press, 2010).

Dósa, Attila, *Beyond Identity: New Horizons in Modern Scottish Poetry* (Amsterdam: Rodopi, 2009).

Dowson, Jane and Alice Entwistle (eds), *A History of Twentieth-Century British Women's Poetry* (Cambridge: Cambridge University Press, 2005).

Draper, R. P., *An Introduction to Twentieth-Century Poetry in English* (Basingstoke: Macmillan, 1999).

Duncan, Andrew, *The Failure of Conservatism in Modern British Poetry* (Cambridge: Salt, 2003).

Dworkin, Craig, *The Consequence of Innovation: 21st Century Poetics* (New York: Roof Books, 2008).

Finch, Annie and Susan M. Schultz (eds), *Multiformalisms: Postmodern Poetics of Form* (Cincinnati: WordTech Communications, 2008).

Gardner, Thomas, *Regions of Unlikeness: Explaining Contemporary Poetry* (Lincoln: University of Nebraska Press, 1999).

Glazier, Loss Pequeño, *Digital Poetics: The Making of E-Poetries* (Tuscaloosa: University of Alabama Press, 2001).

Goodby, John, *Irish Poetry Since 1950: From Stillness into History* (Manchester: Manchester University Press, 2000).

Gregson, Ian, *Contemporary Poetry and Postmodernism: Dialogue and Estrangement* (Basingstoke: Palgrave, 1996).

Hayles, N. Katherine, *Electronic Literature: New Horizons for the Literary* (Notre Dame, IN: University of Notre Dame Press, 2008).

Hinton, Laura and Cynthia Hogue, *We Who Love to be Astonished: Experimental Women's Writing and Performance Poetics* (Tuscaloosa: University of Alabama Press, 2001).

Jeffries, Lesley and Peter Sansom, *Contemporary Poems: Some Critical Approaches* (Sheffield: Smith/Doorstop Books, 2001).

Keller, Lynn, *Re-making it New: Contemporary American Poetry and the Modernist Tradition* (Cambridge: Cambridge University Press, 1987).

Longley, Edna, *Poetry in the Wars* (Newcastle: Bloodaxe, 1986).

McGann, Jerome, *The Point is to Change It: Poetry and Criticism in the Continuing Present* (Tuscaloosa: University of Alabama Press, 2007).

MacGowan, Christopher, *Twentieth-Century American Poetry* (London: Blackwell, 2004).

McGuire, Matt and Colin Nicholson (eds), *The Edinburgh Companion to Contemporary Scottish Poetry* (Edinburgh: Edinburgh University Press, 2009).

McHale, Brian, *The Obligation Toward the Difficult Whole: Postmodernist Long Poems* (Tuscaloosa: University of Alabama Press, 2004).

Mark, Alison and Deryn Rees-Jones (eds), *Contemporary Women's Poetry: Reading/Writing/ Practice* (Basingstoke: Macmillan, 2000).

Middleton, Peter, *Distant Reading: Performance, Readership, and Consumption in Contemporary Poetry* (Tuscaloosa: University of Alabama Press, 2005).

Nielsen, Aldon, Lynn and Lauri Ramey (eds), *Every Goodbye Ain't Gone: An Anthology of Innovative Poetry by African Americans* (Tuscaloosa: University of Alabama Press, 2006).

Perloff, Marjorie, *The Dance of the Intellect Studies in the Poetry of the Pound Tradition* (New York: Cambridge University Press, 1985).

——, *Radical Artifice: Writing Poetry in the Age of the Media* (Cambridge. Cambridge University Press, 1991).

——, *Differentials: Poetry, Poetics, Pedagogy* (Tuscaloosa: University of Alabama Press, 2004).

Perril, Simon, *Contemporary British Poetry and Modernist Innovation* (Cambridge: Salt, 2011).

Roberts, Neil, *A Companion to Twentieth-Century Poetry* (London: Blackwell, 2003).

Rothenberg, Jerome, *Poetics and Polemics 1980–2005* (Tuscaloosa: University of Alabama Press, 2007).

Severin, Laura, *Poetry off the Page: Twentieth Century British Women Poets in Performance* (Aldershot: Ashgate, 2004).

Vendler, Helen, *The Music of What Happens* (Cambridge, MA: Harvard University Press, 1988).

——, *The Given and the Made* (Cambridge, MA: Harvard University Press, 1995).

——, *Souls Says: On Recent Poetry* (Cambridge, MA: Harvard University Press, 1996).

Index